ADVENTURE IN NEW ZEALAND

NEW ZEALAND CLASSICS

ADVENTURE IN
NEW ZEALAND
EDWARD JERNINGHAM WAKEFIELD

an abridgement, edited by
JOAN STEVENS

Golden Press
Auckland, Christchurch, Sydney

First published 1845, John Murray, London, 2 vols.
New Zealand edition 1908, Whitcombe and Tombs, 2 vols.
Abridged edition 1955, Whitcombe and Tombs, 1 vol.
Facsimile reprint of first edition 1971, Wilson
and Horton, 2 vols.

This edition, 1975, reprinting the abridged text
of 1955, with a revised introduction
is published by
Golden Press Pty Ltd
16 Copsey Place
Avondale, Auckland
and
35 Osborne Street
Christchurch
Printed in Hong Kong

Contents

Illustrations

Introduction

EDWARD JERNINGHAM WAKEFIELD was born into a brilliant family. His father, Edward Gibbon Wakefield, was one of the chief advocates and organizers of the colonization schemes associated with the settlement of South Australia and of New Zealand. In our own country, Wellington, Nelson, New Plymouth, and Canterbury—and, at a slightly further remove, Otago—stand to Edward Gibbon Wakefield's credit. Working with him in these enterprises were several of his brothers, notably William, who commanded the expedition to Cook Strait, and Arthur, who led the Nelson colony. The parent bodies of these emigration ventures were the South Australian Association and the New Zealand Company, but behind them were years of struggle and enthusiasm in which Gibbon Wakefield theorized, wrote, and manipulated men.

Jerningham, his only son, was born in 1820, and after a gentleman's education in England and France, accompanied his father to Canada in 1838 in the service of Lord Durham. In 1839, eager for further adventure, he joined his uncle William on board the Tory, which the Company sent out to New Zealand in search of a suitable site for a colony.

He was then nineteen. After almost five years in the Colony, early in 1844, when relations between the Maori people and the settlers were still strained as a result of the Wairau 'massacre', Jerningham's swashbuckling indiscretions drew a public reprimand from the new Governor, Captain FitzRoy. In angry reaction, the young man quitted the country at once. On the long voyage home via South America, the idea ripened of compiling a book about his experiences. During a short stay at Blois, near Bordeaux, his grandfather Edward Wakefield, himself a tireless advocate of the New Zealand Company's schemes, gave Jerningham much encouragement in this plan, and the Journals which he had left in Wellington with a friend were sent for. He finally landed in

England in September 1844, and must have set to work at once.

He remained in England for the next five years, dabbling with more enthusiasm than wisdom in Company affairs, and dissipating his inheritance in dining, wining, womanising, hunting, race-going and the other delights popular in London's play-boy set. Late in 1850, leaving his finances 'in some confusion', he sailed again for New Zealand in the *Lady Nugent* with the advance party for the Canterbury settlement under John Robert Godley. Subsequently he went into politics, both local and national. He was in the first Parliament of 1854, and from 1855–1861 represented the city in the Wellington Provincial Council. His faults of character intensified, however, and his life ended in personal disaster. He died at Ashburton in 1879.

Adventure in New Zealand was put together in six months, appearing on 17 April 1845 in an edition of 750 copies; the famous *Illustrations* for it appeared separately a few days later. The publication date was carefully chosen, as the book was intended to support Edward Gibbon Wakefield's campaign on behalf of the New Zealand Company that year. The Company's case was due to be debated in the House of Commons in the forthcoming session, Charles Buller's Notice of Motion having been lodged on 31 March. The success of the book as Company propaganda was considerable. A number of M.P.s read it, including Sir Robert Peel, and the English and Scottish provincial press quoted it extensively. Old Edward Wakefield was delighted, and prophesied that the book would make Jerningham 'quite a lion'. So indeed it did, for a short year or two, as Jerningham's diary of the time reveals.* He was a persistent journaliser; other diaries which survive include a small pocket-book with notes for 1840–1843, and several journals for periods between 1850 and 1858.

Adventure in New Zealand, then, is closely based on the journals and letters arising from Jerningham's first experience in this country. Most pioneers kept at least some limited record, but Jerningham's material ranges far more widely than was usual. For one thing, he felt himself to be deputising for his father,

*see *The London Journal of Edward Jerningham Wakefield, 1845-1846.* Edited by Joan Stevens, Alexander Turnbull Library, Wellington, 1972

whom he wished to keep fully informed about the progress of the colonising experiment. Some of his earlier letters Home were printed in London in the *New Zealand Journal*, a fortnightly paper issued to publicise the venture. And his letters were read aloud by the family, too, and passed eagerly around the circle of friends who had New Zealand connections.

Almost everything interests Jerningham if it is relevant to successful living in the new land. He makes careful notes of useful facts in his many expeditions—the depth of water at river mouths, the compass bearings of Egmont and other navigational landmarks, the weather, the exact turns and twists of the bush and coastal tracks he followed, the situations of the Maori villages, their tribal affinities, their dominant chiefs. His eye picks out matters of concern to future colonists—that these plains would be good for agriculture, that those uplands would carry sheep, that this river is navigable and leads to good timber. He has great hopes of flax-trading, of steamboats for coastal shipping, of the export of fine native woods, and he notes with an almost personal pride the potatoes, barley, cabbages, rhubarb and flowers which it is possible to grow in the rich Hutt Valley soil.

Equally detailed are his accounts of his dealings with the Maori people. Colonel William Wakefield's vast purchases of land on behalf of the Company were soon the subject of fierce attack by missionaries, governments, and repudiating chiefs. There is a strong element of self-justification therefore in Jerningham's full-dress explanations of the procedure which he and his uncle adopted in these transactions.

Another important part of Jerningham's picture of these years 1839–44 is the political situation, seen by him largely in terms of personalities, 'for' and 'anti' Wakefield. He was not an isolated settler, nor a harassed missionary, but a busy, inquisitive, footloose young man with more brains than balance, and with friends and relations among the ruling 'Gentry'. Politics, moreover, could and did vitally affect his father's colonizing scheme. It is no wonder then, that Jerningham wrote with such one-sided gusto on the political issues of the day. Finally there is the literary motive. Jerningham came from a family of writers, and was well aware that he had a first-class subject. An entry in his 1840–1843 pocket-book reads 'I was more struck than ever at the curious appearance of these large whaling stations. A good description of them would make a graphic and new picture.' 'Graphic' is exactly the word for his self-contained sketch on the whalers, which he has polished into something of a little masterpiece. No wonder he was delighted to find that it interested Peel, as his journal note of 5 May 1845 reveals: 'Sir R. P. reading whale-hunt.' Sometimes Jerningham elaborates his phrasing too much, blurring the vividness of first impressions, as when a jotted note, 'we sat down and had some *Kai*' becomes 'we partook of sustenance'. But on the whole the book gains immeasurably from Jerningham's sense of drama, and he has dovetailed into the narrative with adequate skill the explanatory matter essential for the English reader.

The first edition of *Adventure* ran to over 1,000 pages, in two solid volumes. One reviewer suggested that the work consists really of *two* books: one is 'A History of Partisanship in the New Zealand Colony, by a Partisan', and the other is 'A History of the Practical Working of the Colony of New Zealand, by a Practical Colonist'. This is shrewd judgement. The present abridgement is based on just this fundamental division in Jerningham's subject-matter, except that it proved neither possible nor desirable entirely to omit the 'partisan' element in the book. However distorted Jerningham's versions of some matters may be—as for example his handling of the Wairau 'massacre'—his views were held by others in the colony at the time, and are, therefore, equally as 'historical' as what has later been proved to be the truth. Let the reader take *Adventure* for what it is, one biassed and hot-headed young fellow's record of several exciting years.

Some of the political wrangling has been omitted. Also cut are details of Maori tribal history, geographical data, and repetitive descriptions of the settlements. Minor transitions in the text have been smoothed over without comment, while brief notes indicate more important junctions. Some of Wakefield's footnotes have been retained, some new ones are added, and the spelling of Maori names has been modernised. The aim throughout has been to provide the general reader with a manageable text.

Finally, perhaps, some comments on *Adventure* by the colonists who were its subject matter may alert the reader to the prejudices of the book. Not all who lived in the New Zealand Company settlements from 1839–1844 agreed with Jerningham's picture of the experience, lively and colourful though it is. Here, for instance, is a Wesleyan missionary's opinion. (H. H. Turton, *Wellington Independent*, 4 July 1846.)

'With respect to Mr. Wakefield's work in general, we would simply remark, that from beginning to end, it is one strange commixture of truth and falsehood, plagiary and exaggeration, egotism and vanity; the vehicle of slander and peevishness, and the caricature or exposure of every man's character—*except his own*.'

And on Jerningham's claim that he helped to 'civilise the Maoris', Turton is exceptionally bitter:

'His general intercourse with the natives had but a poor tendency to raise and civilise them. Ridiculing the Missionaries—scoffing at religion—breaking the sabbath—sauntering about in a blanket—singing lewd *hakas* and *waiatas*—galloping about with the females on horseback—and squatting in the warm baths of Taupo, with both sexes, in a state of nudity, for hours together— ... so far from having the least tendency to civilise the Maoris, our Author's general conduct in New Zealand was profligate and debasing in the lowest degree ... open house and midnight orgies at Wanganui ... we compute the number of females whom he has debauched at the awful amount of *half-a-hundred* ...'

and more to the same effect. Turton's reaction is extreme, but it is understandable. Even Jerningham's associates in the New Zealand Company commented on his 'riots and debaucheries' and noted that Colonel William Wakefield, 'although not a Prude or a Puritan, was not altogether pleased at his graceless nephew's pranks'.

Adventure in New Zealand, then, is an informative, vigorous, dashing sort of book, which preserves for us the flavour of the early colonial days. While the historian will always need the full original text, today's general reader should find that this shortened version will provide some admirable reading.

Historical Note

SEVENTY YEARS separate Cook's landfall at Young Nick's Head in October 1769, in the *Endeavour*, and Jerningham Wakefield's at Cape Farewell in August 1839, in the *Tory*. The story of those years is a necessary prelude to Jerningham's record of his adventure.

By 1810, forty years after Cook's discovery, New Zealand was becoming a no man's land, notorious for the lawless violence of white men and of brown. Marsden's Mission at the Bay of Islands in 1814 was followed by those of other churches. Missionary reports, as well as the records of traders and whalers, made New Zealand a name well known in England, where the Ngapuhi chief Hongi was a figure of great interest during his visit in 1820. Hongi returned with muskets, and laid waste much of the North. His example and the pressure of his conquests set all the Maori tribes at war. The guns and ammunition to be gained by trading with the pakeha became a powerful motive in Maori politics.

In 1822 Te Rauparaha, of the Ngatitoa, led his people on their historic migration from Kawhia to the island of Kapiti, which offered a stronghold for both war and trade. Some Ngatiawa from Taranaki and Ngatiraukawa from Taupo joined him and shared in the division of the conquered lands about Cook Strait. With Te Rangihaeata and Te Pehi, Te Rauparaha spread the Ngatitoa terror as far south as Akaroa and Kaiapoi, and by 1839 was the dominant chief from the Wairau to Wanganui.

Meanwhile, in England, men began to think of colonizing these slands of which they heard so much. In 1825 a company was formed in London, and sent out Captain Herd with a party of settlers. He bought land at Hokianga, but the project collapsed. In 1837, with Edward Gibbon Wakefield as its guiding force, a second attempt was made to organize a settlement. Men of ability, wealth, and rank formed the New Zealand Association, later styled the New Zealand Company, and decided to plant English men and the English flag in what was to be a model colony on the Wakefield system. The Hokianga interests were bought up, and the scheme required the purchase of further Maori lands on which the Company could place its emigrants. One feature of the plan on which Wakefield laid great stress was the reservation for the Maoris of one-tenth of the land acquired, a tenth which Wakefield hoped would so rise in value as a result of pakeha settlement that it would compensate the natives for the loss of the rest.

Colonel William Wakefield was appointed agent for the Company to go ahead of the colonists and purchase a suitable site. The plan met, however, with bitter opposition from the missionaries and the Government. The missionaries wanted British law and protection, but they did not want any more white settlement, fearing that it would infringe the rights of the Maori people, and possibly fearing also that full-scale settlement would lessen missionary authority. As for the British Government, it was suspicious of all colonial experiments after the failure of the American one, and felt that it had no legal or moral right to establish a colony in New Zealand without the consent of the natives.

Urged on, then, by the missionaries, the Government consistently blocked Wakefield's plans. But white infiltration into the country continued. Sydney interests were buying in both islands, the French were organizing an expedition to Banks Peninsula. Further extensive land purchases by an organization such as the New Zealand Company threatened to increase the existing disorder. The logic of events convinced the British Government that, however reluctantly, they must take control. Gibbon Wakefield began to fear that there would be a complete prohibition of his enterprise and determined to forestall official action. He probably knew that from as early as December 1838 the Colonial Office had been considering the appointment of Captain Hobson as Consul in New Zealand. In haste, he sent his brother William off in the *Tory* in May 1839, following this up with the despatch in August of the survey ship *Cuba* and in September, of the first immigrant ships. All were to meet at Port Hardy on D'Urville Island in Cook Strait, for it was, of course, not known what land the *Tory* party would buy.

Action on the Colonial Office's proposal of December 1838 was postponed by a change of government, and it was not until July 1839 that Hobson's appointment as Consul in New Zealand was actually made. Then, in terms similar to those drafted six months earlier, Hobson was empowered to treat with the Maoris for the cession to Britain of sovereignty over New Zealand. Maori interests were to be safeguarded. Control of land purchases was insisted on from the outset. Hobson's instructions declared that only those land titles which derived from the Crown or were recognized by the Crown would be valid. The first step was taken on 14th January, 1840, when Hobson was in Sydney. There, Governor Gipps of New South Wales issued a proclamation declaring that after that day any private purchases of land from the Maoris would be invalid.

On his arrival at the Bay of Islands at the end of January two weeks later, Hobson made the next move, negotiating with the Maoris the Treaty of Waitangi, under which sovereignty over the country was ceded to Great Britain. Embodied in the Treaty was a clause prohibiting the buying of land from the Maoris, except through the agency of the Government. News of the Treaty, which was negotiated on 7th February, did not reach the Wellington settlers until early in March. Not long after their arrival, however, they had heard of Governor Gipps's proclamation, which had caused some consternation. Although most of Colonel Wakefield's land purchases had been made fully two months before the date of the proclamation, the Company was nevertheless placed in an awkward position. How much of the land they had bought would be recognized as legally theirs? And how could the settlers, in their turn, be given a valid title to the land they had bought from the Company?

This baffling situation, which developed early in 1840, and which clouded relations between the Government and the Wellington settlers for many years, was not anticipated when young Jerningham Wakefield arrived in New Zealand on 16th August, 1839.

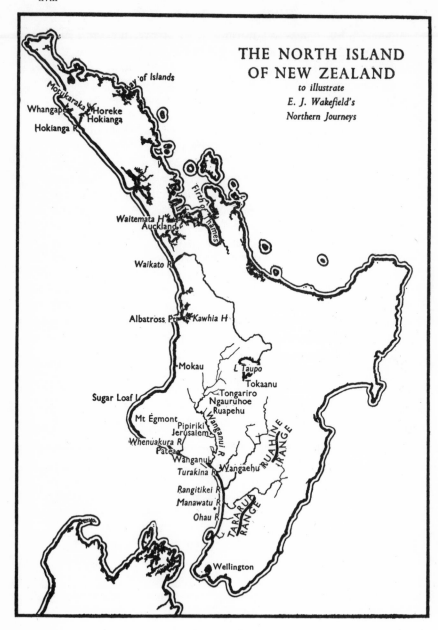

THE NORTH ISLAND
OF NEW ZEALAND
to illustrate
E. J. Wakefield's
Northern Journeys

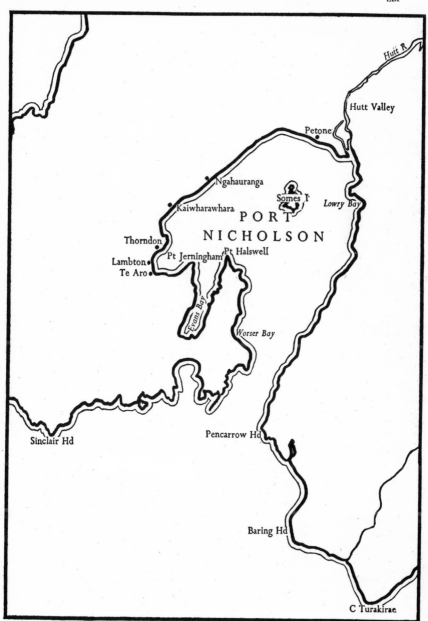

PORT NICHOLSON

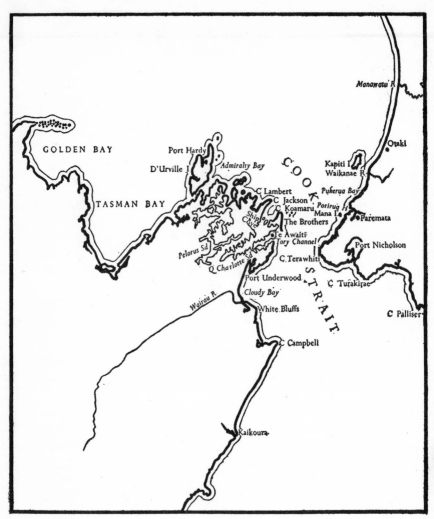

THE COOK STRAIT AREA

CHAPTER I

Beginnings

IN 1837, a society was formed in London, under the name of the New Zealand Association, for the purpose of inducing the British Government to establish a sufficient authority in the islands of New Zealand, and to colonize them according to a plan deliberately prepared with a view of rendering colonization beneficial to the native inhabitants as well as to the settlers.

The author of the plan and founder of the Association was my father, Mr. Edward Gibbon Wakefield; but the members of the Association whose position in public life attracted attention to the project, and whose zealous exertions ultimately saved New Zealand from becoming a French penal colony, were Mr. Francis Baring (the chairman), Lord Durham, Lord Petre, Mr. Bingham Baring, Mr. Campbell of Islay, Mr. Charles Enderby, the munificent promoter of Antarctic discovery, Mr. Ferguson of Raith, the Rev. Dr. Hinds, Mr. Benjamin Hawes, Mr. Philip Howard, Mr. William Hutt, Mr. Lyall, Mr. Mackenzie, Sir William Molesworth, Sir George Sinclair, Sir William Symonds, Mr. Henry George Ward, and Mr. Wolryche Whitmore.

The Association, having matured their plan, but apprehensive of opposition from the Colonial Office, which might nip the project in its bud, addressed themselves to the Prime Minister, Lord Melbourne, with a view of obtaining the sanction of the executive Government: and they imagined themselves to have received such cordial encouragement that they felt justified in collecting a body of intending colonists as an indispensable means of carrying out the undertaking.

Among other steps taken by the Association, were applications to the Church Missionary Society, with a view of establishing a friendly feeling and active co-operation between the two bodies. A deputation waited upon Mr. Dandeson Coates; by whom they were frankly informed, that, 'though he had no doubt of their respectability and the purity of their motives, he was opposed to the colonization of New Zealand in any shape, and was determined to thwart them by all the means in his power.'

When it became necessary to apply to Lord Melbourne the Colonial Minister (Lord Glenelg) spoke on behalf of the Government. He warmly censured every principle of the Association which Lord Melbourne had formerly approved; and above all, disclaimed any right on the part of the British Crown to exercise any sort or degree of authority in New Zealand.

At a subsequent interview, however, Lord Glenelg informed them that very recent dispatches from the Resident in New Zealand, and from the commander of a man-of-war which had visited the coasts, had induced Her Majesty's Government to abandon their objections to the systematic and regulated colonization of the islands; that they still objected to the instrument of colonization proposed by the Association, namely, a Board of Commissioners acting under the immediate control of the Colonial Minister as public officers having no private interest in the matter; but that they were prepared to grant to the Association a Royal Charter of incorporation for colonizing purposes, similar to those under which the English colonies in America were established in the sixteenth and seventeenth centuries. Lord Glenelg further explained, that a condition of the grant of a charter would be the subscription by the Association of a joint-stock capital to be embarked in the undertaking.

Lord Durham declined the offer of a charter, on the ground that members of the Association had invariably and publicly disclaimed all views of pecuniary speculation or interest.

Among the body of intending colonists which had been collected by the Association, were several gentlemen who had disposed of property and abandoned professions with a view to emigrating. These determined to act upon Lord Glenelg's proposal of a charter, and in 1838 exerted themselves to form a joint-stock company. They were joined by many members of the now defunct Association. Thus was formed the New Zealand Land Company of 1839.

The Government, however, exhibited even a greater hostility to this body than to the Association which it succeeded. It only remained, therefore, to adopt the views of the Colonial Office by considering New Zealand as a foreign country, and by proceeding to acquire land and form settlements in the manner hitherto sanctioned by the Crown. With this view, and in accordance with the alleged national sovereignty of the native chiefs, they resolved to send an expedition to New Zealand under the direction of an agent, instructed to adopt the usual method of acquiring land from the natives, but if possible upon a far greater scale than was ever necessary for the purposes of cultivation or even of speculation by individuals. This charge was confided to an uncle of mine, Colonel William Wakefield. He was further instructed to select the spot which he should deem most eligible as the site of a considerable colony, and to make preparations for the arrival and settlement of the emigrants.

A fine vessel of 400 tons, the *Tory*, was bought and prepared for the voyage. She was armed with eight guns, and small-arms for all the ship's company; filled with the necessary stores, provisions, and goods for barter with the New Zealanders; and manned with a strong and select crew.

Such a voyage seemed to offer much novelty and adventure; and I, being then nineteen years old, conceived an eager desire to be one of the party. My father gave his consent to my departure; and I was fortunate enough to obtain a passage in the *Tory* from the patrons of the enterprise.

A body of intending colonists was already collected; and they were to follow the first expedition even before hearing of its proceedings. A rendezvous was appointed for the 10th of January, 1840, in Port Hardy, a harbour in Cook's Strait, which was known to be good for the largest ships. I intended to see the landing of the first body of colonists, and then to return in one of the ships which should have borne them to their destination. So interesting, however, did it become to watch the first steps of the infant colony, and so exciting to march among the ranks of its hardy founders, that I was tempted to postpone my return for four years after their arrival. I can only explain this by the narrative contained in subsequent chapters.

CHAPTER II

Landfall at Cook Strait

ALL OUR equipments and preparations being at length complete, we sailed from Plymouth on the 12th of May 1839.

The ship was commanded by Mr. Edmund Mein Chaffers, of the Royal Navy, who had been acting master of H.M.S. *Beagle* during the survey of Cape Horn and voyage round the world, performed by Captain FitzRoy between the years 1830 and 1836.

Besides Colonel Wakefield and myself, the following gentlemen were passengers on board: Doctor Ernest Dieffenbach, a native of Berlin, who had been appointed naturalist to the Company; Mr. Charles Heaphy, the Company's draughtsman; Mr. John Dorset, who had been promised the appointment of colonial surgeon; Nayti,* a New Zealander, who had been residing during two years in my father's house in London, and who was to act as interpreter; Mr. Richard Lowry, the chief mate; and Mr. George F. Robinson, the surgeon of the ship.

In the steerage were Robert Doddrey, who had formerly visited some parts of the coast of New Zealand in a trading schooner from Van Diemen's Land, and who was engaged as storekeeper and additional interpreter; the second and third mates; and Colonel Wakefield's servant, besides the steward and his cabin-boys.

Petty officers and foremast hands, among whom were a New Zealander and a native of the Marquesas Islands, made up our total muster-roll to thirty-five souls.

The *Tory* sailed remarkably well. We crossed the line, in 26° 50′ W. longitude, on the twenty-sixth day from Plymouth, passed the longitude of the Cape of Good Hope on the 10th of July, and

*Ngatai.

saw the high land of New Zealand on the 16th of August, about noon. We established during the voyage a weekly manuscript newspaper, and a debating society. These recreations, and an ample supply of useful and interesting books, caused the time to pass cheerfully enough. Vocabularies of the Maori or New Zealand language were also constructed from Nayti's dictation; and lessons to him in English spelling, many a deep game of chess, and an occasional *battue* of the albatrosses and other marine birds, which abound in the high latitudes between the Cape of Good Hope and Van Diemen's Land, beguiled the leisure time. These *battues* partook of shooting and fishing; for sometimes we baited large hooks with bits of pork, and caught the gigantic birds by the beak. I remember one day seeing twenty-eight live albatrosses on the deck together, many of them measuring twelve feet from tip to tip of the wings.

The land which we first sighted proved to be the western coast of the Middle Island, not far south of Cape Farewell. A remarkable white fissure in the mountains forms a distinguishing land-mark at a great distance.

Having fairly entered the middle of Cook's Strait by sunset, we hove to with a fresh N.W. breeze till daylight. Once or twice during the night we found soundings in about fifty fathoms. This was conjectured to be near the mouth of Blind Bay.*

In the morning of the 17th we proceeded to the eastward. When I came on deck we had land in sight on both bows. Bearing away for the southern land, we soon made out Stephens Island, and passed within five or six miles of it. As we ran along the coast, D'Urville's Island, the Admiralty Islands, Point Lambert, and Point Jackson were successively recognized from Cook's chart. The high rugged land of the Middle Island, which had at a distance appeared barren and sprinkled with rocks, proved on closer inspection to be clothed with the most luxuriant forest. As we neared Point Jackson, the breeze died away, and we remained for a time becalmed in the entrance of Queen Charlotte's Sound. Cape Koamaru (Koemaroo of Cook) and the Brothers, Entry Island [Kapiti], and the mainland on the north coast of Cook's Strait, were now very distinctly visible; a bright warm sun gave the most charming

* This was Captain Cook's name for what is now called Tasman Bay.

appearance to the romantic shores of the Sound; and we exclaimed against the calm which seemed likely to detain us another night at sea. Two or three of the most impatient got into the cutter, and pulled towards Point Jackson, to try and catch some fish; but they had not got far before a light air sprang up, and we glided into the Sound. The tide favouring us, they had some trouble in over-taking the ship. The scenery became more and more majestic as we advanced into this noble estuary. Its outer mouth is nine miles wide. High wooded mountains rise on both sides; numerous islands and projecting points dot the expanse of still water which penetrates far into the interior; and a glimpse of the Southern Alps is obtained in the extreme distance. We proceeded between Long Island and Motuara. The former, a narrow ridge bare of wood, was crowned with native fortifications; a small *pa* or fort was also visible on the south point of Motuara. As we entered the Sound, we saw four canoes under sail, coming from the westward. Before we anchored for the night in the S.E. entrance of Ship Cove, another canoe came paddling off to us, containing eight natives. We at first thought they hesitated about venturing near us; but it turned out that they were only stopping to bale out their canoe, which was a very ill-constructed affair. As they came alongside the ship, which had almost stopped her way, the canoe was lashed to the chains, and the men scrambled on deck with great activity. We were at first startled by the quickness with which this was done, and by their wild, half-naked appearance. All our anticipations had not prepared us thoroughly for this first meeting; and our friend Nayti was so quiet and silent in his manners, that the contrast of their demeanour was striking. They ran about shaking hands with everybody they met, and seemed to consider their appearance as a matter of course. One of them, a tall muscular young man, ran to assist the helmsman, and seemed proud to display some knowledge of nautical terms and the manœuvres of a ship. They all spoke more or less broken English, and chattered in a sort of authoritative way about the best anchorage, giving themselves quite the airs belonging to a pilot. They had brought on board some fish and potatoes, which we bought for a little tobacco. Night closed in as we let go our anchor, and they returned to their village.

August 18th.—This morning, at daylight, we had warped farther into the cove, and anchored in 11 fathoms, muddy bottom, within 300 yards of the shore, where we fastened a hawser to a tree; thus occupying probably the same spot as Captain Cook, in his numerous visits to this harbour.* There were a good many natives on board already; but, eager to touch the land, I got into a small canoe with Nayti, who paddled me ashore. The hills, which rise to the height of 1000 or 1500 feet on three sides of the cove, are covered from their tops to the water's edge with an undulating carpet of forest. How well Cook has described the harmony of the birds at this very spot! Every bough seemed to throng with feathered musicians, and the melodious chimes of the bell-bird were especially distinct. At the head of the cove is a small level space of land, formed by the alluvial deposit of three rills from the mountains, which here empty themselves into the bay. Landing here, I remained for some time absorbed in contemplating the luxurious vegetation of grass and shrubs, and the wild carrots and turnips which remain as relics of our great navigator. Rich historical recollections crowded on my mind as I tried to fix on the exact spot where Cook's forge and carpenter's shop had stood; and I was only roused from my reverie by the arrival of some more of the party, bent on the same object. We collected some shells, pebbles, and plants, and returned to breakfast on fresh potatoes and some of the fish which had been caught in abundance from the ship in the evening.

The four canoes which we had seen yesterday arrived this morning, and came alongside the ship. They came from Admiralty Bay, and were bound to Cloudy Bay, with pigs and potatoes for sale.

We went ashore again after prayers, and admired the luxurious vegetation. The wood on the sides of the hills appeared almost impenetrable from the thick web of supple-jacks and creepers. We found no natives, the cove being under *tapu*, on account of its being the burial-place of a daughter of Te Pehi, the late chief of the Kapiti, or Entry Island, natives. Those who visited us came from a cove a little farther north, called Cannibal Cove by Cook, and Anaho by the natives. They are called the Ngatihinetuhi tribe, and their principal chief was named Ngarewa, or 'The Straight Trees'.

* Ship Cove.

August 19th.—The work of filling our water-casks and refitting the ship commenced to-day. The storekeeper was very busy laying in a stock of potatoes and pigs from the natives. A pipe bought a basket of potatoes weighing 20 lbs., and a red blanket bought three good-sized pigs. These terms, too, were considered liberal on our part. In the afternoon we went over in the boat to Motuara, the island on which Cook had his observatory and garden. It commands a fine view of the northern part of the Sound, Entry Island, and the high land near Cape Terawhiti. The island had a very gay appearance, being covered with wild shrubs and flowers like an ornamental plantation. We fell in with plenty of pigeons, parrots, and other birds, which our guns soon made to contribute to the table and to the collection of the delighted naturalist. None of the natives live here; but they turn pigs loose on the island, and catch them as they are wanted.

The chief Ngarewa, with his wife, and his son Te Horo, a nice intelligent lad of thirteen, remained to dinner with us to-day. Their behaviour was very respectable: they ate heartily of everything, but drank little, the father warning Te Horo against too much wine. Nayti seemed much pleased at our kind treatment of his countrymen. He was at first ashamed of their rude appearance, and often apologized to us for it. He seemed, too, suspicious and afraid of them, and inclined to cling to us in consequence.

During the next few days we made great friends with the natives. The barter went on alongside; Ngarewa remained on deck or in the cabin amusing himself with a pipe and a book of prints, or trying to understand and answer our inquiries about his place and people. He did not appear to have much influence on the latter, and at any rate never exerted it. Te Horo guided us on shooting excursions up the sides of the hills, or joined our fishing parties to the next cove to the south, where we always had a good haul with our sean.* The women of the village had almost all removed to Ship Cove, where they eagerly undertook the task of washing our clothes.

On the 22nd we took Ngarewa home to his village in our whale-boat, after he had received from my uncle a gun and some other small presents. We found the village of Anaho in a level piece of ground at the head of Cannibal Cove, and were much amused by

* Seine net.

seeing the *whare puni*, or sleeping houses, of the natives. These are exceedingly low; and covered with earth, on which weeds very often grow. They resemble, in shape and size, a hot-bed with the glass off. A small square hole at one end is the only passage for light or air. I intended to creep into one of them to examine it; but had just got my head in, and was debating within myself by what snake-like evolution I should best succeed in getting my body to follow, when I was deterred by the intense heat and intolerable odour from proceeding. One large house in the village, with wattled walls plastered with clay, we were told belonged to an Englishman then in Cloudy Bay. The natives use it for a common habitation during the day, and assemble in it to prayers every morning and evening. They all came out to greet us with the constant shake of the hand.

A mischief-making native tried to annoy us by threats and extortions of payment for wood and water, on account of the *tapu* of Ship Cove. He persisted in his violent demands; and early one morning came alongside in a canoe, and carried away our fishing-sean, having first pushed over one of the apprentices who was in the boat. Captain Chaffers went on shore with an armed boat to demand instant restitution of the net; and found that our tor-mentor had enlisted the feelings of the other natives in his favour. They were sullen and reserved, and refused to give it up at first.

Their appearance, and the fact that many fresh natives were ashore, induced Captain Chaffers to return on board, and prepare the ship for an emergency. The guns were shotted, the crew armed, sentries placed at the gangways, and a spring put on the cable so that the ship's broadside might be brought to bear on the beach where the natives were encamped. During these pre-parations, one or two large war-canoes came round the northern point of the cove, and dashed in to the beach at great speed, the rowers singing in time with their paddles. A single canoe, full of natives, now came off to the ship. As they silently paddled round the stern, we observed that some carried their tomahawks and greenstone clubs or *mere pounamu*. The others kept their blankets and mats wrapped over everything but their heads. Our original persecutor was the first who attempted to ascend the ladder, tomahawk in hand; but he was startled to find at the top a sentry with a musket and bayonet, and my uncle, who quietly but firmly told him to go ashore, and that he would allow no natives to come on board armed. 'Dogskin', as we had nicknamed him from his wearing a mat of that material, seemed inclined to persist in his intention of getting on deck; but the sight of the end of a pistol sticking out of my uncle's coat-pocket suddenly made him change his mind; and he descended into the canoe, which pulled slowly back to the shore. A smaller canoe next came off, with only a boy paddling, and an old chief whom we had not yet seen, who showed that he was unarmed, and requested to be allowed to come on board. This was complied with; and the old gentleman introduced himself as Te Whetu, or 'the Star'. He told us that he came from Rangitoto, which we afterwards discovered to be in D'Urville's Island, and that he was waiting in a bay north of Cannibal Cove for fair weather to cross the strait to Kapiti, in order to be present at a grand *tangi*, or mourning feast, over the death of a sister of Te Rauparaha, the great chief at that place. He explained to us that every one would cry very much, and that then there would be much *kai kai* or feasting. He asserted, though, that we ought to pay for the *tapu*; but suggested as an amendment, that the *utu*, or 'payment', should be handed to him instead of 'Dogskin'. We therefore concluded that the demand was altogether unjust, and a mere bullying attempt at extortion.

Te Whetu appeared to be about sixty years old, but he was still wiry and strong. He was very amusing and fond of conversation. He declared himself 'no missionary', and said he had four wives, the fifth having lately died. Having inquired how many the Kings of England had, he laughed heartily at finding that they were not so well provided, and repeatedly counted 'four *wahine*' (women) on his fingers. We gave the natives a small present of tobacco, recovered the seine, and soon restored friendship, as they had become tired of being excluded from their market on board. Te Whetu took kindly to the cabin-table, where covers were always laid for him and Ngarewa's family, who had taken no part whatever in the disturbances. The natives were rather puzzled at our display of force, and my uncle's firmness on the occasion excited general respect among them. They had previously described us as a missionary ship; many of them having taken notice of our observance of the Sunday, and some having attended our service on that day. They now, however, said we were half-missionary, half-soldier. A native missionary teacher, named William, assembled the natives who were on board to prayers several evenings. Te Whetu always sat apart when this took place. No further attempts at extortion were made; and Te Whetu told a canoe-full of his people, who attempted to come on board one morning, that they were not wanted, and that he was very comfortable where he was.

On the 28th, my uncle sent Doddrey, the storekeeper, with a native guide, to a village at the southern entrance of Queen Charlotte's Sound, which Nayti and also the resident natives described as containing a hundred white men, with three *rangatira*, or 'chiefs'. In the afternoon of the following day, he returned in a whale-boat with two Englishmen. One was named Williams, and was carpenter at the village in question, where he said there were about sixty Europeans or Americans living by whaling. The other was named Arthur [Elmslie], and owned the meeting-house in Anaho village. Both brought their native wives with them. That of Arthur belongs to the village, and he generally lives there in the summer. It was now, however, the season for whaling, in which pursuit we learnt that he was engaged; and he was in consequence living at Te Awaiti, whence the boat came.

The crew of the whale-boat consisted of young native men, dressed in the costume of European seamen; and we heard that a great many of them are employed in the boats by the whalers.

The arrival of our countrymen produced a great change in the deportment of the natives. They now cringed to our new guests, who took but little notice of them; and the obnoxious 'Dogskin' disappeared. The newcomers confirmed our idea that the demand of *utu* was a mere extortion, and were much amused at the relation of our alarm and warlike demonstration. They told us that the natives were always ready to take advantage of inexperienced visitors in this way.

We could do nothing here towards attaining our object, which was to select and purchase a location suitable for the emigrants whom we expected to follow us in January. Neither Ngarewa nor

Te Whetu could give us any distinct information as to the owner-ship of the land in this neighbourhood. They both spoke of Te Rauparaha as the great chieftain to whom they were in a measure tributary; but they seemed to agree that Te Hiko, the son of Te Pehi, had the best right to the land here. Neither, however, was described as having an absolute right to dispose of land; and the vested rights appeared to us to be involved in much confusion. Our white friends could not clear up our doubts; and, moreover, it was plain that although the immediate vicinity of Ship Cove could boast of excellent harbours and sublime scenery, it was not at all suited for a large European colony. My uncle therefore determined to avail himself of the services of Williams and Arthur in piloting the vessel to Te Awaiti, where we might acquire more information.

While we remained at anchor in Ship Cove, Dr. Dieffenbach had ascended two of the hills which bound the bay. On the first expedi-tion he was accompanied by Mr. Heaphy, the artist, and Te Horo. They emerged from the forest into a coppice of fern, ten feet high, which clothed the upper part of the hill. After a tedious scramble through this, they reached the summit, and were rewarded by a panoramic view of the numerous bays and coves of Queen Char-lotte's Sound, dotted with many islands, and the northern shore of Cook's Strait. It was impossible not to be struck by the majesty of this primæval forest.

August 31st.—The weather, which had been very boisterous, with much rain, during the last few days, cleared up this morning. Having completed most of our refittings, and laid in a good stock of potatoes and water, we weighed anchor at 10 in the morning, and stood up the Sound with a light wind and favouring tide. We bade adieu to our friends the natives, and set Te Whetu and Ngarewa ashore as we got under way. We were, however, accom-panied by the native teacher William, and by the native who had sprung to the wheel on our first·arrival. The latter, whose native name was Whare, had made himself a general favourite on board, and had apparently taken a fancy to the ship; for he installed himself among the men without any agreement, and joined in all the work without any recompense but his meals and a little tobacco. His activity and mirth, together with the rich humour

which he displayed in executing some of the native dances, as
well as in mimicking almost every one on board, earned for him
the sobriquet of 'Jim Crow', which he retained during the whole
time that he stuck to the ship.

At 3 p.m. we reached the entrance of the channel which joins
the Sound with Cook's Strait to the eastward. The entrance is
about a mile wide; and the channel, which was christened Tory
Channel after Captain Chaffers had surveyed it, turns first to the
east, and then to the north-east, thus insulating but a narrow
strip of land, and running nearly parallel to the Sound for the
greater part of its course. At sunset we anchored off the village
of Te Awaiti, or 'The Little River'. The whalers, who have a
rough way of pronouncing the native language, have hardened
this name into Tarwhite.

As soon as we arrived, Mr. Richard Barrett,* who was at the
head of one of the whaling parties, came off in his boat to us.
We had been highly amused at the comfortable obesity of Williams,
and considered him a promising sample of the good effects of New
Zealand feeding. What was our surprise on finding Dicky Barrett,
as he is generally called, as much stouter in person as he was
shorter! Dressed in a white jacket, blue dungaree trousers, and
round straw hat, he seemed perfectly round all over; while his
jovial, ruddy face, twinkling eyes, and good-humoured smile, could
not fail to excite pleasure in all beholders. And a merry party it
was to look upon, as we sat round a bottle of grog on the cabin-
table, listening to the relation of the wild adventures and 'hair-
breadth 'scapes' of Barrett and his two fellow-whalers.

Barrett had been in New Zealand for ten or twelve years: first
as a flax-trader at the Sugar-loaf Islands near Taranaki, or Mount
Egmont, where, with ten other white men, he joined the native
inhabitants in their desperate resistance to the invasion of the
Waikato tribes; and during the last five years as a whaler at this
spot.

The acquaintance and assistance of Dicky Barrett promised to

* Richard Barrett was an English sailor who settled at the Sugar Loaf Islands, New Plymouth, in 1828, among the Ngatiawa people. He married the chief's daughter, and with
Jack Love, Te Wharepouri, and Te Puni, held out in the famous siege of Ngamotu *pa* in
1831, during the Waikato invasions of Taranaki. In 1834, with the survivors, he migrated
to the Cook Strait area, first to Port Nicholson, then to Te Awaiti.

be most advantageous to us, as he was related by his wife to all the influential chiefs living at Port Nicholson. This was one of the spots to which the instructions of the Company particularly directed the attention of their agent, as being likely, from the description given by Nayti and other persons who had visited it, to prove a suitable spot for the establishment of the future colony. Barrett's account fully confirmed this idea; and he, after having been made acquainted with our views and projects, expressed himself willing to second them with all his ability. He was thoroughly acquainted with the feelings and customs of the natives, as well as their language.

We also learnt from him in how unsettled a state was the proprietorship of land about Cook's Strait. The country had been conquered about fourteen years before by the Kawhia tribe [the Ngatitoa]. They had almost exterminated the Muaupoko, Rangitane, and Ngatiapa, who were the original occupiers. And even the spots now occupied were in dispute between the conquerors and the Ngatiawa, who followed nine years afterwards in their track. As we did not propose to take possession of any territory without a positive sanction on the part of the natives, it was determined that Barrett should explain our views to them. He confessed that they would be sure to accept a payment, and that certainly they had a right to it, as we should probably include villages and cultivations in such large districts as we proposed to buy. A very important part of our projected plan was, to reserve a tenth portion of the land bought by us for the benefit and use of the natives. We had it in view thus to secure a valuable property to them, which might preserve their chiefs in circumstances equal to those of the higher order of settlers in future times.

September 1st, Sunday.—After prayers on board, we landed and visited the whaling-town of Te Awaiti. Dicky Barrett's house was on a knoll at the far end of it, and overlooked the whole settlement and anchorage. There were about twenty houses presented to our view; the walls generally constructed of wattled supple-jack, called *kareao*, filled in with clay; the roof thatched with reeds; and a large unsightly chimney at one of the ends, constructed of either the same materials as the walls, or of stones heaped together by rude masonry. Dicky Barrett's house, or *whare* as it is called in

Maori or native language, was a very superior edifice, built of sawn timber, floored and lined inside, and sheltered in front by an ample veranda. A long room was half full of natives and whalers. His wife Rangi, a fine stately woman, gave us a dignified welcome; his pretty half-caste children laughed and commented on our appearance, to some of their mother's relations, in their own language. He had three girls of his own, and had adopted a son of an old trader and friend of his named Jacky Love, who was on his death-bed, regretted by the natives as one of themselves. He had married a young chieftainess of great rank, and his son Dan was treated with that universal respect and kindness to which he was entitled by the character of his father and the rank of his mother.

We found Williams's *whare* in the centre of the town; and Arthur Elmslie's perched up on a pretty terrace on the side of the northern hill which slopes from the valley. A nice clear stream runs through the middle of the settlement. Some few of the whalers were dressed out in their clean Sunday clothes: but a large gang were busy at the try-works, boiling out the oil from the blubber of a whale lately caught. It appears that this is a process in which any delay is injurious. The try-works are large iron boilers, with furnaces beneath. Into these the blubber is put, being cut into lumps of about two feet square, and the oil is boiled out. The residue is called the scrag, and serves to feed the fire. The oil is then run into coolers, and finally into casks ready for shipping. The men were unshaven and uncombed, and their clothes covered with dirt and oil. Most of them were strong muscular men. The whole ground and beach about here was saturated with oil, and the stench of the carcasses and scraps of whale-flesh lying about in the bay was intolerable.

Another man, heading a whaling-party here, was nicknamed 'Geordie Bolts'. His real name was Joseph Toms; but being crippled in an encounter with a whale, he had the fame of never having been able to face one since; and hence the *nom de guerre*. He was married to a near relation of Rauparaha, and by means of this alliance maintained another whaling station at a harbour called Porirua, on the main between the islands of Kapiti and Mana.

In a bay separated by a low tongue of land from the main valley of Te Awaiti, we found another whaler named Jimmy Jackson, who had a snug little cove to himself. He was positively equal in dimensions to Williams and Barrett both together. He had been, we found, ten years here, being one of the first settlers. He declared the Pelorus river to be an excellent place for a settlement; and offered to introduce my uncle to an old friend of his in Cloudy Bay, Jack Guard, who knew the native owners of that district, and who piloted H.M.S. *Pelorus* in her trips about the Strait. We had read an account in the papers, just before we left England, of the discovery by this vessel of a large river and fine district opening into Cloudy Bay; and we were anxious to examine it for ourselves.

During the next four days we had ample opportunities of observing everything remarkable at Te Awaiti and its neighbour-hood, and of learning many particulars of its first foundation and subsequent history.

The above-named John Guard was the first who entered the south-eastern mouth of the channel, two miles east of our present anchorage, in a small sealing vessel. This was in 1827. Having been driven in by a gale of wind, he built a house, and carried on sealing and whaling, with great risk and annoyance from the natives, and no great profit for a long while. The natives, in a constant state of war (for this was just at the epoch of Rauparaha's invasion), were so ill-provided with potatoes or indeed any kind of provisions, that our adventurers subsisted for some time on whale's flesh and wild turnip-tops; and often, for want of workmen and tools, they could not save the oil, having no casks, and kept only the bone, which they sold on the rare occasions when they could find a market on board vessels from Sydney. The Ngaitahu tribe, in their predatory incursions, frequently destroyed their houses and all their property, along with that of the natives. One old hand, now in Te Awaiti, had had his house burnt down no fewer than four times.

Since 1831, however, when whaling-ships began to resort to Cloudy Bay, Sydney merchants worked the stations there and at other places on the coast by means of agents. They paid nominally £10 per ton for the oil, and £60 per ton for the bone, finding casks and freight themselves. The wages of the whalers, however, were paid in slops, spirits, and tobacco, at an exorbitant profit. A pound of tobacco, worth 1s. 3d. in Sydney, was valued at 5s. and sometimes 7s. 6d. here, and other things in the same proportion. The men, a mixture of runaway sailors and escaped convicts, sign an agreement at the beginning of the season, in which these prices are stated, so that they cannot go elsewhere to work, and must submit to these terms. The season lasts from the first of May to the beginning of October. In these five months, a whaler can earn £35 if the season be good; but all depends on the success of the fishery; as, if there were no whales caught, there would be no pay, and the only wages consist in a share of the produce.

The artisans seemed to be the best off. Carpenters and black-smiths get 10s. a day, and insist upon payment in money. Williams had amassed a good deal in this way, and having laid it out in purchasing goods of all sorts from whale-ships, he drove a good trade on shore, knowing whom to trust.

We were told that the different whaling parties on both shores of Cook's Strait, near Banks's Peninsula, and still further south, were reckoned to procure 1200 tons of oil annually, and that about 500 white men were employed in the pursuit.

The more industrious of the whalers, during the summer, pro-cure supplies of pigs and potatoes from the natives, and make large profits by disposing of them again to the whale-ships which look in at the different harbours previous to going out on the whaling-grounds, or returning home full. The less active spend the summer at the village of their native women, either cultivating a patch of ground which the natives have tacitly allowed them to take possession of, or depending entirely on their native connexions for fish and potatoes, and drinking out the extent of their credit with the agent in the strongest and most poisonous liquors.

Much rivalry is of course engendered by the nature of the whaler's occupation. Fierce quarrels and wild orgies were to be met with both day and night; and never, perhaps, was there a community composed of such dangerous materials and so devoid of regular law. The law of the strong in mind and body was, however, in force. Some few men of iron will and large limb ruled to a considerable degree the lawless assemblage, and maintained a powerful influence by their known courage and prowess, whether in the whale-boat or the fight on shore. Some few, too, though very few, like Dicky Barrett, were respected for their kindhearted-ness to all.

The redeeming quality of hospitality we found unbounded among them; a stranger was always welcome to a share of the meal, a drop of the grog, and a seat on a stool, made of a whale's vertebra, in the ample chimney-corner.

There were about twenty-five half-caste children at Te Awaiti. They were all strikingly comely, and many of them quite fair, with light hair and rosy cheeks; active and hardy as the goats with which the settlement also swarmed. The women of the whalers were remarkable for their cleanliness and the order which they preserved in their companion's house. They were most of them dressed in loose gowns of printed calico, and their hair, generally very fine, was always clean and well-combed. It was evident that the whaler's seamanlike habit of cleanliness had not been abandoned; and that they had effected that change at least in their women, who seemed proud of belonging to a white man, and had often, we were informed, protected their men from aggres-sion or robbery.

§

September 6th.—Mr. Guard having arrived from Cloudy Bay in a strong sailing-boat, I determined to accompany my uncle, and we started for the Hoiere or Pelorus river.

September 7th.—We now perceived the entrance to the estuary of the Pelorus river [i.e., Pelorus Sound]. Half-way up the hill which forms the south head, we saw five head of wild cattle, the descendants of some given to the Kapiti natives a few years before by a Sydney merchant, in payment for a cargo of flax. The estuary is about a mile wide at the entrance, but immediately expands. For forty miles we continued to advance along this magnificent arm of the sea, which only differed from Queen Charlotte's Sound in the grander scale on which are the mountains, the woods, and the spacious bays and harbours branching out in every direction. So numerous and varied in their forms are these ramifications, that it would be easy to mistake the track to the fresh-water river. The whole scene forms a labyrinth on an immense scale, in which you may lose your way among tortuous paths of water two or three miles broad, and between hedges composed of mountains from 2000 to 3000 feet in height, clothed to the summits with the most luxuriant and majestic timber. Even our pilot guided himself in some of the most intricate passes by watching the set of the tide. Having reached at sunset to within a mile of the spot where H.M.S. *Pelorus* anchored, we again encamped on a shingly beach in a bay on the east side of the Sound. At this spot there were some ten or fifteen acres of level ground, on which we were shown the remains of a large *pa*, once the head-quarters of the tribe conquered and almost exterminated by Rauparaha. Our friend Charley borrowed one of the fowling-pieces to shoot a pigeon which was perched close to us. He would not fire until he had got the end of the gun six yards from it, and consequently blew it to pieces. He seemed proud, however, of his dexterity in having crept so close without disturbing the bird. The wood-pigeons of this country are as stupid as the tree-partridges of North America, and, especially in these unfrequented parts, are not easily disturbed. We therefore indulged in some good-natured raillery at Charley's expense. These birds are very large, of brilliant plumage, and extremely well flavoured. We had laid our blankets on the shingly beach, which makes an excellent mattress; and were rather alarmed in the night by the tide, which, on rising, extinguished the fire at our feet.

September 8th.—Soon after starting this morning, we passed the mouths of two deep bays, which stretch far to the east and south-east. The natives told us that at the head of these are necks of land over which the natives haul their canoes into the head of Queen Charlotte's Sound and the Wairau river respectively. This latter empties itself into Cloudy Bay, south of Port Underwood. We had now reached the fresh water, and were steering between extensive mud-flats, from among which we disturbed countless flocks of wild ducks of different sorts.

We were soon ascending against the current of a rapid and narrow stream, forming numerous islands covered with an abundance of shrubs and scattered trees; the hills close in upon the valley in places. The *pitau*, or tree-ferns, growing like a palm-tree, form a distinguishing ornament of the New Zealand forest. In these natural shrubberies, too, and especially in wet situations, a kind of cabbage-tree, called *ti* by the natives, flourishes in great abundance. Its branches are covered with distinct bunches of long fibrous leaves, which grow in an erect position. The *kowhai*, too, a species of mimosa, covered with bright yellow blossoms, abounds in such situations. As we proceeded, the boat had frequently to be tracked over shallows and rapids, the natives leaping readily into the water for this purpose. Just before we reached our destination for the night, we fell in with a party of the Rangitane, or tributary natives. These came to our assistance at the last severe rapid, and obeyed, in apparent fear and trembling, every direction of Charley and the other members of the victorious tribe. They had ascended hither from Anakoha Bay, in order to collect flax and work it into mats as part of their tribute to Rauparaha; and had formed a temporary encampment on a shingly island covered with high flax of the finest kind.

When we lay down for the night, our attendant natives begged us to examine our fire-arms and hatchets, and to keep them close to our hands, ready for use. As Jacky Guard himself did not neglect the injunction, we also complied; but we were not disturbed from a sound sleep until early daylight, when I was awoke by some heavy drops of dew falling on my face from the overhanging branches, where they had collected during the night. The birds, too, had begun their cheerful hymn.

My uncle and I took our usual morning plunge, and experienced the sharp cold of the stream, which takes its source among snowy mountains. The natives and Guard stood in great astonishment on the bank, and had a hearty laugh as we rushed out, shivering and nearly blue. As the boat could proceed no further on account of the shallowness of the river, we obtained a canoe and experienced guides from among the slave tribe, and pushed slowly up the stream, wishing to ascertain whether the valley, now narrowed to little more than a mile, expanded into the interior, as we had been led to expect from the account of the officers of the *Pelorus* and the unbounded praises of Jacky Guard. The canoe was hollowed out of a single tree, and propelled by alternate paddling, poling, and tracking, as the different parts of the river required. Our guides seemed much astonished at everything new about us and our equipments. At a halt which we made about mid-day for a meal, some of them wished to taste the brandy which we put into the water. The scene that ensued baffles description. They made frightful grimaces, held their throats with both hands, and rushed down to the river with a yell, to plunge their gaping mouths and watering eyes into the clear stream. I am convinced that they had never before tasted ardent liquors, and that they would not readily acquire the taste for them. The river was no longer navigable even for our small canoe, after getting, with great trouble, eight miles from last night's camp. We reached some miles further than the officers of the *Pelorus* had penetrated with Guard, and then retraced our steps, after setting fire in pure mischief to the fern. The blaze spread far and wide, and its glare was perceptible all night from our camp. On the way up we had passed the remains of another large *pa*, built on a spot apparently safe from inundation. Old painted posts and carved monuments rose mournfully from among the tangled grass and briars, claiming respect for a certain venerable appearance of antiquity. The pretty situation under the hill-side, the rich vegetation of the spot under a glowing sun, and the solitary and decaying relics, told the whole history of Rauparaha's devastating raid, which was not belied by the dejected air with which our guides pointed out the resting-place of their fathers.

Moving down a little further to-night, we made a tent of the boat's sail close to the flax-collecting encampment. We here saw this magnificent plant in perfection. Each plant consisted of some forty or fifty leaves resembling those of our flag, from two to four inches in breadth, and reaching to the length of eight or nine feet. The leaves diverge from the root, and two or three flower-stems also shoot from the ground. These, however, had only begun to sprout. The leaves are all folded in two longitudinally, thus giving an inner and outer side to the leaf; but when it has attained its full growth, it sometimes opens out, although never so as to lie perfectly flat. The inner side has a natural gloss, while the outer side is dull. The natives seemed to prefer the innermost leaves, cutting them at about a foot from the ground with a sharp mussel-shell, of which they had brought a large stock from the sea-side. When a quantity of leaves had been collected, they proceeded to a division of employments. Some split the leaf longitudinally along the fold above mentioned, and a second gang cut the dull or outer side of each half-leaf nearly through transversely about midway along its length. For this operation, which is rather delicate and requires experience, a small cockle-shell was used. The art appeared to be to cut through all but the fibres, which border closely on the glossy portion. The half-leaves, thus prepared, were handed to a third workman. He, taking a bundle of them in his left hand at the transverse cut, and spreading them out like a fan, with the glossy side upwards, took a mussel-shell between the finger and thumb of his right hand to perform the next operation. This consists in giving each half-leaf a longitudinal scrape from the transverse cut in the middle to each end. He held the leaves extended by seizing the ends of each in succession with his big toe. Flax-scraping is always performed in a sitting posture, and one foot works quite as hard as either of the hands. The dexterity and quickness with which this whole operation was performed drew from us repeated exclamations of delight, of which the performers seemed not a little proud. The result of the scrape is to make about five-sixths of the leaf, beginning from the dull side, drop off on to the ground in two pieces. The fibres which compose the glossy surface remain in the hand of the operator, of the full length of the leaf, and he puts them aside, and proceeds with another bunch. The splitters and transverse-cutters worked faster than the scrapers, and when they had operated on all that was gathered, they also took up their mussel-shell and scraped in their turn. The short pieces which I have described as dropping on to the ground were treated as refuse, and allowed to dry or rot; the full-length fibre of the glossy side alone being preserved to undergo further processes previous to manufacture into mats. The only use that I have ever seen made of the short refuse is for the outer portion of a rough mat, much resembling the thatch of a house. These leaves being woven in close rows, hanging downwards one over the other, into the interior texture of the mat, are perfectly impenetrable to rain. I have often braved with impunity the heaviest rain, sleeping under no other shelter.

The plant is called *phormium tenax* by naturalists. The general native name for the plant, we were told, was *korari;* but each sort, and there are ten or twelve, has its distinctive name. Any portion of the leaf, when gathered, becomes *harakeke;* the fibre when prepared, *muka.*

We descended the river in company with four or five canoes, in which the flax-workers stowed themselves, with their women and children, cats, dogs, and pet sucking-pigs, who all took their places among the baskets of flax and potatoes, and seemed as much at home when shooting a ticklish rapid as on shore. One boy of twelve years old made himself a canoe of two bundles of soft bulrushes, called *raupo,* which he bound together with flax, and guided with great dexterity from his perch in the middle.

[*Held up for several days by contrary winds, the party did not reach the* Tory *again until 16th September.*]

We could not fail to perceive, on our return, that the population of Te Awaiti were watching our movements, apparently intent upon purchasing land for themselves in the neighbourhood of whatever location Colonel Wakefield might select for the expected colony. Information also arrived that a missionary schooner had visited Port Nicholson, with a message to the natives not to sell their land, and that Mr. Williams (the chairman of the Church Mission) would soon arrive from the Bay of Islands.

My uncle, therefore (who had intended to proceed to Cloudy Bay, where Guard and Wynen* engaged to prepare the natives for disposing of the 'Hoiere' to us) determined to go to Port Nicholson as soon as the wind should be fair. On the morning of the 20th September we left the Sound with fair wind and tide, having weighed anchor at day-light.

We had got on board Barrett, and his wife and children, with several attendant natives of both sexes, who formed a sort of colony in our ample 'tween-decks. Dicky had long been too fat and heavy to go out himself in the whale-boats, and left the affairs of the station in the hands of a sort of clerk during his absence. We also took over a steady trader, named Smith, who knew the natives well, and was to be left in charge at Port Nicholson, should we succeed in purchasing it. He had been mate of two or three vessels about the South Seas, and was a little of whaler, sawyer, carpenter, and trader.

To the south of the entrance of Te Awaiti, the bleak, barren hills which bound the Tory channel to the east run down into successive

* A land-buyer from Sydney.

points, round one of which lies the harbour of Point Underwood. Further east we could distinguish the low land at the mouth of the Wairau river, the remarkable cliff called the White Bluff, which forms the eastern extremity of Cloudy Bay, and the land trending along down to Cape Campbell, all backed by a rugged mass of hills that seem to augment as they retreat into the interior, from the tablelands near the coast, till they swell into the volcanic and snow-clad range of Kaikoura. Looking north, the hills above Te Awaiti terminate in an abrupt bluff, some 300 feet in height, called Wellington Head by the Europeans. This is the nearest land to the North Island, here seventeen miles distant; and it was not until we had got some offing that we saw Cape Koamaru and the Brothers. The latter are two rocky islets, standing forty feet out of water at the distance of a mile from the main. As our eyes wandered across the Strait, they were met by Kapiti, Mana, and the adjacent mainland, the high lands about Cape Terawhiti, which is the nearest point to the Middle Island, and the coast on either side of Port Nicholson Bay, extending about thirty miles from Terawhiti to Cape Palliser. As both coasts recede from the narrowest part of the Strait, it is about thirty miles from the entrance of Te Awaiti to that of Port Nicholson. As we drew under the high land east of Cape Terawhiti, the north-west breeze blew fresh over the hills, and we flew along under all sail past the long reef of pointed rocks which lies off Sinclair Head. This is the bluff termination of a range of mountains called Rimurapa, and lies about six miles from Terawhiti.

CHAPTER III

The New Zealand Company
Buys Wellington

THE COAST now forms a semicircular bay, at the north-east end of which is the mouth of Port Nicholson. A low table-land jutting out into a headland which we christened Baring Head, and the bluff end of a ridge called Turakirae, which divides Port Nicholson from Palliser Bay, form the eastern side of the semicircle. The western side slopes down from Sinclair Head into bare hills of moderate height, which, with a hilly fern-covered peninsula, form the western head of the harbour. The cove, at the head of which is the low sandy isthmus joining the peninsula to the main, might be mistaken by an inexperienced person for the real entrance. Piloted, however, by Dicky Barrett, we soon opened out the true channel, which lies between a two-headed bluff now called Pencarrow Head, a mile inside of Baring Head, and the peninsula. A reef of low black rocks is situated about mid-channel; and this seemed, as we approached from the westward, to close the passage. We found it, however, a mile in width between the reef and Pencarrow Head, and beat in against a good working breeze. Two islands inside the harbour formed distinguishing marks.

Captain Cook once anchored in the entrance of this magnificent harbour. Being anxious to rejoin the other ship in company with him, he was unable to examine it, but spoke highly of its promising appearance as a port. It was christened Port Nicholson by the captain* of a Sydney trading vessel some years ago, after his patron and friend the harbour-master of Port Jackson, in New South Wales.

Captain Herd of the *Rosanna*, 1826.

As we advanced up the channel, which continues from two to three miles in width for four miles from a little inside the reef, we were boarded by two canoes, containing the two principal chiefs of the tribe living on shore. One of mature years, named Te Puni,* or 'Greedy', advanced with much dignity of manner to greet Barrett as an old and respected friend, and was joined in this by his nephew Te Wharepouri,* or 'Dark House', a fine commanding man of about thirty-five. They were both nearly related to Mrs. Barrett, and had been Dicky's companions in the dangerous wars of Taranaki. The old man, Barrett told us, was as famous for his wisdom in council as for his former deeds of war. Wharepouri exercised the more immediate direction of the tribe, having acquired a more modern reputation by recent warlike exploits, by his attractive eloquence, and by his perfection in the native accomplishments of canoe and house making, clearing, and marshalling his followers in the field.

The harbour expanded as we advanced, two deep bays stretching to the south-west from the innermost end of the entering channel. From their western extremity the land trends round to a valley lying at the northern end of the harbour, about eight miles from the reef, while the hilly shores of the eastern side continue nearly straight to the mouth of the valley; thus leaving the upper part of the great basin four or five miles in width. In this upper part lie the two islands, behind the largest and most northerly of which we anchored at the distance of half-a-mile from the sandy beach at the valley's mouth. Te Puni eagerly inquired the motive of our visit, and expressed the most marked satisfaction on hearing that we wished to buy the place, and bring white people to it. Wharepouri also expressed his willingness to sell the land, and his desire of seeing white men come to live upon it.

When the followers of Te Puni and Wharepouri formed part of the extensive migration from Taranaki about the year 1834, they found this district occupied by the Ngatimutunga who determined to seek a new location. They partly forced and partly paid the captain of an English vessel to carry them to the Chatham Islands, which they conquered and occupied. Before they departed, Pomare,

* Wakefield uses the spellings 'Epuni' and 'Warepori', which are still retained in Wellington place-names.

their head chief, formally ceded the place to Wharepouri in exchange for some clubs of green-stone or *mere pounamu*. The Ngati-awa had since that period been much harassed by parties of the old occupants, and also by invasions from Rauparaha's 'boiling-water' allies,* who had sometimes come overland down the northern valley which I have noticed.

The two chiefs passed the night on board. They told us that the schooner of which we had heard had left some native missionary teachers, and that, in compliance with Mr. Williams's instructions, they had built houses and chapels in readiness for his arrival. They then discussed the merits of the missionary labours. 'We want,' said they, 'to live in peace, and to have white people come amongst us. We are growing old, and want our children to have protectors in people from Europe. We do not want the missionaries from the Bay of Islands; they are *pakeha maori*, or "whites who have become natives". We have long heard of ships from Europe. Here is one at length; and we will sell our harbour and land, and live with the white people when they come to us.'

Te Puni also asked us to explain what the missionaries meant by saying, 'that all the white men not missionaries were devils.'

September 21st.—In the morning the two chiefs renewed the conversation about the land; and told Colonel Wakefield to go and look at the land, and see how he liked it. They did not wish to talk any more about it until this had been done; and Wharepouri said he should go and finish a large canoe which he was working at, and that in two or three days he should have done, and my uncle would know whether the land was good. A chief named Amahau was appointed to take him up the river which flows through the valley of which I have spoken; and they started, with Barrett and some natives, in a small canoe.

Several of us landed at a large village opposite our anchorage, and witnessed the ceremony of crying over Rangi, [Mrs. Barrett] whom many of her numerous relations had not seen for five years. The village lay, as its Maori name (Pito-one, or 'End of the Sand') implied, at the western end of the sandy beach, which is about two miles long. The main river falls into the sea at the eastern end, about a quarter of a mile from the hills which bound the

* Ngatiraukawa, so called because they came from the Taupo thermal regions.

valley to the east, and is called the Heretaunga. A merry brawling stream, called the Korokoro, or 'throat', flows between the village and the western hills. The valley seems to preserve an average width of two miles to a considerable distance, bounded on either side by wooded hills from 300 to 400 feet in height. It was covered with high forest to within a mile and a half of the beach, when swamps full of flax, and a belt of sand-hummocks, intervened.

The *tangi*, or crying, continued for a long period. The resident natives raised the most discordant whining lamentations, streaming at the eyes, nose, and mouth, and lacerating every part of their bodies with sharp cockle-shells until the blood flowed. This was done, however, with considerable regularity and attention, so as to leave scars rather ornamental than otherwise after the affair was over. Those who wish to commemorate one of these scenes of mourning or rejoicing (for the ceremonies and native word are precisely the same in both cases), apply a black dye to the scar, and thus retain a sort of slight *tatu.**

We started with a native guide to look for pigeons, strongly impressed with the wish of escaping to a respectful distance from the melodious greeting.

Along the foot of the western hills we passed through numerous flourishing potato-gardens, and were greeted and stared at by those at work in them, who eagerly collected all the news from our guides. We found abundance of pigeons, and returned laden to the *pa*. The *tangi* had terminated; the *umu*, or 'cooking-holes', were smoking away for the feast; and eager groups of inquisitive faces were gathered round the proud narrators of our doings in Queen Charlotte's Sound. Our friend Jim Crow found many old friends and relations at Pito-one,† and his audience was by no means the least numerous or attentive. Nothing can remind one more forcibly of the monkey who had seen the world, than a Maori thus relating news. He is an incorrigible exaggerator, and swells each minute circumstance into an affair of state, taking delight in drawing repeated exclamations of amazement from the surrounding *badauds*, who admire and envy the red night-cap or trousers with which he may be adorned, with quite as much zeal as they drink in his metaphors and amplifications.

* Tattooing
† The modern spelling, 'Petone', is used hereafter.

Nayti, who belonged to a different tribe, the Kawhia, had not yet had much opportunity of indulging in this universal propensity; he seemed shy and reserved among these people, and they appeared to regard him with more suspicion than respect.

We found one solitary white man, named Joe Robinson, living in a village [Hikoikoi] near the mouth of the river, having taken a native wife from the tribe. We saw a proof of his industry and ingenuity in the shape of a boat, the planks for which he had cut with a hand-saw; and he had made all the nails himself out of iron hoop. This boat* earned many a pound in later times by trading round the coast.

Colonel Wakefield returned on board in the evening, having ascended the main branch of the river until some snags prevented the further progress of the canoe. He described the banks as of the richest soil, and covered with majestic timber, except where fertile but scanty gardens had been cleared and cultivated by the natives. He found some fifty people at work there, who had concealed themselves in the bush the day before on hearing our guns when we saluted the New Zealand flag as we anchored. They greeted him on his ascent, and presented him with potatoes cooked in readiness on his return. At one spot they inquired of the guide whether the white men in the ship were missionaries. Upon his answering that they were all *devils*, 'shouts of laughter,' Colonel Wakefield afterwards wrote, 'betrayed their acquaintance with his allusion, and their opinion of the uncharitable tenet which had given rise to it.'

September 22nd, Sunday.—The breeze of yesterday had increased into a gale, and blew with great violence from north-west. The ship, however, was not affected by it. Several canoes came off with natives, to be present at our Church service. One of them, a low skimming-dish thing without topside planks, filled and turned over, ducking six or seven natives, including a woman, who were passengers. They seemed to be perfectly used to such accidents, and some hung on to the bottom of the canoe while the others swam with one hand and gathered the paddles which had gone adrift. One of our boats soon rescued them, and they were furnished with dry blankets and sent to warm themselves at the galley.

* The *Venture*

In the evening a messenger arrived from abreast of Kapiti, with news that a fight might be expected; the 'Boiling-water' tribe having mustered in great strength near to that place, and being set on by Te Rauparaha to attack the Ngatiawa along the intervening coast. As there seemed some probability that this invasion might reach Port Nicholson, the natives one and all went ashore in defiance of the gale to gather the particulars and consult on measures of defence.

23rd.—I accompanied Colonel Wakefield and Barrett in an excursion to the different settlements round the harbour. At one about half-way along the west shore, called Ngahauranga, we found Wharepouri at work with an adze on a large canoe. The bottom of this vessel consisted of a single tree hollowed out, and was sixty feet long. The long planks to be added on to the sides were placed between pegs stuck into the ground so as to give them the requisite curvature. We had not been there long before two large canoes from the southern end of the harbour put in at his call. They were on their way to Petone, whither two chiefs were going in order to discuss the sale of the land. When they had landed, there were about sixty men assembled, and they proceeded to hold a *korero* or 'talk', on the all-important subject, while the women prepared a feast in the native ovens, and the children gathered round us to examine our clothes and other equipments, and to stare at our white faces.

Wharepouri put aside his adze, and introduced the matter shortly, saying that this white man (Colonel Wakefield) had come to buy all their land and give them white people to befriend them.

A chief named Puakawa,* or 'Bitter Milk-thistle', now rose, and opposed the intended sale with great energy. He objected to it on the score of the bad treatment which he urged might be expected from the white settlers, and represented the folly of parting with the new home of which they had acquired so good and secure possession after the long sufferings and dangers of their migration. He spoke for an hour, most vigorously, and with admirable emphasis and gesticulation. Although I did not then know enough of the language to understand all his words, and only gathered the substance from Barrett at each pause, his expression and action

* Te Puwhakaawe.

sufficiently explained the spirit and sense of his oration. An old sage named Matangi now rose and favoured the sale. He was once the most influential chief of the tribe, and was a near relation of Wharepouri's father. His extreme old age and consequent physical debility had impaired his influence, but his experience and venerable dignity still gave great weight to his words. His silver-white hair and long beard, and benignant countenance, gave him the air of a Priam or a Nestor, and he almost wept for joy when he dwelt on the prospect of white people coming to protect his grandchildren against their enemies.

Wharepouri followed in the same strain; talking, however, about himself a great deal. He said that he was known in Europe, and that the ship had been sent to him. This is the usual habit of a powerful chief, who always seizes upon any opportunity of maintaining his personal consequence among his people. No native ever 'bounces', as it is called by the whalers, at one of these public *korero*, unless he is confident that no other member of the tribe dare contradict or ridicule his assumption. The perfect silence maintained during Wharepouri's somewhat bombastic speech, proved to how great an extent he might rely upon his authority. He was left, however, with no audience but the leader of the opposition, Puakawa, as soon as the cooks displayed their bill of fare. We also partook of the meal, having assigned to us two or three newly made basketsful of birds and potatoes cooked deliciously.

The Maori *umu*, or cooking-hole, is a very complete steaming apparatus, and is used as follows. In a hole scraped in the ground, about three feet in diameter and one foot deep, a wood fire is first lighted. Round stones, about the size of a man's fist, are heaped upon the faggots, and fall among the ashes as the fire consumes the wood. When they are thus nearly red-hot, the cook picks out any pieces of charcoal that may appear above the stones, turns all the stones round with two sticks, and arranges them so as to afford a pretty uniform heat and surface. She then sprinkles water on the stones from a dried gourd of which the inside has been hollowed, and a copious steam rises. Clean grass, milk-thistle, or wild turnip leaves, dipped in water, are laid on the stones; the potatoes, which have been carefully scraped of their peel with cockle-shells, and washed, are placed on the herbs, together with any birds, meat, or fish that may be included in the mess; fresh herbs are laid over the food, flax baskets follow, completely covering the heap, and the mass is then buried with earth from the hole. No visible steam escapes from the apparatus, which looks like a large mole-hill; and when the old hags, who know how to time the cookery with great accuracy from constant practice, open the catacomb, everything is sure to be found thoroughly and equally cooked.

The little birds were chiefly the *tui* or mocking-bird. This bird has been often described. It resembles a blackbird in size and plumage, with two graceful bunches of white feathers under the neck. It abounds in the woods, and is remarkably noisy and active. Its most common note is a mixture of two or three graduated notes on a flute, a sneeze, and a sharp whistle; but it imitates almost every feathered inhabitant of the forest, and, when domesticated, every noise it hears. It is of a particularly sweet flavour, and very tender.

We were struck, during the discussion above-mentioned, with the natural dignity and becoming regularity with which the deliberations were carried on. With the exception of an occasional exclamation of '*Korero! Korero!*' (speak! speak!) which was used like our 'hear! hear!' in either an encouraging or an ironical sense, or an earnest but low expression of approval or dissent, no interruption of the orators ever took place; nor was there any contention as to the order in which the different chiefs should speak. Even while Wharepouri was employing each of his feet to rub off the other a cloud of small, troublesome sand-flies which annoyed him while he was speaking, not a smile was to be observed even among the children. No consulting among themselves took place; each speaker seemed to have come with his words prepared, or to rely on his own capacity for expressing the ideas of the moment or meeting unexpected arguments. Puakawa, although far from convinced, seemed to acquiesce partly in the general decision adopted in favour of the sale, and moved off with the rest of the travelling orators to Petone, where a similar discussion was to take place. We took the remains of our meal with us into the boat, and visited one or two settlements at the southern end of the harbour before we returned on board. It is absolutely requisite, in order to comply with the forms of Maori etiquette, for the guest to take away his dish and all that he has not eaten. It would give lasting offence to leave on the spot any part of what is set before him. A compliance with this custom would cause some astonishment at a large London banquet.

24th.—The discussion was renewed at Petone to-day; many chiefs being present from the other settlements. It ended, as yesterday, in the thorough approval of the measure by a very large majority; Puakawa and a few adherents still looking with a doubting eye upon the transaction. When the speeches were concluded, and the whole nature of the proposed transaction, including the provision for the Native Reserves, had been explained to them, Colonel Wakefield asked the chiefs, through Barrett, whether they had made up their minds? They asked in return, 'Have you seen the place? How do you like it?' He answered that he had seen it sufficiently, and that it was good: upon which they replied, that it would be for him now to speak, as they had decided upon selling their lands on their own judgment, aided by the advice of their people in the neighbourhood. They referred to Puakawa and his people, who were the only dissenters, and said that they had but little right to speak about the land, and had shown no solid argument against its sale. Their chief one had been that the white people would drive the natives away, as they had done at Port Jackson; and this the others over-ruled by adducing the Native Reserves, and saying that they would live with the Englishmen as with each other.

After the serious discussion had closed, some of the warlike chiefs amused us and themselves by sham-fighting, and their exercise with the spear and tomahawk. One, named Te Kaeaea, diverted us much by his active menacing gestures and hideous grimaces of defiance, leaping about like a monkey, and bringing a long pointed wooden spear within an inch of our bodies; then retreating with a roar of laughter every time he saw us shrink from the thrust. He is nicknamed Taringakuri, or 'Dog's-ear', and professed great hatred for Rauparaha, whose name he frequently shouted out as he brandished his hatchet against thin air. I repaid him his surprise the first day that he came on board. I had got an accordion under a large cloak, and kept time to its notes with my mouth, so as to deceive him and twenty other natives into the idea that I was uttering the various sounds. They showed a profound respect for my oratorical talents, until I let them find out the trick, a day or two after. The accordion in question was called my mouth for a long time afterwards.

25th.—This morning, the goods which Colonel Wakefield intended to give the natives for their land were got upon deck, in the presence of about a hundred of the natives.* Except incessant chattering, they offered no obstruction or inconvenience to this process; but as they filled up a good deal of room on deck, which was wanted in order to assort the various things, my uncle requested Wharepouri to explain this and get them to go ashore until all was ready. He instantly addressed them from the hurricane-house, and set the example of going on shore himself, which was readily and expeditiously followed by all

On the 26th September, when all the articles had been selected and arranged, a message was sent on shore for all the chiefs, who came accompanied by their sons. They examined the stock of goods strictly and carefully, and approved of the quality and quantity. They seemed, however, embarrassed as to the distribution among the six minor tribes of which the population was composed. It

* The goods paid for the Wellington lands were—

100 red blankets	50 steel axes
120 muskets	1,200 fish hooks
2 tierces of tobacco	12 bullet moulds
48 iron pots	12 doz. shirts
2 cases soap	20 jackets
15 fowling pieces	20 pairs trousers
21 kegs gunpowder	60 red nightcaps
1 case ball cartridges	300 yards cotton duck
1 keg lead slabs	200 yards calico
100 cartouche boxes	100 yards check
100 tomahawks	2 dozen handkerchiefs
40 pipe tomahawks	2 dozen slates
1 case pipes	200 pencils
2 doz. spades	10 doz. looking glasses
10 doz. pairs scissors	10 doz. pocket knives
1 doz. pairs shoes	2 pounds of beads
1 doz. umbrellas	100 yards ribbon
1 doz. hats	1 gross Jews harps
1 doz razors	10 doz. dressing combs
6 doz. hoes	2 suits superfine clothes
1 doz. shaving boxes and brushes	1 doz. adzes
1 doz sticks sealing wax	

By the values of those days, these goods represented about £400.

was therefore proposed to them to divide the lots on our deck. Colonel Wakefield also sent for the principal native missionary teacher, a young man who had been christened Richard Davis, after his master and patron at the Bay of Islands, and who had arrived in the missionary schooner mentioned formerly. It was hoped that his presence as a witness to the transaction might give it weight and force; but on his arrival, we found him so importunate for presents to himself, and so totally devoid of influence or authority among the chiefs, that we did not regret his returning to tend a sick child at home.

It was plainly contrary to the custom of the Maori to dispose of so important an affair without plenty of talking; so they debated in due form as to the course to be adopted in distributing the goods; and Wharepouri, as he had been repeatedly urged by us, used his best endeavours to prevent the occurrence of one of those fierce and sometimes fatal scrambles which Barrett and the other white men told us were the universal consequence of a large present of goods to any of these tribes. Puakawa addressed another violent harangue to the assemblage, dissuasive of the whole measure. He seemed most earnest and wilful in his opposition, and used the energetic action suited to his words. 'What will you say,' urged he, 'when you find that you have parted with all your land from the Rimurapa to the Turakirae, and from the Tararua to the sea?'

These were the boundaries which had been pointed out by Wharepouri from the deck in the hearing of the assembled chieftains. He had followed with his finger the summit of the mountain ranges mentioned, and told me their names, in order to their insertion in the deed, which I had been employed in preparing in the course of the day. Tararua is the name of a high snowy range, at the head of the great valley, from which the two other ranges branch off to the sea.

It was extremely difficult—nay almost impossible—to buy a large and distinct tract of land, with fixed boundaries, from any native or body of natives of this part of New Zealand, perfectly unused as they were to any dealing in land according to our notions. These people had no distinct boundaries marked when they received the cession from the Ngatimutunga, and would have been puzzled to walk round or point out accurately any particular limit between the waste land under their jurisdiction and that at the disposal of another tribe. The Kawhia tribe, indeed, laid a claim to this whole neighbourhood, also without exact boundaries. The Ngatiawa chiefs knew that they had a right to occupy any portion of the land near Port Nicholson, because Pomare had told them to do so, and because they maintained by their own gallantry and strength their right to clear new patches where they pleased and to live unejected by their enemies. But they knew not of any further right to a district covered with primæval forest, far too vast for the use of any descendants of their tribe whom they could look forward to, and likely, as far as they thought, to remain both unvisited and useless for ages to come. No hunting ever led to disputes concerning limits in the forest, there being no beasts to hunt; and the only disputes respecting land which had yet occurred between the natives themselves arose from the invasion of lands already cleared or likely to be wanted soon, or the taking of trees from a forest already marked out by another savage for a supply of canoes or house-timber. The first clearer became the acknowledged owner of a tract of hitherto intact land: the first axeman in a primæval forest laid claim to the surrounding trees. But a claim to waste land beyond this natural one of seizure and occupancy was unknown among them at this time.

'What will you say,' continued Puakawa, 'when many, many white men come here, and drive you all away into the mountains? How will you feel when you go to the white man's house or ship to beg for shelter and hospitality, and he tells you, with his eyes turned up to heaven, and the name of his God in his mouth, to be gone, for that your land is paid for?'

These long and repeated discussions were most interesting and satisfactory; as they proved how thoroughly the most dissentient natives understood the force of the transaction, and how gratefully they would welcome the subsequent disarming of their suspicions.

The debate had lasted till sunset; and all but the elder chiefs returned to the shore for the night.

September 27th.—This morning the distribution on the deck of goods commenced, Wharepouri superintending it with much formality, and several of the chiefs addressing the numerous spectators at intervals. Some trouble arose from the desire not to open the cases of muskets, of which there were only five, that some might be sent to each of the six settlements. In these large acquisitions of property, the natives always like to receive a bale, a case, or a cask whole, as the transaction assumes a more opulent appearance in the opinion of the other tribes among whom the news travels. For instance, more pigs can be obtained for an unbroken cask of tobacco, than for the contents divided into many small portions, and exchanged against single pigs. My uncle, on becoming aware of the difficulty, at once gave them a sixth case, which made things quite smooth.

Wharepouri placed equal portions of all the other goods on each of the musket-cases, till they were expended. He reserved but little for himself; keeping some powder and cartridges, in order to be ready for war. Several of the other chiefs showed equal disinterestedness, and declared that their principal object was to get white people to live among them. A handsome young man, named Wi Tako, who was nearly related to Mrs. Barrett, received the share for his father, the chief of Pipitea and Kumutoto, two contiguous settlements at the south-west end of the harbour; and he arrayed himself in a good suit of clothes selected from the heap. He had taken an active and eager part in promoting the agreement, and bringing it to a conclusion. Old 'Dog's-ear' received the share for his settlement, which is called Kaiwharawhara; Te Puni received that for Petone; Wharepouri himself took charge of the portion assigned to his immediate followers at Ngahauranga, and dispatched a share which had been made purposely smaller to the *pa* Te Aro, the most southerly of the settlements, where a tributary tribe, called the Taranaki, had their habitation. The sixth share was assigned to Puakawa and his followers, who had determined, when they saw the others receiving their shares satisfactorily, to desist from any further opposition. He accordingly took charge of the goods, and, though in silence, followed the example of the others.

I had prepared a deed according to Colonel Wakefield's instructions, nearly in the words of some deeds which we had on board, that had been drawn on the model of those used by missionary land-buyers in the northern part of the island. The boundaries and native names being inserted from Wharepouri's dictation, the deed was brought on deck, and laid on the capstan. As I read it through, sentence by sentence, in English, Barrett interpreted into Maori; and he was repeatedly urged by Colonel Wakefield to explain fully each important provision contained in it. The Native Reserves were especially dwelt upon. Although the natives had repeatedly discussed every point, and this was therefore only a repetition of the agreement to which they had all given an ample assent on several occasions, and though they were anxious to get the goods on shore, and the distribution there ended, they listened with great attention and decorum to the recapitulation of the deed in both languages. The chiefs then came up in succession to the capstan, in order to make their marks. As each one's name was called, I wrote it down, and held the pen whilst he made a mark opposite. They all brought their sons with them, in order, as they suggested, to bind them in the transaction, and to prove that they looked forward to the future.

The boats were then sent away with the goods to the settlements; the chief of each accompanying them, and undertaking to distribute them at his own place. The officers in charge of the boats reported on their return, that not the slightest tumult had attended the landing, and that the greatest quietness and order had prevailed while the chief apportioned the lots of each head of a family.

Wharepouri and Te Puni appeared at our dinner-table to-day, dressed in their newly-acquired suits of clothes, and looked very respectable. The former, however, soon came into my uncle's cabin to undress, as he found the coat and shoes made him very uneasy. Both these chiefs had been to Sydney, and were exceedingly desirous of becoming like an English gentleman.

During the time taken up in discussions, I had acquired a great many words of Maori, and began to understand a good deal and make myself understood a little. I had become very good friends with the natives in various excursions ashore, and was designated by a nickname while here, which remained from this time my only name among them till I left the country. Some of the young people had made many attempts to pronounce 'Edward Wakefield', on receiving an answer to their question as to my name. The nearest approach they could make to it was 'Era weke', and some wag immediately suggested 'Tiraweke', the name of a small bird which is very common in the woods, and known for its chattering propensities.* As I had made it a point to chatter as much as possible with them, whether according to Maori grammar or not, they agreed that the *sobriquet* would do, and reported their invention at the *pa*. The old men and chiefs were not a bit behind their juniors in their hilarity and fondness for a joke, and never called me otherwise afterwards. They also christened Colonel Wakefield 'Wide-awake', after some chief who had been so called by the flax-traders in former times; and this name also has clung to him ever since.

Dr. Dieffenbach and Mr. Heaphy engaged some native guides one day to go and look for some birds called *huia*, which were said to abound in this part of the country.

The *huia* is a black bird about as large as a thrush, with long thin legs, and a slender semicircular beak, which he uses for seeking in holes of trees for the insects on which he feeds. In the tail are four long black feathers tipt with white. These feathers are much valued by the natives as ornaments for the hair on great occasions; and are highly esteemed as presents from the inhabitants of this neighbourhood to those of the north, where the bird is never found. Near the insertion of the beak, a fleshy yellow wattle is placed on either side.

Our sportsmen crossed the mouth of the Heretaunga river, and ascended a steep ridge of the eastern hills. Among the forests on the top they remained ensconced in the foliage, while the natives attracted the birds by imitating the peculiar whistle, from which it takes the name of *huia*. They only shot two or three, which had followed the decoy almost on to the barrels of their guns.

I had formed one of several shooting parties and fishing excursions. The former were generally conducted in the different creeks into which the river divides from a kind of tidal lagoon inside the sand-bar, and we fell in with numerous pigeons and wild-ducks while exploring their courses as high as our boat could proceed. The grandeur of the forest which overshaded these clear creeks, the luxuriance and entanglement of the underwood, and the apparent richness of the soil, could nowhere be exceeded. We longed to see the time when the benefit of the latter should be reaped by industrious English yeomen.

* *Tiraweke* is a variant of *tiraueke*, the saddleback, now uncommon.

Our fishing parties were generally directed to a snug cove about a mile south-east of the river's mouth, which we christened Lowry Bay, after the first mate, who used to be head fisherman, and direct our bungling exertions in the management of the seine. In this place we generally had a fine haul of plaice, sole, and several other kinds of fish. On the beach near Petone we obtained several immense hauls, whenever a shoal of *kahawai* came into that part of the bay. The natives catch large quantities of them with a bone hook at the end of a fish-shaped piece of wood, inlaid with the shell of the mutton-fish, or *haliotis*, which bears the lively colours and brilliancy of mother-o'-pearl. This hook requires no bait, and a dozen of them are dragged along the water by a canoe which pulls at full speed through the shoal.

Sunday, 29th September.—After prayers, Colonel Wakefield went round the harbour with Wharepouri to visit the different settlements, in order to see how the people were satisfied, and to invite them to a sort of festival which was to be held on the occasion at Petone on Monday. At the slave settlement, Te Aro, Wharepouri addressed the occupants, who had the same abject dependent appearance which we had remarked in the Rangitane at the Pelorus River. He told them what benefits would accrue to them, and excused himself for having sent them a smaller share of the goods, as the free settlements had required a large proportion; but encouraged them by reminding them that they were now armed, and in a position to defend themselves, should they be attacked by Rauparaha and the 'Boiling-water' tribes.

At this place Colonel Wakefield proposed to pay for the chapels and houses which the missionary delegates had built on a piece of flat land where he intended to fix the site of the town; but Wharepouri objected, saying that he had already paid for the whole of the land and everything upon it.

At each of the other settlements Colonel Wakefield engaged the natives to be active in collecting provisions, clearing land, and bringing timber for building to the site of the town. Wharepouri supported the request, and then asked the young men to collect at Petone, in order to join in a war-dance to be given in the morning. Colonel Wakefield was universally treated as a benefactor, and we had the satisfaction of hearing on all hands expressions of contentment at the purchase-money, and eager hope for the speedy arrival of the settlers.

September 30th.—This morning we observed the natives gathering from all parts of the harbour. Canoes and parties on foot, glittering with their lately acquired red blankets and muskets, were all closing in upon the place of rendezvous; fresh smokes rose every moment on shore as a new oven was prepared for the feast; and Wharepouri and the other chiefs who had slept on board went on shore early to make the necessary preparations, accompanied by our carpenter, who was to superintend the erection of a small tree which the natives had procured for the purpose, as a flag-staff, close to the Petone *pa*. In the afternoon, on a signal from the shore, we landed in our boats with all the cabin party, and all the sailors that could be spared, to take part in the rejoicings. We were joyfully received by the assemblage, which consisted of about three hundred men, women, and children. Of these, two hundred were men, and had armed themselves with the hundred and twenty muskets they had received from us, spears, tomahawks, pointed sticks, stone and wooden clubs, etc. Even a dozen umbrellas, which had formed part of the payment, figured in the ranks. Every one was dressed in some of the new clothes; their heads were neatly arranged, and ornamented with feathers of the albatross or *huia*; handsome mats hung in unison with the gay petticoats of the women and the new blankets of the warriors; the latter were bedizened with waistcoats and shirts, and belted with cartouch-boxes and shot-belts. It was high holiday with everybody; and a universal spirit of hilarity prevailed among the excited multitude.

As we landed Colonel Wakefield ordered the New Zealand flag to be hoisted at the staff; and the same was done at the main of the *Tory*, which saluted it with twenty-one guns, to the great delight of the natives at the noise and smoke.

Wharepouri then asked if we were ready; and told us that many men were absent, some at their distant gardens, some on an expedition to the westward, and some deterred by the bad weather which had prevailed during the morning. He then took his station at the head of one of the parties into which the fighting-men were divided, 'Dog's-ear' having marshalled the other at a little distance.

Wharepouri was dressed in a large hussar cloak belonging to my uncle, to which he had taken a fancy, and brandished a handsome green-stone *mere*. His party having seated themselves in ranks, he suddenly rose from the ground and leaped high into the air with a tremendous yell. He was instantly imitated by his party, who sprang out of their clothes as if by magic, and left them in bundles on the ground. They then joined in a measured guttural song recited by their chief, keeping exact time by leaping high at each louder intonation, brandishing their weapons with the right hand, and slapping the thigh with the left as they came heavily upon the ground. The war-song warmed as it proceeded; though still in perfect unison, they yelled louder and louder, leaped higher and higher, brandished their weapons more fiercely, and dropped with the smack on the thigh more heavily as they proceeded, till the final spring was accompanied by a concluding whoop which seemed to penetrate one's marrow. After this preparatory stimulant, the two parties ran down to the beach, and took up positions facing each other at about two hundred yards' distance. They then repeated the dance; and at its conclusion the two parties passed each other at full speed, firing their guns as they ran, and took up a fresh position nearer to each other.

A small reinforcement was now brought up from Puakawa's village at the mouth of the river to one of the parties; and we were much surprised to see at the head of it Richard Davis, the missionary teacher, dressed in warlike costume, and his head bedecked with *huia* feathers. He took an eager part in the proceedings, and was the bearer of a sort of sham challenge from one party to the other. They now for a third time went through the *peruperu*, or 'war-dance'; but dispensed with any sham-fighting, as the day was nearly at an end, and they wished everything to terminate in an amicable way. Many of the women had joined in the wildest part of the dance, yelling and grimacing with as demoniacal a frenzy as any of the men. We were shown some natives from Wanganui, a settlement some distance north of Kapiti, who distinguished themselves by their ferocious appearance. They had blackened all round their eyes with charcoal, and painted themselves copiously with streaks of red ochre and oil; they performed their part with excessive vigour and *gusto*, and looked, when in the ecstasy of the dance, like demons incarnate. Barrett and Wharepouri told us that these Wanganui natives were looked upon as the most savage and warlike even by the other tribes, and that they spoke a different dialect from the Ngatiawa. They were closely allied, at this time, with the latter.

A *haka* was now performed by about one hundred and fifty men and women. They seated themselves in ranks in one of the court-yards of the *pa*, stripped to the waist. An old chieftainess, who moved along the ranks with regular steps, brandishing an orna-mented spear in time to her movements, now recited the first verse of a song in a monotonous, dirge-like measure. This was joined in by the others, who also kept time by quivering their hands and arms, nodding their heads and bending their bodies in accordance with each emphasis and pause. These songs are often made impromptu on various subjects; but those selected for the present occasion were principally ancient legends.

At the conclusion of the *haka*, we were served from the ovens with the joints of a pig, which had been sacrificed for the occasion, and the whole assemblage partook of an ample meal. We drank the healths of the chiefs and people of Port Nicholson in bumpers of champagne, and, christening the flag-staff, took formal possession of the harbour and district for the New Zealand Land Company, amidst the hearty cheers of the mixed spectators. The whole scene passed with the greatest harmony, and we were sensibly struck by the remarkable good feeling evinced towards us by the natives.

This disposition continued unabated during the three days more that we remained at this place. The natives, whether chieftains, inferiors, or slaves, treated us with the greatest kindness and affection. Wharepouri suggested that a deputation should proceed in the ship to assist us in buying the district of Taranaki, from which they were driven, and of which all who had been there, whether natives or white men, spoke in the highest terms. He also spoke of a flat fertile district to the eastward, called Wairarapa, which opens into Palliser Bay. He declared it *tapu* for Colonel Wakefield, and swore by his head that no one else should have any of it till he had been to see it. Barrett told us that it answered his description, and had a fresh-water stream running through it into Palliser Bay.

c

Te Puni's eldest son, Te Whare, and a young chief named Tuarau, nephew of a former head chief of the Ngatiawa tribes, were selected to go with us to Taranaki, and took up their berths on board. Te Whare had accompanied Captain Chaffers in a surveying expedition in one of the boats during the last week, of which an excellent chart of the harbour was the result. As soon as this was drawn, Colonel Wakefield proceeded to name the various points and bays. The south-western bay, where the most secure anchorage exists, and where the town was to be built, was named Lambton Harbour, in honour of the Earl of Durham, who was Governor of the Company, and had been a warm patron of the project in England.* A piece of level ground, over which the town was to extend, was named Thorndon Flat, from Thorndon Hall in Essex, the residence of Lord Petre, who had also forwarded with his unceasing support the intended colony. The river Heretaunga received the name of Mr. William Hutt, another of the most energetic friends of the undertaking. The large island Matiu was christened Somes's Island, after Mr. Joseph Somes, the then Deputy-Governor of the Company. The most remarkable headlands at the entrance were named after Mr. Francis Baring, Sir George Sinclair, and Pencarrow, the residence of Sir William Molesworth; and the names of other places were selected from among those likely to be respected and honoured by the future inhabitants as memorials of the disinterested founders of the colony. Barrett's Reef must not be omitted in this list, as commemorating our worthy and honest co-operator.†

The utmost satisfaction prevailed among all on board, at the conclusion of all the arrangements, as well as among the natives. We felt that we had secured, by an honourable bonâ fide transaction with the natives, an unexceptionable harbour and site for a town; and although the neighbouring land, with the exception of the valley of the Hutt, was rather rugged, we considered this as no lasting obstacle to the fitness of the place for a colony. Indeed, compared with the land on the Middle Island, the hills here appeared both low and easy of cultivation. We were moreover convinced, by the numerous accounts which we had gathered from white adventurers as well as natives, that this was the only harbour

* The Earl's family name was Lambton.
† Colonel Wakefield also named Point Jerningham after his nephew.

MEETING OF THE SHIPS *TORY* AND *CUBA* IN COOK STRAIT, 1840

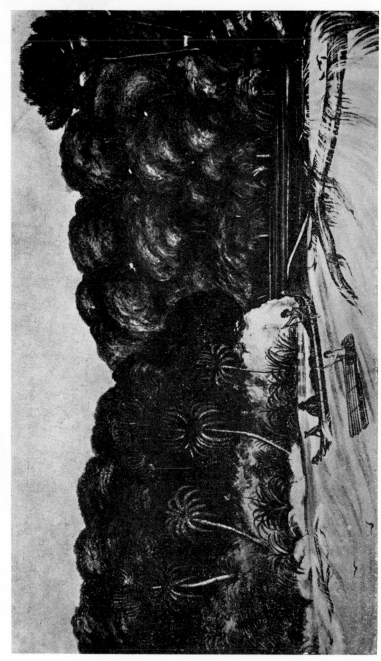

accessible to large shipping between Manukau on the west side of the North Island and the Thames on the opposite coast; and that the shipping and trade of that extensive coast-line must be sure to centre here.

Colonel Wakefield left with Wharepouri, Mr. Smith, whom I mentioned above, with a stock of garden-seeds and carpenter's tools, and a few goods with which to encourage the natives in the work of preparation for the arrival of the settlers. Wharepouri promised to put him in a new house at his own settlement, and to take care of him till our return. We also landed some pigs of a superior breed before we sailed. Some boards bearing the words 'New Zealand Land Company' were put up in conspicuous places on the shores of the harbour.

CHAPTER IV

Te Rauparaha

O N THE morning of the 4th of October, we sailed from Port Nicholson, and anchored at night in the mouth of Port Underwood in Cloudy Bay. The lofty and more barren mountains beneath which it lies struck us as cheerless and desolate after the shores of Port Nicholson; and rude flurries of wind from the high peaks whistled among our rigging.

In the morning of the 5th we warped further into the harbour; we found here the *Honduras*, barque, taking in oil and bone from the stations; and we were very busily employed in making up our letters for England. Dicky Barrett left us at this place, proceeding to Te Awaiti in a sealing-boat with all his family and train. He agreed to return to us here in order to proceed to Taranaki. We found several whaling-parties on the different beaches; which are separated from each other by such steep ridges that boats are the more common means of communication. In Ocean Bay, in which the swell causes a good deal of surf, we saw the timbers of some small vessels which were being built there, and found an old trader named Ferguson who had the reputation of never being sober. On the sides of the impending hills are the remains of some clearings made by the crew of a whaler under the direction of a Captain Blenkinsopp, who purchased this bay from the natives, and was also said to have bought the plains of Wairau, a few miles further south, from Te Rauparaha and Te Rangihaeata, his fighting general, for a ship gun, some years since.

In Kakapo Bay, we found Jacky Guard and all his family, including his wife, a fine buxom-looking Englishwoman, and the children who were with her prisoners among the natives. They all looked healthy and rosy. Still further north on the west side was another bay, also inhabited by white people. These two bays are much better sheltered than Ocean Bay. One party, conducted by a Portuguese, were established in a cove just inside the eastern head.

On the 13th we sailed for Te Awaiti, to look for Barrett. Arthur was again on board of us as pilot. As we approached the mouth of the Tory Channel, the wind fell light, and we consequently lost the flood-tide. We had been hove-to for half-an-hour, when a fresh breeze from south-east sprang up, and Arthur, who knew the sailing qualities of the *Tory*, told Captain Chaffers that he might 'put her at it', and we rattled in against a four-knot tide. We flew past the southern head, on to which you might have flung a biscuit, with the tide-rip fizzing and smoking on either side of us. A handy ship is requisite to effect this entrance.

We found that Barrett had been detained by the illness of his wife; and as she was still too ill to come on board, Colonel Wakefield determined to cross over the Strait and effect an agreement with Rauparaha, and then return to the north entrance of the Sound for Barrett. We took with us an interpreter named John Brooks, who had been engaged in Cloudy Bay as a sawyer. He was thoroughly acquainted with the native language and habits, having been eight years among the wildest Waikato natives.

On October 16th, we stood over to Kapiti, leaving the Channel with the ebb tide. About four miles N.E. of the Brothers, we saw a dangerous rock, looking like a boat at a short distance. As we neared the north shore, we could distinguish the opening nearly abreast of the flat table island of Mana, where a small harbour called Porirua indents the wooded hills. These incline inwards from the coast a little to the south of Kapiti, and a sandy beach succeeds the rock-bound shore which extends from Cape Terawhiti.

As we approached Kapiti, which has a high peak in its centre, and is covered with forest to the water's edge, we made out some small islands lying off its south-eastern extremity. These form a very excellent anchorage for a limited number of ships. A whale-boat from the easternmost island soon boarded us; and the 'headsman' or commander of the boat, piloted us into an outer roadstead in twenty-two fathoms, which is reckoned more convenient for a large ship than the inner one, as a vessel can more easily get under way in case of accident. He told us that a sanguinary battle had taken place at a village called Waikanae on the mainland, about three miles from our anchorage, the same morning. Many of the whalers had witnessed the contest from their boats outside the surf. We afterwards gathered the full particulars. The feast to which Te Whetu had told us he was going, had taken place on Mana, where the funeral obsequies of Waitohi, a sister of Rauparaha, had been celebrated by some thousand natives of different tribes. On this occasion, Rauparaha had killed and cooked one of the unfortunate Rangitane slaves, who brought him tribute from the Pelorus; and had shared the flesh among his most distinguished guests. Among these were the Ngatiraukawa, a tribe who were induced several years before by Rauparaha to come from the interior of the North Island in order to assist him in his conquest of these parts, and who were led by a renowned chief named Te Whatanui, or 'the Great Store'. They commonly reside at Otaki, about twelve miles north of Waikanae, and had been incited by Rauparaha to annoy the Ngatiawa on their first arrival from Taranaki. Feuds, bloody wars, and a bitter hatred of each other, had been the consequence; and some of their old grievances had been revived by their meeting at Mana. Rauparaha cunningly fanned the flame; and mutual insults and recriminations followed, on the passage of the Ngatiraukawa past Waikanae to their homes after the feast. Shots were fired in defiance over their heads as they passed along the beach, and even some pigs which they were driving were taken from them and killed by the Ngatiawa. They prepared for a contest, were marshalled by their chiefs the same evening, and, by previous concert with Rauparaha, attacked the Waikanae *pa* at daylight.

Two rivers meet there, the Waimea and the Waikanae. A small out-lying village, situated on the sandy tongue of land between the two, sustained the first brunt of the attack. A fierce and bloody contest ensued, ending in the retreat of the invaders, and their total rout along the sandy beach.

Rauparaha, who had failed to bring the assistance of men and ammunition which he had promised to Te Whatanui, landed from his canoe late in the skirmish, but swam through the surf to it on the first symptoms of defeat, the Ngatiraukawa losing many men in a vigorous rally made to cover his escape.

The numbers engaged had been, from all that we could gather, about equal on both sides, to the amount of 400 or 500 men each; but the defeated had left fifty dead on the field, and the conquerors only eighteen. The beaten party had managed to carry off their wounded, of whom there were a much larger number on both sides.

We had just made up a boat's crew from the cabin party, to go over and see the field of battle, the surgeons taking their instruments with them, when a message arrived from Rauparaha. He was on Evans's Island, the nearest to the ship of the three islets, and expressed a desire to see Colonel Wakefield. We therefore pulled round and went to see him.

As we leaped from our boat he advanced to meet us, and, with looks of evident fear and distrust, eagerly sought our hands to exchange the missionary greeting. During the whole of the ensuing conversation he seemed uneasy and insecure in his own opinion; and the whalers present described this behaviour as totally at variance with his usual boastfulness and arrogance. He made us a pious speech about the battle, saying that he had had no part in it, and that he was determined to give no encouragement to fighting. He agreed to come on board the next day; and departed to one of the neighbouring islands.

He is rather under the average height, and very dignified and stately in his manner, although on this occasion it was much affected by the wandering and watchful glances which he frequently threw around him, as though distrustful of every one. Although at least sixty years old, he might have passed for a much younger man, being hale and stout, and his hair but slightly grizzled.

His features are aquiline and striking; but an over-hanging upper lip, and a retreating forehead, on which his eyebrows wrinkled back when he lifted his deep-sunken eyelids and penetrating eyes, produced a fatal effect on the good prestige arising from his first appearance. The great chieftain, the man able to lead others, and habituated to wield authority, was clear at first sight; but the savage ferocity of the tiger, who would not scruple to use any means for the attainment of that power, the destructive ambition of a selfish despot, was plainly discernible on a nearer view.

The life of this remarkable savage forms an era in the history of New Zealand.

Previous to 1825 he had lived among his tribe, the Ngatitoa, in the neighbourhood of Kawhia. Hongi returned from his visit to England in 1820, provided with muskets and devoured with restless ambition. His followers became, by their possession of fire-arms, the most powerful tribe in New Zealand. At their head he ravaged the whole northern end of the North Island. In consequence of these devastating wars the Waikato and Kawhia tribes pressed upon each other, and the latter were obliged to give way in the struggle.

Rauparaha had already gained a great name by his warlike achievements; and he was thought worthy of a place second only to the head chief Te Pehi in the guidance of the expelled tribe, which came southward to seize upon a new home.

Te Pehi Kupe was the same man who, early in 1826,* went on board an English ship which was going through the Strait; and obtained a passage to England, in order to bring back, like his old conqueror Hongi, a stock of fire-arms from that country. He left his son Te Hiko o te rangi, or 'the Lightning of Heaven', to take his station among the tribe. [During Te Pehi's absence Te Rauparaha's influence was greatly increased. Soon after his return from England he was killed by the Ngaitahu near Banks Peninsula.]

Since Te Pehi's death, Rauparaha had become the sole *ariki* or ruler of Cook's Strait; easily weighing down the balance of Hiko's higher descent by his own superior talents of deceit and knowledge of their little world.

[*Here Wakefield recalls many of Te Rauparaha's bloodthirsty exploits. He goes on to speak of the relations between Te Rauparaha and his fellow-chief and nephew Te Rangihaeata.*]

Their respective stations were pithily described by one of the whalers, who told us that 'the Robuller', as he mispronounced his name, 'cast the bullets, and the Rangihaeata shot them'. Rauparaha was the mind and his mate the body on these blackmail-gathering rounds. They had both acquired a violent taste for grog; and this, and fire-arms and powder, were the principal articles demanded.

The whaling-station on Evans's Island we found to be more complete, and under more thorough discipline and efficient manage-

* In 1824 (not 1826) on the *Urania*.

ment, than those in Port Underwood or at Te Awaiti. The boats put off after a whale just as we arrived, and struck us by their precision and good appointment. The head of the party was a determined-looking man of middle age, named Tommy Evans. He was obliging and hospitable in the extreme to us during our stay; and was reckoned the best master at Kapiti.

On one of the other small islands was a station conducted by an American, who is a renowned enemy of the whale; and two other stations were situated on the northern part of the great island of Kapiti. All these stations seemed to us to bear a more favourable aspect than those on the other side of the Strait. Evans's party had taken 250 tons of oil, and he told us that his own profits alone would amount to £300.

On October 17th I accompanied our three surgeons to Waikanae, to carry succour to the wounded. We proceeded to the main *pa*, at the mouth of the Waikanae river. We were loudly greeted, and conducted into a large court of the village, where five hundred men, women, and children were assembled in a row to shake hands with us. This was no small task; but in order to show them that we approved of their newly-acquired missionary principles, we carefully went through the whole ceremony.

This was the largest *pa* we had yet seen. The outer stockades were at least a mile in circumference; and the various passages between the different courts and divisions formed a perfect labyrinth. A numerous train of youths guided us to the houses of the wounded men. As we passed, we observed one of the dead chiefs laid out in state in the court before his *wharepuni*. His body was wrapt in his best mats; and his head, with the hair neatly arranged and copiously ornamented with feathers, reclined against a carved post, which was painted with *kokowai*, or red ochre. In circles around stood or sat his friends and relations, wailing and lacerating their faces and limbs.

Our surgeons were all three hard at work for some hours, extracting bullets, binding up wounds, and setting broken limbs. We found the wounds bound up by the natives generally with the leaf of the flax, and bark splints on the broken limbs. The patients bore pain with the most perfect stoicism.

The inhabitants of this village professed to be all Christians, having been converted by native teachers. Accordingly, they buried their fallen enemies on the field of battle; adhering, however, in some degree to the native superstitions, by burying a stock of tobacco and pipes with each, to console him on his way to the *Reinga*, or future life according to their belief.

On our return to the ship we found that Rauparaha had been on board. The chiefs were at first much opposed to selling any land, saying that they had been told the white people would drive them away from their future settlements. They were also exceedingly jealous of our purchase of Port Nicholson.

Colonel Wakefield, after much discussion, appeared to convince them of the friendly intentions of the white people towards them, and that they would be much benefited by their arrival; and they finished by saying, 'Look at the land! if it is good, take it!'

Rauparaha stayed on board to dinner, with his wife, a tall Meg-Merrilies-like woman, who had a bushy head of hair, frizzled out to the height of six inches all round, and a masculine voice and appetite. She is the daughter of his last wife by a former husband.

Rauparaha and several other of the Kawhia chiefs drank ardent spirits freely, repudiating the use of water, and refusing with great contempt anything less than a full tumbler. It did not seem, however, to have the same effect upon them that it would have upon a person unhardened to the use of liquor.

Rauparaha sat for his portrait to Mr. Heaphy, and made a noisy demand for a waistcoat in payment as soon as the sitting was over. Indeed, he asked shamelessly for everything which he saw, and he seemed well used to being refused.

On the 18th, the chiefs were again on board. Tungia, who was the father of Tommy Evans's native wife, and nicknamed 'the Wild Fellow' by the whalers, was remarkable for his noisy and turbulent manner. All the others, except Hiko and his uncle Te Rangihiroa, had the same bad qualities which we had observed in the Cloudy Bay natives. They united the uncontrolled ferocity of the savage to the acquired indifference to honour and the degrading vices of the white outcasts among whom they had dwelt.

Hiko struck us forcibly by his commanding stature, by his noble intelligent physiognomy, and by his truly chieftain-like demeanour. His descent by both parents pointed him out as a great leader in

Cook's Strait, should he inherit his father's great qualities. He was sparing of his words, and mild of speech. He had carefully treasured up his father's instructions, and the relics of his voyage to England. He showed us a volume of the Library of Entertaining Knowledge on the New Zealanders,* in which is contained a portrait of Te Pehi, on which he placed great store. He was said to pay his slaves for their work, and to treat them with unusual kindness, and the white men spoke of him as mild and inoffensive in his intercourse with them.

Te Rangihiroa, the younger brother of Te Pehi, was also a worthy old chieftain. He was free from the vices of the other Kawhia chiefs, and was universally well spoken of as kind-hearted to all his fellow-creatures of both races by even the most depraved of the white men.

A gale from south-east detained the natives on shore until the 21st, when they came off, and the proposition was again made to them of purchasing the whole of their rights and claims of whatever sort to land on both sides of the Strait.

They again discussed the matter very fully, and asked to look at the goods. This was complied with; and though they evidently considered the quantity as far beyond anything they had yet seen or heard of in payment for a thing so great a drug as land, they could not refrain from haggling and bargaining for an addition to the heap. Hiko requested more soap, women's clothing, slates, and such useful articles; while Rauparaha and his party pressed for more fire-arms and powder. This was arranged, after some trouble and disagreement; and Colonel Wakefield proceeded to explain to them, by means of the interpreter, the whole force of the bargain into which he wished to enter with them. A plan of those parts of the two islands over which their conquests extended was carefully examined by them; and it was fully explained to them that, after this transaction, they would have no more land, or rights over land of any sort to sell, and that they could not receive any further payment whatever hereafter for any land if they joined in this agreement. They were also told that a suitable portion for the maintenance of the chiefs, with their families and successors, would be made *tapu* for them for ever; and that those

* *The New Zealanders*, by G. L. Craik, published in 1830.

natives who worked for the white people would be paid by them for their labour. All this was repeated to them over and over again in different forms, till they showed themselves perfectly acquainted with the bargain which they were to accept or refuse. They ended by agreeing fully to every provision; and Rauparaha dictated to me the native names of all the places on both coasts to which they had any claim, whether by conquest or inheritance. This operation took some time, as I made him repeat some of the names several times, in order to write them down clearly, and as he showed me the position of each on the map before mentioned. He then joined with the others in consenting to cede the whole of his rights whatsoever to land in those places. They all agreed to come on board to sign the deed, and receive the payment, the next day.

Hiko, however, fell ill, and bad weather prevented the others from leaving the shore. Rauparaha, who is not to be deterred by anything from his own selfish objects, came off through a rough sea, in a substantial, strong-built, well-manned canoe, and tried to induce Colonel Wakefield to conclude the transaction without Hiko. 'He is only a boy,' said he, 'and has nothing to do with the land. Give me the goods, with more powder and arms. Of what use are blankets, soap, tools, and iron pots, when we are going to war? What does it matter whether we die cold or warm, clean or dirty, hungry or full? Give us two-barrelled guns, plenty of muskets, lead, powder, cartridges, and cartouch-boxes.' His proposition was of course quietly refused.

October 23rd.—The *Tory* having shifted her berth nearer to the two small islands on which the natives principally reside, the chiefs again came off, Hiko and his uncle in a nice whale-boat belonging to the former. A third *korero* took place before about twenty white witnesses and a numerous attendance of natives from the shore, so that the deck was quite crowded. All expressed their perfect consent to the sale, and asked for the payment to be made. The goods were accordingly got up and placed on deck. Colonel Wakefield had added a bale of clothing, and several other useful articles, at the request of Hiko, who had persuaded the others to cease their clamours for fire-arms. A dozen fowling-pieces, included in the payment, were brought up and placed, ready for distribution, on the companion-hatch.

Rauparaha, Tungia, and the other warlike chiefs, rushed at these in the wildest manner, each attempting to seize one; but they were all immediately removed out of their reach; and Hiko, who had been trying on one of the coats preparatory to the distribution, no sooner saw the selfishness and ill-faith of his rivals, than he took off the coat, called to Rangihiroa, who had remained an unmoved spectator of the whole scene, and steered his boat to the shore in high dudgeon.

Colonel Wakefield immediately declared the negotiation at an end, and ordered the goods below. The turbulent chiefs loudly vented their disappointment at this aspect of the affair, laid the blame on each other and on him, and accused him of partiality to Hiko. They asked why he was to be set before the old men, and what he had to do with the land, to be considered for so much? Some of them even made some of their customary grimaces at Colonel Wakefield, expressive of defiance and contempt; and Tungia began dancing about and uttering a violent harangue, which seemed to indicate an intention to attack the ship. Some few small articles were pilfered from the heaps in the confusion, and taken ashore under the mats of slaves who had been set to do this.

They threatened, and tried every means to intimidate Colonel Wakefield into proceeding with the affair. They said they would sell the land to the French and Americans, or to the ships from Port Jackson, of which they said plenty would come presently; and, finally, they expressed their determination to go to Port Nicholson and kill all our natives there.

Throughout this critical scene Colonel Wakefield displayed the most admirable courage and presence of mind. He laughed at their taunts, and treated their threats with indifference; and at length told them that they must leave the ship, whether the affair went on or not, if they could not behave more quietly. He refused their repeated proposals to buy their lands, and to leave Hiko to deal for his own; and managed, by exemplary command of temper and countenance, and by a due mixture of firmness and mildness in his replies, not only to subdue their riotous disposition, but to bring them round to as friendly a spirit as they had been in before the disagreement arose.

On October 24th, Rauparaha and Hiko determined to make up their difference, and, unsolicited by Colonel Wakefield, came on board unattended. They looked for some time over some books of plates in the cabin, talking on different subjects, and then requested that the deed of conveyance might be read to them. This was done, and the whole translated and fully explained to them. The map was also again placed before them, and they pointed out the places to which they had a claim, saying, that no one lived on a great part of it, and that this part was of no use to any one, and least of all to them.

They then both signed the deed; Hiko making a cross opposite his name with the pen which I held for him, but Rauparaha making a peculiar mark of his own with the pen in his own hand. They then left the ship, each with his two-barrelled gun, and promised that the rest of the chiefs should sign the deed on the morrow, when the rest of the goods were to be delivered.

On the next day this was done. Rauparaha and Charley signed by proxy for their relations in Cloudy Bay, and old Te Whetu, for his son Mark, who was said to be of great authority in the neighbourhood of D'Urville's Island.

It was agreed that a share for Rangihaeata should remain on board, and that his signature should be obtained at Mana, where he then was. He arrived, however, in a canoe, on the 26th; and after some blustering and speechifying, he signed the deed, and took his allotted share.

Nayti left us here, wishing to go and stop with his relations near Mana till the emigrant ships should arrive.

Colonel Wakefield, having visited Waikanae, was eagerly received by the missionary natives there, who offered to sell their land; but for no consideration except the munitions of war, as they wished to defend themselves against the Ngatiraukawa.

Te Patu, and some other chiefs deputed from their number, went over with us to Queen Charlotte's Sound; where we intended to effect a contract with the Ngatiawa residing there, similar to that which we had concluded with the Kawhia at Kapiti.

A strong gale of wind off the entrance of the Sound, on October 29th, carried away our foreyard and some of our rigging, and left us in a very dangerous position in the midst of a boiling tide-rip, driving fast on to the Brothers. We escaped, however, by means of the superior sailing qualities of the *Tory*, and the admirable management of Captain Chaffers, and ran under the shelter of Mana to repair our damages.

We found this island flat on the top, with high cliffs all round, except on the side towards the main, where a snug amphitheatre contains the *pa* in which Rangihaeata and a few followers usually reside, and also the establishment of the white man owning the island. A small flock of sheep and fifty head of cattle, with two draught-horses, are attached to this sort of half-farm, half whaling-station.

§

We proceeded to Dicky Barrett's at Te Awaiti. During our absence, Jacky Love, the trader whom I mentioned as having obtained the affection of the natives by his kindness and generosity, had died. Two hundred natives followed his body to the grave; and they subsequently erected a monument over it such as usually graces the tomb of a great chieftain. This was a canoe stuck upright in the ground, some 20 feet high; painted in fanciful designs with red and black dye, and edged all round with a fringe of feathers.

From the 1st to the 8th of November was spent in negotiating with the natives, who collected to the number of three hundred, and formed encampments on the different islands and beaches near the ship, for a total cession of all their rights and claims. The same full explanations were made that had been used in the two former cases; and the same care taken that ample deliberation and due calmness should insure the perfect validity and truth of the transaction.

Much difficulty occurred, both during these discussions and at the distribution of the goods, in consequence of the absence of chieftains of great influence to take the lead in treating and speaking for the others. Innumerable petty disagreements had to be put an end to, and jealousies to be appeased; and as no one chief possessed sufficient authority to undertake this task, much more trouble and annoyance necessarily devolved upon Colonel Wakefield. His usual patience, determination, and good temper did not fail him; and he fully succeeded in conciliating their universal goodwill.

The result of this equality of authority among so wild a rabble gave rise to a disagreeable scene, during the distribution of the goods after the execution of the deed by the numerous chiefs.

One of the many smaller tribes composing the Ngatiawa, namely the Puketapu, consisted of particularly quarrelsome and unruly members; and, after the other tribes had taken their shares ashore, this one found it impossible to arrange the distribution without a *taua* or 'scramble'.

I was in the 'tween decks when it began; and, hearing a loud and continued stamping on the deck, thought the natives were 'rushing' or attacking the ship. Under this impression, I sprang aft to obtain a weapon of defence from among those always ready in the cabin. On my way, I met Te Whiti, one of the chiefs of a tribe which had effected a quiet division; and he reassured me by telling me that no harm would be done to the white people, and that I had better go up in the rigging and look upon the way in which the natives divided their goods.

Following his advice, I clambered up into the longboat between the masts, and was at first bewildered at the sight. About one hundred and fifty natives were piled above the various heaps of goods, writhing, struggling, stamping, pulling each others' hair and limbs, tearing blankets, shivering whole cases of pipes and looking-glasses, and withal yelling and screaming in the most deafening manner. Some of the wildest had stripped naked. Disengaging themselves for a moment from the mass, they tightened the thong of their tomahawk-handle round their wrist, and prepared to plunge into the thickest of the mass, where some dearly-prized article was in contention among a heap of furies. Barrett, however, and some other white men well known to the natives, pinioned the arms of two or three of the wildest with their own, and gradually restored order and peace. The combatants looked exceedingly crestfallen as they gathered up the remains of the broken things; but took especial pains to tell us that it was no fault of ours, but the *porangi* or 'foolishness' of the Maori. Others, who had assumed a quiet, watchful attitude during the disturbance, smilingly produced from under their mats some chain-hook, sounding-lead, or other handy weapon, with which they had armed themselves in case of the worst.

During the negotiations, our old tormentor at Ship Cove, 'Dog-skin', once appeared alongside; but upon our recognizing him, although his costume was much altered, and pointing him out to the attention of Barrett and the surrounding natives, he was evidently much ashamed, and went right away. Nor did he ever return on board. Ngarewa attended the whole proceedings, and received his share of the payment.

On the 9th November, Colonel Wakefield landed and took formal possession in the name of the Company.

We had now obtained the rights and claims of a large proportion of the owners of land on both sides of Cook's Strait.

The Kawhia claimants by conquest, and the Ngatiawa or actual occupants, had both been satisfactorily dealt with in a general way. It remained to satisfy the tribes resident along the sea-coast of the northern shore, between Waikanae and the Sugar-loaf Islands. Colonel Wakefield left it to future times to deal with the Ngatiawa of Waikanae, many of whose chiefs had been concerned in this last affair, and who had seemed moreover well inclined to join in the transaction on the occasion of Colonel Wakefield's recent visit to them. He also postponed to a less disturbed season the idea of dealing with the Ngatiraukawa. And he resolved next to proceed to Taranaki, in order to satisfy the now scanty occupiers of that extensive and fertile region by the mediation of Barrett and the ambassadors from Port Nicholson.

Considering a large district as secured on each side of the Strait, only subject to satisfying the least important inhabitants, Colonel Wakefield named the two provinces respectively North and South Durham, in honour of the then Governor of the New Zealand Land Company.

Having promised a passage across to Waikanae to some of the chiefs, we sailed for Kapiti on the 11th November.

We found that during our absence a barque had been here from Sydney, with an agent sent to purchase land for Messrs. Cooper and Levi,* merchants in that place. The whalers told us that he had purchased Kapiti, which we knew to have been purchased

* Cooper and Levy, after whom the two northern harbours of Banks Peninsula were named. The ship appears to have been the *Eleanor*, Captain W. B. Rhodes, who went on to leave cattle, with a stockman in charge, at Akaroa.

already so many times, that we omitted both that and Mana from the list of places to which we had bought the natives' rights.

We were detained a week here by a succession of light baffling winds and calms. During this interval, Wharepouri and several other chiefs from Port Nicholson, who had joined the muster at Waikanae, came across in their war-canoes to see us. On one occasion, three, well manned and armed, bearing together nearly one hundred men, came alongside. They look very pretty when at full speed. The finely-carved head and stern of the canoe are ornamented with feathers of the pigeon and albatross; and bunches of the latter plumage, or of that of the gannet, are disposed along the batten which covers the joint of the bottom and top side of the canoe. The men are placed at equal intervals along either side to paddle; and they keep excellent stroke to the song of two leaders, who stand up and recite alternate short sentences, giving the time with a *taiaha* or long wooden spear. Two experienced hands in the stern use larger paddles for steering.

The *taiaha* is rather a long-handled club than a spear. It is generally made of *manuka*, a very hard, dark, close-grained, and heavy wood. When polished with oil, it becomes nearly black. The *taiaha* is about six feet long. At one end is carved a representation of a man's head, thrusting out his tongue, which forms a sort of spear-head. His eyes are represented by small pieces of the mother-o'-pearl-like shell, which I have before alluded to as used for their fish-hooks, let into the wood. The tongue and face are all minutely carved so as to represent the *tattoo*. Above the forehead, a part of the stalk of the weapon is covered with the bright-red feathers from under the wing of the *kaka* or large parrot, to represent the hair; and an abundant tuft of long, white dog's-hair imitates the feathers or head-dress. The *taiaha* is held just above the dog's-hair, and flourished in the right hand with the tongue downwards. From this place the stalk gradually expands into a flat, sharp-edged blade, about three inches wide at the end; and this is the part used to strike in fighting, both hands managing the weapon like a quarter-staff.

Wharepouri could hardly talk about the prospect of the settlers arriving at Port Nicholson. His mind was quite unsettled by the warlike aspect of affairs, and he spoke of the probability of his

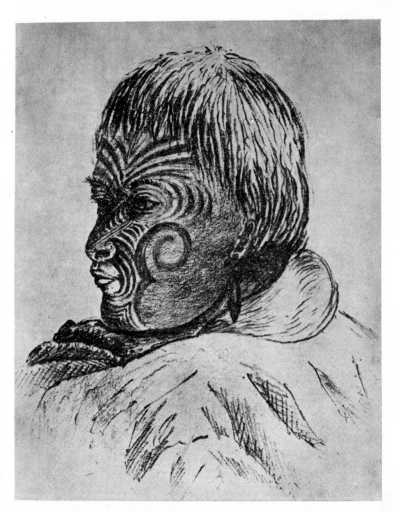

TE RAUPARAHA

EDWARD JERNINGHAM WAKEFIELD, 1820-1879

death in the approaching contest. We ascertained that about 800 fighting-men had mustered at Waikanae, and that there would soon be 600 more of the Ngatiawa tribe from different parts of the Strait.

Rauparaha had been for some time at Otaki, as it was supposed inciting the Ngatiraukawa to renew the attack.

On the 17th November, we had got our anchor up, and sailed a little way before a light southerly breeze, which failed, however, when we had got opposite the Waikanae.

While we were anchored with a kedge, three chiefs, belonging to the Wanganui tribes, came off from Waikanae to commence negotiations for the sale of their district. They were allied to the Ngatiawa, and had taken great part in the defence of the place on the 16th of last month. They heard all the usual explanations, described the boundaries within which their claims lay, and, after receiving a fowling-piece each in part payment, signed a deed which had been translated to them. Two of them, Te Kirikaramu and Te Rangiwhakarurua, returned on shore. Kurukanga, the son of the latter, and principal chief of Wanganui, remained on board to show us the entrance of the river, and that we might land him to prepare his people for the completion of the purchase on our return. He was an active, intelligent man; and seemed highly anxious to have white men among his people. He was attended by a slave, who acted famously as valet-de-chambre, anticipating the slightest want of his master. This chief had taken a distinguished part in the battle of Waikanae. He was universally known as a brave warrior and skilful general.

On the morning of the 18th November, as we lay nearly becalmed off the sandy beach between Waikanae and Otaki, Rauparaha came on board, on his way from the latter place to Kapiti. He seemed ill at ease, although we greeted him kindly notwithstanding our aversion for his character. He asked for some grog, and then took an early opportunity of stating, in the most barefaced way, that he should sell some land to the vessel from Port Jackson, as he wanted more guns, and had only sold us Taitapu and Rangitoto; that is, Blind Bay and D'Urville's Island!

Colonel Wakefield reproached him instantly, and in the strongest terms, with his falsehood and duplicity; making Brooks, the interpreter, repeat to him several times that he had behaved as a liar and a slave, instead of a great chief. Rauparaha maintained, however, an imperturbable silence, giving no answer to this severe attack, or to the reproaches which all the cabin-party addressed to him. He demanded and drank another glass of grog, and then got into his canoe, which pulled for Kapiti.

We were of course much hurt by this rapid repudiation of his bargain; and, though we depended entirely upon the perfect justice and openness of the agreement which we had made with him, before so many witnesses and in such explicit terms, for our justification before the world, we foresaw some obstacles already arrayed against the peaceful settlement of the Strait during the life of this deceitful old savage.

CHAPTER V

A Dangerous Voyage : Taranaki
and Hokianga

IN THE evening a fine breeze swept us past Otaki; and in the morning we were far north of the Wanganui river. Kuru* and his attendant were now fairly puzzled; they had never seen their country from further out at sea than they go in their canoes; and as all the land north of Waikanae is level and low for a great distance inland, so as not to bear any distinguishing features from the Strait, they confounded different parts of this monotonous coast.

Dicky, however, recognised the land as being between Patea and Wanganui. We therefore took advantage of a fine north-east breeze off the land to run along close to it, towards the place we sought. I remained in the main-top most of the day, gazing with delight on the extensive tract of level plains which stretched back far as the eye could reach from the edge of the cliffs which form the shore. Smokes from two or three bays to the northward appeared to invite our approach. As we ran along under all sail in the smooth water sheltered by the land, in some places within less than a mile of the shore, we at one place got into shoal water, six and then four fathoms as we neared a stony point. Kuru warned us to stand off before his caution was confirmed by the lead. The weather was too thick for us to distinguish the mountains, which lie far distant to the east and south-east. We stood off for the night under easy sail; and found ourselves in the morning abreast of the river's mouth, about three miles off.

During the next seven days we were tormented by fresh gales from between west and north during the day, and calm moonlight

* Kuruhanga.

nights. In our various tacks towards the coast we could frequently distinguish breaks in the cliff, which Barrett recognised as the locations of Te Namu, Waimate, and other spots rendered famous by the visits of the *Alligator*,* and at which he had reposed during the great migration of the Ngatiawa.

We enjoyed magnificent views of Tongariro, a high snowy mountain about ninety miles from the coast, in which the Wanganui takes its rise, and also of Mount Egmont or Taranaki. The latter forms a beautiful object from the sea. It rises gradually and evenly from a circle thirty or forty miles in diameter, one-third of which circle is formed by the sea. With the exception of a small group of low hills near the Sugar-loaf islands, the land between the sea and the mountain forms an inverted amphitheatre, wooded down to within six or seven miles of the cliffs. The open ground seemed also interspersed with wooded portions. The Ngatiawa natives on board with Barrett almost cried with joy as they looked once more on what all the natives agree in describing as the garden of the country.

We at length anchored to the north of the middle Sugar-loaf island, on the morning of the 27th November, in eight fathoms. A long swell from S.W. made us roll very heavily.

A volcanic peak at Sugar-loaf Point shoots up to the height of 500 feet. Two islands lie at the distances of one and two miles respectively to the westward; and several islets and extensive reefs are scattered about on the southern side of the point. Barrett went off in a whale-boat, accompanied by Te Whare and Tuarau, the two young deputies from Port Nicholson; but he found the surf too heavy for landing. They succeeded in making themselves known to some natives on the beach, two of whom swam off through the surf, and came on board the *Tory*.

An interesting scene now took place: Maori custom had prevented any communication in the boat; and even for some time after they had got on board, all four sat weeping on the deck, with their heads buried in their mats.

One of the two strangers at length rose, and after the ceremony of rubbing noses had been performed by all, he related in a recitative

---

* In 1834, with unnecessary violence, H.M.S. *Alligator* rescued from the Maoris Jack Guard's wife and children, who had been taken prisoner at the wreck of the ship *Harriett*.

dirge, beautifully affecting in its tone and expression, the hardships and dangers which had been endured by those on shore since the retreat of the main body of their relations. Their numbers, he said, had been woefully diminished by the predatory incursions of the Waikato war-parties. They had repeatedly been besieged in their strongholds on the peak or the islands; and, unable to trust themselves so far from places of refuge as to cultivate to any extent, had lived in a great measure on fish and fern-root. 'But,' he said, 'though we muster now no more than threescore, we have determined to remain on our dear native land, and to struggle on through fear and hunger. We are glad to see our brothers from Port Nicholson, and our old white friend.'

Tuarau answered them in an encouraging strain; telling them how he had brought white men to pay them for their land, and to protect them from their enemies; and how a like protection had been needed and secured by his fathers in the south. He drew a short sketch of our progress and intentions, and then delivered the advice of Te Puni and Wharepouri, that they should sell Taranaki to their good *pakeha*, or white man.

The next morning we landed Barrett and his train, including Tuarau. It was declared impossible to collect the different chiefs connected with the district of Taranaki in less than a week, as some of them resided far off. Colonel Wakefield, therefore, determined to leave Barrett here to prepare the natives for the sale, and to proceed himself at once to Hokianga and Kaipara, two harbours in the north of the island, where he had to discover and take possession of certain districts which had been acquired by the Company from former purchasers before we left England.

Dr. Dieffenbach was also persuaded by my uncle to land here, and seize the opportunity of examining Mount Egmont and the surrounding country, so highly interesting to the geologist, and of which so little was yet known from authentic sources. The surf was still exceedingly high on the beach; but the whale-boats landed Dicky and all his goods and chattels, animate and inanimate, by an early hour in the afternoon, and we weighed anchor and stood to the northward, before a fine fresh breeze.

Te Whare had determined to accompany Colonel Wakefield in his peregrinations; Jim Crow considered himself now as much attached to the ship as her figurehead,* and a native of Rotuma (one of the South Sea Islands), named 'Saturday', who had been whaling under Barrett, also made his choice for the *Tory*.

On the evening of the first of December, we came in sight of what we supposed to be the heads of Hokianga. We had on board some printed directions, given us in England, stating that a regular pilot lived at the entrance, and that a flag-staff on the south head was used to direct ships, by its signals, over the bar. As we could see no flag-staff, and as the sea appeared to break right across the entrance, we fired several guns, but received no answer. Accordingly, we stood off all night, and in the morning ran down about ten miles to the south, and found the real place. We had been last night off Whangape harbour, a place sometimes called False Hokianga, on account of its great similarity to this harbour. The thick weather had prevented any observations, and our dead reckoning had led us into this error. We passed safely over the bar, directed by the flag-staff, which is very ingeniously arranged, so as to incline to the right or left as may be required. A vessel entering or going out has to obey its motions by standing in the corresponding direction.

Immediately at the entrance were high sand-hills; but the appearance of the banks improved, being clear and level for some way back as we advanced. About twenty miles up the river the banks had become irregular and wooded. At a place called the Narrows they approach one another within two ships' lengths, having been as much as a mile or two apart up to that place. Two or three miles above the Narrows, and twenty-six miles from the river's mouth, we anchored close to two other barques which were loading *kauri* timber for New South Wales. On the bank to our left was the house and store of a timber-dealer and general storekeeper. In front was a small flat island, on which were some sawyers' and blacksmiths' workshops. On either side of this island a tributary of the Hokianga flowed into the pool in which we lay. To the right a point of land just hid from us the buildings of the head Wesleyan mission. In ascending the river we had passed Herd's Point. This is a tract of land that was purchased by the agent of the Company of 1825.

* The figurehead of the *Tory* was an effigy of the Duke of Wellington.

We found the whole country about the Hokianga river very irregular; and though there is a good deal of valuable and available land, it is much dispersed among steep hills, and intersected by innumerable creeks and mangrove-swamps. At low water the banks of the rivers have a most dismal appearance; these swamps and extensive banks of mud drying out to a considerable distance from the sound bank, and thus making the operation of landing extremely difficult and inconvenient.

During the next two days we visited different parts of the river. At Mangungu, the Wesleyan Missionary station above mentioned, we met with Mr. Bumby, then Chairman of the mission.

We found in this gentleman a truly worthy teacher of the Christian religion. He had visited Port Nicholson in the schooner which I before mentioned; and we now felt more than ever convinced that the native teachers left there had been led by jealousy to exceed their duties. He imagined, however, that he had secured the piece of ground at Te Aro, on which the houses and future chapel had been built. Colonel Wakefield told him how the natives had disregarded this verbal agreement unaccompanied by payment; but assured him that he would be at all times ready, in fulfilment of his instructions from the Company, to reserve a sufficient place in the future town for the location of a chapel and mission-house of each of the two stations.

At the mission were some poor farm-buildings; a press, which was worked by natives under the direction of Mr. Woon, the printer; and a very nice chapel. The buildings were of *kauri* timber, which works up very well. The rooms lined with this wood, carefully planed, had the neat appearance of a work-box.

In different places along the banks of the river, huge logs of this valuable wood lay ready for sale or embarkation. The few natives about the settlement were extensively employed in lumbering, and made large profits by this work and the sale of the trees. We were much struck, however, by the difference of character as well as physical appearance of the natives here in comparison with those of our friends in Cook's Strait. The latter had appeared far superior in stature and muscular power. There was here, moreover, none of the same eagerness to supply a ship with provisions. In all the harbours of Cook's Strait, we had always been surrounded by canoes, bearing more than sufficient for our consumption. Here, on the contrary, it was difficult to procure fresh provisions, even by sending to the residence of the chiefs. Entirely borne away by the high profits arising from the great competition between white men for the *kauri* logs, they neglected to cultivate the ground, and disdained going in their canoes to catch any of the fish which abound near the heads. During the whole time that we lay here, we had not a single canoe come alongside for the purpose of barter, and were obliged to procure our fresh provisions at an exorbitant price from a haggling white dealer.

The rest of the natives, who are all professed Christians, were accustomed to collect from different parts of the neighbourhood on the Saturday afternoon, in order to be in readiness for the morrow's services. They occupied a collection of temporary huts at the foot of the gentle slope on which the chapel and mission are built. I was much struck by their miserable outward appearance. They were wretchedly clothed, covered with dirt, badly supplied with food, generally speaking weak and sickly-looking, and altogether more abject in their manners and miserable in their condition than the slaves at Pelorus River, who, however poor and degraded, had at least some lightness of heart and physical energy. The missionary natives showed no curiosity as to us, and hardly turned their heads to answer a question; they seemed to have lost all the Maori's natural vivacity and inquisitiveness, and to be a generation whose feelings and natures were blunted.

In a word, they appeared tamed without being civilized. Together with the ferocity they had lost the energy of the savage, without acquiring either the activity or the intelligence of a civilized man.

They performed, however, their part of the religious ceremonies on Sunday with great order and decorum; joining universally in the responses and hymns, and listening with marked attention to the sermon which followed.

On the Monday they again disappeared; having excited no feeling in my mind but that of sincere pity for their degraded physical state.

About two miles above Mangungu, we found the establishment of Lieutenant McDonnell, who had been some years in this country, and who had sold his claims to certain districts of land here and at Kaipara to the Company. A brig was loading *kauri* spars at the river-side. A nice wooden house, belonging to Lieutenant McDonnell, stood on a terrace about fifty yards back from the river. Mr. Marriner, his agent, had a comfortable cottage on the bank below, buried in the midst of flourishing gardens. The fig and prickly pear were growing well in the open air; and a vineyard, with three hundred and fifty vines of different sorts, promised great things. Some cattle belonging to Mr. McDonnell were running on the tops of the hills, and one of these, which we bought for the ship, was very fair meat.

We saw nothing of the Roman Catholic Bishop, Monseigneur Pompallier, who, we were told, had lately bought land for a missionary station on the banks of the river, and made many converts. He had been attacked by both sects of Protestant missionaries in the most intolerant manner.

Colonel Wakefield took formal possession for the Company of Herd's Point, and of a district of land opposite called Motukaiaka, bought of Mr. McDonnell, who had obtained from the chiefs of the Ngapuhi a promise in writing to sell him a tract of land on the Kaipara, which was also bought by the Company.

The chiefs assembled at Horeke, Mr. McDonnell's station; and they confirmed the agreement, and deputed a chief named Taonui to go with us to Kaipara and show us the land in question.

Previous to sailing, Colonel Wakefield purchased from a lady, representing herself to be the widow of Captain Blenkinsopp, some deeds professing to be the original conveyances of the plains of Wairau by Rauparaha, Rangihaeata, and others to that gentleman, in consideration of a ship-gun. They were signed with elaborate drawings of the *moko* or *tattoo* on the chiefs' faces.

On the 16th of December, we set sail for Kaipara. On the evening of the 18th, we anchored in ten fathoms, on the tail of one of the extensive banks which lie outside the entrance of that harbour to the distance of five or six miles from the land. We caught in two hours enough snapper to last the whole ship's company for many days.

19th December.—This morning I was awakened by Dr. Dorset, who told me that we were aground. As I was swinging in a cot,

I could not feel any bumping, and treated his announcement as a joke. On his repeated statements, however, I put my foot on deck, and soon felt a tremendous bump. I dressed in haste and hurried on deck. The usual measures to get the ship off were taken, but in vain. Captain Chaffers and the well-disciplined crew exerted themselves most creditably. Five of our guns, three or four anchors and cables, a deck-load of spare spars which we had taken in at Hokianga, and several other heavy articles, were thrown overboard. Kedges were carried out and hauled upon, but with no effect. Some heavy mill-stones and paving-flags were got up out of the hold and rolled overboard. One of them was carelessly sent through our best whale-boat, which lay at the gangway.

During half-an-hour the ship continued to bump heavily. An old man-o'-war's man, who had joined us in Plymouth Sound, amused me much by his determined *sang froid* on this occasion. He happened to have been in the *Pique* frigate, on the famous voyage which she made across the Atlantic without a rudder after striking on a rock on the coast of Newfoundland. He was now at the helm; and coolly rolled his quid in his mouth, as he related in a low tone the more appalling dangers of that adventure, or warned me to keep further from the wheel, each time that a bump of the rudder made it spin round like the fly-wheel of a steam-engine. 'This is only soft sand,' said he; 'I've been bumping on hard rocks for a day and night and no harm done: shear a *little* further off the wheel, sir, and mind your legs with them chains,'— then a bump and whir-r-r-r went the wheel—'only soft sand, sir!' as he rolled his quid over, and again handled the wheel. 'All right, sir,' to an inquiring glance from the captain as to the feel of the rudder—then another great bump, and warning, and whirling, and rolling of the quid, and then he resumed his yarn as quietly as if nothing were the matter.

The tide having ebbed, it became impossible that the vessel should come off until the next flood. Colonel Wakefield mustered a crew of volunteers from the cabin to pull ashore in the whale-boat which remained whole, and obtain assistance from the *Navarino*, a vessel which we had been told at Hokianga was loading spars about thirty miles up the river. We thus left the most useful men on board, with the longboat and cutter, the two best boats.

Te Whare, Saturday, Mr. Heaphy, Dr. Robinson, Dr. Dorset, and myself were to pull at the oars, thus having one spare hand to relieve the tired; and Colonel Wakefield steered.

We were no sooner out of the eddy formed by the ship, than we were hurried along seawards, notwithstanding all our efforts, by the fierce ebb tide. The heavy swell had now begun to break on the outer edge of the shoals, and the roar sounded louder and louder in our ears as we drifted nearer to the breakers. The day was cloudless, and the sun, nearly at the zenith, distressingly hot. The chronometers and deeds had been placed in the stern-sheets for safety, but not a drop of water. We worked until we could perspire no longer, and then the toil was excessively painful. An ineffectual attempt to anchor in one of the channels had only lost us ground, the line having proved too short; and we were soon within a quarter of a mile of the outer breakers, which seemed to menace certain destruction.

Just as we had given ourselves up for lost, a faint breath of air was felt from seaward; one of the natives' blankets was extended between two stretchers in the bow; and this, with the unremitting efforts of the rowers, kept us in about the same position for two or three hours, till the flood-tide made.

Even then we were not in perfect safety; the flood set so strongly to the northward that we became involved among new breakers. Saturday, however, here took the steer-oar, and steered us with great presence of mind through a threatening line of surf; when we found ourselves in a smooth channel, gliding towards the harbour at the rate of five knots. Each rested on his oar, and we now paused, to establish a better mast and sail with a blanket stretched on two of them.

I shall never forget the pleasure of the first drink of water at the rill on a beach near the North Head.

We pulled and sailed about twenty miles up the harbour, which is a great estuary, five or six miles wide, receiving the waters of several rivers; and had just gained sight of the vessel's masts about ten miles from us, on rounding a point to the north, which opened a view of the Wairoa or 'Long-water' river, when the tide turned against us. We were thus obliged to land on the nearest beach, and encamp till the flood. As we had worked hard since the morning, without even breakfasting, this arrangement was agreeable enough to us; and some tin cans of preserved meat, and our small store of biscuit, were soon finished. Clouds of mosquitoes, however, defeated our attempts to sleep. The smoke of the fire had scarcely any effect on them, and while our eyes were filled with wood-smoke, they were stinging our knees and every other part of our bodies that was unprotected by anything thicker than duck. Half-burying oneself in the sand, smoking, expeditions to distant parts of the shore, or among the fern at the back of the beach, and up the small hills by which it was skirted—all proved unavailing to get rid of these terrible enemies; and at the first dawn of day, as soon as the tide had turned, we were glad to leave the inhospitable beach and get into the boat, stiff and unrefreshed. Even the natives had exclaimed against the numbers and perseverance of the *naenae*, as the mosquitoes are called in Maori. Saturday's stolid unconcerned face was rich to behold, as he sat by the fire stirring them out of each ear with a small twig.

A few hours' pull brought us alongside the *Navarino*; where we were most kindly received by Captain Warming, as soon as we had told our doleful tale. He treated us with the most genuine hospitality, and immediately dispatched his mate, with an efficient boat's crew, to the assistance of our shipmates.

After some breakfast and a refreshing bath, I slept soundly for some hours; and, soon after getting up, had the satisfaction of seeing the *Tory* come full sail round the point near to which we had passed the night. She had forged over the bank into deep water, after being exposed for some hours to heavy seas which broke over her.

The vessel was so much injured as to require heaving down, and thus it became necessary to take out all the cargo and ballast. It was plain that she would not be again fit for service for a month or two; and the time was fast approaching when Colonel Wakefield had engaged to meet the first fleet of emigrant-ships at Port Hardy in Cook's Strait. Colonel Wakefield therefore determined to proceed overland to the Bay of Islands, in order to charter a small vessel to take him to Port Hardy, and then join us here. He started in one of our boats up the Wairoa river on the 26th December.

On the 29th, the boat returned, having landed Colonel Wakefield about one hundred miles up the river. The party described the river as navigable for shipping up to that point, and the banks as clothed with the finest *kauri* timber, from twenty miles above our anchorage. They had passed several sawyers' and lumberers' stations, and also stations of the Wesleyan and Catholic missions. They described the mosquitoes to be in great numbers and extraordinary vigour in every place where they had stopped.

All the cargo was now landed and stored under tents ashore. The cabin-party also established an encampment under a cliff nearly abreast of the anchorage. The *Tory* was hove down on a sand-bank at the first spring-tide, on the 4th of January; and, after a survey by Captains Chaffers and Warming, the necessary repairs were proceeded with.

The land in the neighbourhood of Kaipara harbour and its tributaries is far from promising in appearance. The part near the anchorage is chiefly table-land clear of timber; and the barren clay of which it consists seems to refuse sustenance to anything but stunted fern. In the valleys cut out of the table-land by sluggish streams there are dull swamps which might furnish more available land when drained.

§

About the middle of January, (1840), the *Guide* brig arrived, bringing letters from Colonel Wakefield to Dr. Dorset and myself. These informed us, shortly, that he had reached Port Hardy on the 11th of January, without finding any ship from England; and he instructed Dr. Dorset to put some goods on board the *Guide* and proceed to Taranaki, in order to complete the purchase there, and bring Barrett and Dr. Dieffenbach to Port Nicholson. If we reached the latter place before him, we were to get the natives to build plenty of temporary huts, in readiness for the emigrants. He had chartered the *Guide* by the month.

This brig was an old whaler belonging to Sydney; originally a Calcutta pilot-brig, teak-built, of about 150 tons burden, and swarming with cockroaches.

A crew had been collected by the great personal exertions of Colonel Wakefield and Mr. Blackett, at the Bay of Islands, and consisted of the worst class of runaway sailors, and probably worse regular 'beachcombers' of Kororareka. The captain was a lazy, indolent old man, fond of grog, and of sleep, and of a good charter by the month. The mate was the former doctor of the vessel when whaling, perfectly ignorant of navigation and seamanship, and, like the captain, perfectly devoid of influence over the rascally crew.

Dr. Dorset, Doddrey the storekeeper, and I, were the only ones who took up our berths on board. The necessary quantity of goods being on board, we proceeded down the river; and, on the morning of the 29th of January, left the heads with a light south-east breeze and ebb-tide.

We at length, after constant southerly gales, managed to come in sight of the Sugar-loaf islands on the 1st of February, and anchored to the north of the inner one, Moturoa, or 'High Island', in the afternoon. Barrett came off from the island and piloted her to the anchorage.

Dr. Dorset and I landed on Moturoa, and clambered up the sides of this conical rock to a terrace about 100 feet above the sea, where our friends had taken up their abode. We found ourselves in a niche about twenty yards in circumference, sheltered by an over-arching rock. In one corner was a *wharepuni*, occupied by Barrett and his family, and in the middle a *whata*, or 'storehouse', stuck upon four poles about six feet high, and only approachable by a wooden log with steps cut in it. We were received cordially by Rangi and the children, Barrett's black cook Lee, Dr. Dieffenbach, 'Worser', the whaler, and six or seven natives of both sexes. Barrett related to us all that had occurred since we left him there.

I ascended Paritutu, or 'Obstinate Cliff', the Sugar-loaf Peak on the main, accompanied by Dr. Dieffenbach. It is nearly five hundred feet high; and almost perpendicular on the side next the sea, whose sullen roar against its base sounds diminished to the ear. The two islands, Moturoa, and Motuomahanga, or 'Isle of Refuge', appear like rocks to seaward. Inland, a magnificent extent of country meets the eye. For some miles from the coast it seemed clear from wood; then were extensive park-like glades and groves on the edge of the forest, which rolled far eastward in soft undulating lines. Mount Egmont's snowy peak towered out of the clouds at fifteen miles' distance, and Tongariro, at least ninety miles distant, appeared more to the north, glistening over the most distant forest ridge. Cape Egmont to the south-west ran down gradually to a point, one gently curved line extending from the sea to the summit of Mount Egmont. To the north a spacious bay extended to near Albatross Head at the entrance of Kawhia, dotted in its centre by some remarkable white cliffs, called Parinunui, or 'Large Cliffs'. On the top of Paritutu we observed two or three pits, the remains of places of refuge of the Ngatiawa from their enemies.

This evening a strong north-west gale set in. In this case the anchorage becomes dangerous, and the cutter, whose captain was warned by Barrett of the approaching storm, hove up her anchor and walked away to windward in the first of it. Our skipper, who had irresolutely postponed his determination to the last, at length slipped his anchor, and stood under easy sail to the northward. Unable to tack, he came back after wearing, evidently in a worse position than before; and dusk, accompanied by a whirling tempest of wind, lightning, and rain, hid the brig from our sight. Clinging hard to the rock in one of the crannies on the northern side of Moturoa, we lit a beacon-fire, and made out a light on board which proved her to have anchored again just outside the surf.

We crept into the *whata*, appointed for the sleeping-place of Dr. Dorset, Dr. Dieffenbach, myself, and two natives, with no pleasant anticipations as to the fate of the brig. The gale had come on so suddenly that we had not had time to remove anything from the brig, and all the Company's deeds were on board in my desk. Doddrey, however, was in charge of it, and 'Worser' was fortunately on board with one or two whaling natives.

We were rather cramped in our elevated bed-room; which was so small that the only way of sleeping five in it was to lie across the narrow way, about four feet wide, and double up our legs. The violence of the storm, which beat right into the niche, precluded, however, any idea of sleeping outside; and we made the best of it.

In the morning the brig had disappeared; much to our contentment, for we had expected to have seen her lying wrecked on the beach. She did not again make the anchorage until the 13th February.

During this interval we lived in the niche on Moturoa, plentifully fed by the natives. 'Black Lee', the cook, had a knack of

D

making excellent dishes of pork, potatoes, pumpkins, leeks, and fish, of which we got plenty. Then Dicky was never at a loss for a yarn, and kept us all in good humour. A clamber to the top of the island two or three times a day to look out for a sail afforded some employment; as the path was anything but easy, and the footing on the worn rock rather precarious. About half a dozen huts were perched about on different parts of the rock, and caves were hollowed out wherever the ground had been soft enough, and neat wooden doors placed to shelter the stores in them.

We landed twice on the main during these twelve days; but were glad to return to the island to sleep, the mosquitoes being in myriads on shore. We did not walk far from the landing-place, as the natives had no great store of food on the main, and it was necessary to embark before the surf should be too heavy for our small canoes.

Dr. Dieffenbach related to us his adventures in two attempts, the first of which had been unsuccessful, to reach the summit of Mount Egmont, which he had calculated to be about 9000 feet above the level of the sea. He had also been along the coast as far as Mokau about halfway to Kawhia, where he had been received by the natives with primitive hospitality. He has since given, in a publication of his own,* an interesting journal of these expeditions.

It was here, that I was first struck with the absurdity of maintaining the native language, and the extent to which this was done by the missionaries. Some of the latter, on their recent visits, had baptized and christened most of the children, and many of the grown people. They gave them English names; but, instead of spelling these names in English and teaching the natives so to spell, write, and pronounce them, they taught them to pronounce them in Maori in the way nearest approaching to the actual sounds; and then commemorated this adaptation by a printed card, on which the transmogrified name appeared, with the date of baptism. Thus 'Caroline' was printed '*Kararaina;*' 'Edward', '*Eruera*'; 'Charlotte', '*Harata*'; 'Judith', '*Urihi*'; 'Solomon', '*Horomona*'; 'Paul', '*Paora*'. This seemed indeed an advance in order to retrograde: it would surely have been preferable to baptize them by *native* names, if they would not teach them the English lan-

* Dieffenbach's *Travels in New Zealand*, London, 1843.

guage in the missionary translations of the Bible. The Maori language is essentially a poor one, and possesses in particular but few words which express abstract ideas. The translators have overcome the difficulty by coining words, written according to the Maori pronunciation which nearest approaches to the word sought to be represented. All proper names, too, are transformed in the native Bible like those given to the natives.

Examples of these manufactured words* are:

glory	*kororia*
victory	*wikitoria*
amen	*amine*
Jerusalem	*Hiruharama*
minister	*minita*
devil	*rewera*
hymn	*himene*
book	*pukapuka*
king	*kingi*
bishop	*pihopa*
Jesus Christ	*Ihu Karaiti*

We had begun to despair of the reappearance of the brig; and thought it extremely probable that the disorderly crew had taken possession, and carried her off with her cargo to some other country.

On the 13th February we made out a sail to the west-south-west. Barrett launched his whale-boat, and we boarded the old *Guide* about six miles off the islands. She had fortunately left a buoy to her first anchor; and to this we fastened her in the evening.

14th February: The natives came on board to-day, and after some hesitation on account of a desire for more fire-arms, agreed to sign the deed on the morrow.

15th February: This morning I took the deed, drawn up like the former ones, ashore. Barrett translated it, and explained its provisions. Forty-seven signatures were than appended to it, including the women and the children, whom the chiefs compelled to come and touch the pen, as they would be the future chiefs. Two or three young men, who had acquired the knowledge of

* This list has been considerably abbreviated from that appearing in the original edition of this book.

writing, signed their names in full. The others made a cross opposite to their names, as had been done on former occasions.

A party of fifty or sixty natives, who had arrived from a settlement further south, now expressed a desire to sell another tract
of land adjoining that sold by the Ngamotu chiefs; and a large
number of them signed a second deed after a short negotiation.
The goods were then landed in whale-boats through the surf.

The Ngamotu natives got quietly through the distribution of
their share; but those from the southward, who were extremely
wild and uncouth in their manners and appearance, although professing to be strict *mihinare*, or 'missionaries', could not effect it
without a scramble.

The two purchases extended from a spot half-way between the
mouth of the Mokau river and the Sugar-loaf islands, to a river
called Wangatawa, south of Cape Egmont; and inland, to the
summit of the mountain, and thence to a spot on the banks of
the Wanganui river, high up its course. Had we been provided
with a handier vessel and good crew, we should have proceeded
to extend the transaction by treaties at Mokau, and at Patea
between Cape Egmont and Wanganui; the chiefs of those places
having been prepared for such an arrangement by deputations
which had travelled to Ngamotu in order to treat with Barrett
during our absence. We were forced, however, by the inferior
sailing-qualities and appointments of the *Guide*, to renounce these
expeditions on a dangerous lee-shore; and turned her head towards
Port Nicholson on the evening of the 16th. The whole menagerie
from Moturoa was transferred on board; three Mokau chiefs
accompanied us, in order to urge upon Colonel Wakefield the
purchase of their country; and we bade farewell to our friends at
'the Islands', promising that they should soon have *pakeha* to live
amongst them.

Just as it fell dark on the 20th, we rounded Cape Terawhiti,
with a freshening breeze from north-west. The skipper got very
nervous when the squalls came whistling off the high land about
Sinclair Head; and, ignorant of this coast, seemed to dread the
long lines of black reefs with which it is fringed. We all, however,
supported Dicky Barrett in his earnest declarations that it was
necessary to carry on; and made all sail to windward. A fine moon,

peeping every now and then through the driving scud, lighted us on our way; and by daylight on the 21st February we were beating up within port Nicholson, close to Somes's Island.

CHAPTER VI

Petone Pioneers

W E SOON distinguished with great delight some large vessels at anchor between the island and the main; and, when nearer, shouted with joy as we made out white tents and new reed-houses along the line of beach at the foot of the Hutt valley. At about 9 a.m. we anchored north of Somes's Island, close to a newly-arrived emigrant ship. Two others, apparently discharged, also lay in the anchorage. Landing opposite Petone, I was delighted to meet Colonel Wakefield, safe and well. He was accompanied by Captain William Mein Smith of the Royal Artillery, to whom he introduced me as the Surveyor-General of the New Zealand Land Company. We were also greeted by several other gentlemen, whose tents or huts were pitched in the neighbourhood.

Colonel Wakefield was living in one corner of a large store-house built by Te Puni in the *pa* at Petone. On my way to this grand residence, I was affectionately greeted by the old chief and his people, who screamed our names, 'Tiraweke' and 'Takuta' or 'Doctor', in most dolorous strains. A perfect *tangi* or lamentation took place in the *pa* over Rangi and the rest of Barrett's train; and they all expressed their unfeigned delight at our happy meeting, and their satisfaction at the arrival of our friends from England.

While Saturday cooked some salt pork and potatoes at the fire in the court-yard, I sat down and listened to a brief account of my uncle's doings since we parted at Kaipara.

[*As already related, Colonel Wakefield had travelled in the* Guide *from the Bay of Islands to Port Hardy, in D'Urville Island, Cook Strait. Thence he had sent the brig to fetch Jerningham and Dr. Dorset,*

*while he went on to Port Nicholson, which he reached on 18th January,
to find that the Company's survey ship Cuba had arrived, and was
anchored off Somes Island.]*

On the 20th January, a sail had been reported outside; and he
boarded the *Aurora* at the heads. This was the first emigrant
ship that arrived. A strong north-west wind obliged her to anchor
at the entrance of the harbour until the 22nd, when Colonel
Wakefield left a pilot on board and returned to the *Cuba*. During
the next week, the work of disembarking had been going on. A
small jetty was run out by the surveying men; locations were
allotted near the beach for the pitching of tents and temporary
huts, in the erection of which the natives assisted; and some
wooden houses in frame sent out by the Company for the reception
of the labouring emigrants, were also set up. At this time a Mr.
Buller, a Wesleyan missionary, visited the place, and performed
divine service on board the *Aurora* on Sunday the 26th January.

More than one competitor, however, for land had visited the natives since our departure, and had attempted to buy patches of land
over our heads. One of these was a Mr. Robert Tod, who had
arrived in a schooner from South Australia, and had immediately
looked about for any chance of laying claim to a portion of the
land, which he understood from Smith, whom we had left here,
to be intended for the occupation of a large English colony.

A more influential and dangerous rival had also been here, in
the person of the Rev. Henry Williams, the chairman of the Church
mission in New Zealand, who had arrived in a schooner from the
Bay of Islands but a short time after our departure. Under the
pretence of securing a piece of land for the native teacher, named
Richard Davis, whom I have before mentioned, he had obtained
an assignment to himself of 40 acres in the best part of the proposed
site.

The natives repeatedly stated that Mr. Williams had, during
his visit, told them that the white settlers expected by us would
drive them to the hills, and that they ought to have disposed of
their land at the price of a pound a foot; advising them to claim
money on the return of Colonel Wakefield. Their good faith, however, was as yet unimpaired.

We afterwards heard that Mr. Williams had proceeded in our track about Cook's Strait; always forestalled by us a few days in our purchases of the land. At Kapiti he had expressed much disappointment at his inability to catch us.

On the 31st of January, the *Oriental* had arrived at Port Nicholson, bearing some of the leading settlers, as well as an additional number of emigrants. They had selected the banks of the Hutt river, about a mile from the sea, as a temporary location, and set to work on tents and houses. On the 7th of February, a sail being reported outside, Colonel Wakefield had gone out to the Heads in the *Cuba*, and brought in the *Duke of Roxburgh*, the third emigrant ship, whose captain had been lost overboard accidentally in a gale of wind off Stephens Island.

A few wanderers from South Australia, New South Wales, and Van Diemen's Land, had arrived between our departure and my arrival in the *Guide;* some with Mr. Tod, some in other small schooners and cutters. They applied themselves to make the most of the new colony by means of their colonial experience. One, named Coghlan, had established a grog-shop half-way along the beach, where a disorderly assemblage of sailors, stray whalers, and other bad characters from the different stations, had become accustomed to assemble, and caused some annoyance to the quiet settlers by their drunkenness and wild orgies. As there was positively no law or authority to prevent this, Colonel Wakefield's warning to Coghlan against a repetition of the disturbance had been treated with some contempt. Upon this he had explained his views to Wharepouri and Te Puni; and they, with several other chiefs of authority, had accompanied him, with their arms and mats of state, to the den in question. They then confirmed Colonel Wakefield's statement that he acted by their authority; and threatened to send Coghlan on board ship again if he should not, for the future, carry on his business in a more decent manner. This demonstration had had as good an effect as a caution from a bench of Magistrates.

In the evening of the day on which we arrived, February 21st, a fourth ship, the *Bengal Merchant*, anchored in the harbour. This vessel came from the Clyde, and was laden with Scotch emigrants. These seemed in high spirits; and, although the weather began to be wet for some time, they only remarked that it was 'rather saft', and worked away at temporary habitations like the rest.

During the next few days, I was busy visiting various old friends, who had squatted along the banks of the Hutt. The sand-hummocks at the back of the long beach were dotted over with tents of all shapes and sizes, native-built huts in various stages of construction, and heaps of goods of various kinds, which lay about anywhere between high-water mark and the houses. Thus ploughs, hundreds of bricks, millstones, tent-poles, saucepans, crockery, iron, pot-hooks, and triangles, casks of all sizes and bales of all sorts, were distributed about the sand-hummocks. The greatest good-humour prevailed among the owners of these multifarious articles; the very novelty and excitement of their employment appeared to give them high spirits and courage. They pitched their tents and piled up their goods in rude order, while the natives, equally pleased and excited, sung Maori songs to them from the tops of the *whare* or huts where they sat tying the rafters and thatch together with flaxen bands. As I passed along, I was greeted by many an old acquaintance among these, who would jump down from his work with a shout of joy, and inquire anxiously whether 'Tiraweke' had forgotten him. Then would come a merry congratulation at my having returned safe from the *pakaru* or 'broken' ship, and generally, to conclude, a proud sign towards the house erecting for his *pakeha*, and another cheer as he scrambled up again to his work. Thus I advanced through a running fire of kind greetings. At the back of the hut occupied by Coghlan, whither a flag-staff and New Zealand flag invited the sailors, a rough and new-made track struck off to the settlement on the river-bank, across a miry swamp. After about a quarter of a mile of this, I reached the junction of a small creek [Moreing's] with the Hutt; and soon found myself at the beginning of a little village of tents and huts, among the low scrubby coppice wood which covered this part of the valley. A rough path had been cleared by the surveying men along the bank; and on either side of this the colonists had been allowed to squat on allotted portions until the survey of the town should be completed.

The expected surveying vessel, the *Cuba*, had made a very long passage; and, after touching ineffectually at Kaipara and Port

Hardy, had come on to Kapiti, where those on board heard from the whalers that Colonel Wakefield had fixed on Port Nicholson as the site of the first settlement. They had accordingly arrived here on the 4th of January. Captain Smith, the Company's Surveyor-General, had preferred the lower part of the valley of the Hutt to Thorndon and its neighbourhood for the site of the town: as the whole 1100 acres, with sufficient reserves for promenades and other public purposes, could be laid out on perfectly level ground in the alluvial valley; while the hilly nature of the country at the south-west extremity of the harbour precluded the possibility of placing much more than half the town and reserves on flat ground. He had, accordingly, neglected the instructions given by Colonel Wakefield to the man whom we left here, to have the town laid out at Thorndon [the level piece of land at the south-west extremity of the harbour] and had proceeded with the survey on the banks of the Hutt.

I found, however, among several of the landholders already on shore a disposition to prefer Colonel Wakefield's first choice.

The site now under survey was found, as new lines were cut through its matted vegetation, to be in many places swampy, and much intersected by sluggish creeks, the land being so level as to want drainage. The distance from the sea, too, seemed a great objection; especially as the river was only navigable at high water, and the anchorage was exposed to a strong sea from the heads when the wind was southerly, and the long, shoal beach was in that case lined by an inconvenient surf, which interfered with the dry landing of goods. At Thorndon, on the contrary, the anchorage was landlocked; and the largest long-boats might run their noses on to a beach on which no surf could ever break, opposite the spot on which the town could be built. Looking forward to future times, it became evident that Lambton Harbour would become the seat of commerce by means of its natural capabilities; and it was feared that the possessors of the few earliest choices of country sections of 100 acres each might become the sole land-owners of a successful rival to *the* town, and *the* town itself sink gradually into disuse. The question, however, was postponed until the whole of the land-owners representing the preliminary settlement of 1100 sections should have arrived to give their opinion.

I found the squatters on the Hutt no less busy and merry than their fellows on the beach. I met and welcomed two or three old friends whom I had not seen since I left England, and made several new acquaintances among the young capitalists who were working with their retinue of labourers at putting their goods and chattels into some order and security. Three gentlemen, whom I was much pleased to see again in New Zealand, had formed themselves into a commercial firm, and had brought with them, among other things, the complete machinery of a steam-engine of twenty horse power, adapted for sawing or flour mills. These were Mr. Edward Betts Hopper, of Dover, Mr. Henry William Petre, and Mr. Francis Alexander Molesworth. They were as busy as the rest, landing and arranging their goods. At high water, the ships' long-boats and private cargo-boats brought quantities of goods up to the owners' locations; the labourers and masters worked altogether at the casks, and bales, and other heavy things; the natives lent their willing aid, being very handy in the water, and then returned, either to a job at hut-building, or to hawk about their pigs and potatoes, which they brought in canoes to this quick market.

I walked some distance along the surveyor's line, and made the acquaintances of such of the new-comers as I did not already know. Each capitalist appeared to have a following of labourers from his own part of the country. Cornish miners and agricultural labourers had pitched their tents near Mr. Molesworth; Kentish men dwelt near Mr. George Duppa, a little higher up; and many of the Scotch emigrants were collected near a point between two reaches of the river, where Mr. Dudley Sinclair and Mr. Barton were erecting their dwellings. At the latter place Mr. Sinclair's English cow was browsing on the shrubs of her newly-adopted country.

Small patches for gardens were already being cleared in various spots; ruddy flaxen-haired children were playing about near the doors; and the whole thing made an impression of cheerfulness and contentment.

Then the mildness of the climate, the good preparations made before leaving England, and the hearty good-feeling existing among the colonists themselves as well as between them and the natives, all tended to give the extensive bivouac the air of a picnic on a large scale, rather than a specimen of the first hardships of a colony.

For, although all were often wet in the numerous boat-excursions and fording of streams and creeks, or occasional showers of rain, no one felt any injury to his health; master and man toiled with equal energy and good-will; and both enjoyed a good meal, often served up with all the comforts of civilized life. Thus, in a little, cramped, but weather-tight tent, you found a capitalist in shirt-sleeves, taking a hasty meal of preserved meat and good vegetables (the latter grown from the seeds we had left with Smith), and drinking good beer or wine; and this from excellent glass and crockery, with plate, and clean table-cloths, and cruet-stands, and all the paraphernalia. The labourer ate an equally comfortable dinner from the *pot-au-feu*, full of ration-meat and potatoes or cabbages, which had been prepared by his wife at the gipsy-fire outside.

Each English family had got a native or two particularly attached to them. They supplied their guests with potatoes and firewood, and with an occasional pig; shared in the toils and meals of the family, delighted at the novelty of every article unpacked, and very quick at learning the use of new tools and inventions; chattered incessantly in Maori and broken English; devoted themselves, each to his own *pakeha*, with the greatest good-breeding, patience, and kind attention; and soon accustomed themselves to observe and imitate almost every new habit, with a striking desire of emulating the superiority of their white brothers.

Even this first step in colonizing their country must, however, have been a startling contradiction to all their previous ideas.

Although we had often explained to them that many hundred white men would come and cover the country, their minds had evidently not been of sufficient capacity to realize the idea of such numbers. The Maori language has no word for a number above *mano*, a 'thousand'; and even this is generally used indefinitively to describe any large amount.

Accordingly, soon after the emigrants from the two first ships had landed to look about them, Wharepouri came to Colonel Wakefield's hut one morning, and showed him the war-canoes hauled down to the water's edge ready for launching, in front of Petone. Upon being asked his meaning, he said he was come to bid farewell. 'We are going,' said he, 'to our old habitation at Taranaki. I know that we sold you the land, and that no more white people have come to take it than you told me. But I thought you were telling lies, and that you had not so many followers. I thought you would have nine or ten, or perhaps as many as there are at Te Awaiti. I thought that I could get one placed at each *pa*, as a white man to barter with the people and keep us well supplied with arms and clothing; and that I should be able to keep these white men under my hand and regulate their trade myself. But I see that each ship holds two hundred, and I believe, now, that you have more coming. They are all well armed; and they are strong of heart, for they have begun to build their houses without talking. They will be too strong for us; my heart is dark. Remain here with your people; I will go with mine to Taranaki.'

After some ineffectual attempts at dissuading him, Colonel Wakefield thought he had better not interfere any more with this sudden panic; and told him that if he doubted the power and wish of the white people to make the life of the natives happy, he had better go, although he should much regret the separation.

On Wharepouri's return to the *pa*, however, he found the council of chiefs, from which he had come with this message, totally dispersed. The emigrants had eagerly urged the natives to assist them in building temporary shelter. Some were gazing with delight on the liberal offers of blankets, guns, and tobacco made by the new-comers for materials and labour; while others had already started off to the woods to cut rafters and ridge-poles. Others were assisting to land goods, and could not be persuaded to remain idle enough to talk about going while good pay attended smart work. They unanimously refused to start until they should have reaped the abundant harvest to be obtained by working for the *pakeha hou*, or 'new white men'; and when they found that this harvest was continual, and that they were not only well paid for their work, but treated with uniform kindness and gratitude for their prompt services—when they found, too, that the visitors were not all stalwart, well-armed men, but many of them good-natured women and smiling children, while the very men proved kinder than they had expected—the canoes were hauled up, and the whole Taranaki scheme was treated as a vagary of which they were much ashamed. Wharepouri himself often laughed at this sulky fit with Colonel Wakefield and myself; and had domesticated himself as the particular friend of a family on the banks of the Hutt, whom he supplied with food and the labour of his slaves.

Old Te Puni had attached himself especially to Colonel Wakefield. The stores had been placed entirely under his care, of which he was not a little proud. He and his people were engaged on a good-sized house near the store-house for my uncle. Another Petone man had built a house for me; but as I was not sure of remaining very long, I had declined the honour of a residence of my own. I made the house, Maori retainer, and all, over to Dr. Dorset, who had taken shelter at first under the roof of an old friend of his, a passenger in the *Aurora*.

A brisk northerly wind and rain continued from the evening of the 23rd February to the morning of the 27th; but the squatting still went on with great vigour.

On the 26th, Captain Heale of the *Aurora* gave a farewell dinner on board to the principal settlers; and I, among others, accepted his invitation. The bright hopes and good prospects of the young colony formed the subject of several animated speeches, and various sanguine conjectures were hazarded as to the future history of the New Zealand flag.

The rain continued, with but few intervals, till the 1st of March, with a heavy south-east gale, which threw a heavy surf on to the beach, and tried the strength of several of the tent-ropes.

During this time, I either wandered about among the squatters, or chatted with the natives at Petone *pa*.

Colonel Wakefield and I lived in a room, partitioned off from the large barn-like store, which faced the south-east, and was anything but warm during the gale, the only window being a piece of canvas, and the door a rickety and badly-fitted one from a ship-cabin. A large dresser along one side of this room, which was about eight feet broad and twenty long, served for table and writing-desk. At the end furthest from the door, a 'bunk', or wooden shelf, supported Colonel Wakefield's bed. Mine was a cot, placed on the top of a pile of musket-cases and soap-boxes against the partition. The floor consisted of the natural grey shingle which formed the beach; and the roof, which was luckily waterproof, bent and yielded to every puff of wind. The plan of tying everyting together with flax, in both the walls and the roof, makes these Maori houses so elastic that no wind can blow them down. The thatched walls are highly airy, and a copious ventilation circulates through them in every direction.

We had, however, plenty of thick blankets, and used to sleep soundly and turn out fresh and hearty at daybreak. Then a sea-bath was close to the door; and wonders were done in the cooking way by Saturday, the Rotoma man, who officiated as Jack-of-all-trades until the return of my uncle's servant in the *Tory*. I used also to be constantly in and out of the tent of Mr. Henry Moreing, which was close by.

Next to his two tents was the camp of a Mr. Crawford, who had been one of the first overlanders from New South Wales to Adelaide, and who seemed determined to 'rough it' as roughly as possible. He dwelt in a low hut, into which it was necessary to crawl, in common with some uncouth-looking Australian servants, who made one think at once of bushrangers and banditti.

A brig arrived from Sydney with thirty head of cattle. She was stated to be chartered by a company formed in Sydney with a large capital to buy land and occupy it. The agent on board laid claim to a large tract of land nearly opposite the island of Mana, bought from some former purchaser; but the operations of the agent had been stopped by a proclamation made at Sydney on the 14th of January against any further purchasing of land in New Zealand.

On the 2nd of March, the first meeting of the Committee of Colonists* took place, in a wooden frame house belonging to Captain Smith, which was then situated in the sand-hummocks about half a mile east of Petone. Nothing could, however, be done beyond preparatory measures.

A report was brought, just at dusk on the same day, that the Hutt was overflowing its banks in many places; and we started in Barrett's boat to ascend the river in order to give assistance. The attempt proved ineffectual, owing to the force of the current swollen by the rains. In the morning, Colonel Wakefield went up the valley, and found that many of the reports had much exaggerated the real state of things. There had been, however, as much as eight inches of water in some of the houses on the river-bank.

* This was a body appointed to maintain order in the settlement.

In the afternoon, the *Cuba* returned from Kawhia [whence she had gone on 7th February], and anchored in Lambton Harbour, as a strong south-east gale was blowing, which made the roadstead at Petone inconvenient.

On the 4th March at noon, the gale ceased, the weather cleared up, and the sun shone out bright and warm. There is nothing more cheering than the convalescence of the weather in Cook's Strait after an attack of cold rainy weather from south-east. The atmosphere is rare and clear; everything dries quickly; and the plants seem to grow visibly as the wind shifts gradually round to a genial breath from north-east. I walked along the banks of the Hutt, to see what damage the flood had done. The people were all joking about the fright which it had caused them, and still appeared to treat it as a picnic casualty. Notwithstanding the long-continued rain and rough weather, no colds or rheumatisms were complained of, and the work of squatting went on as cheerfully as ever. Some, however, who had learned by the flood in how low a situation their first dwellings had been placed, determined to remove in time. About thirty or forty people, chiefly followers of Mr. Molesworth from Cornwall, erected a long row of reed and flax cottages on an elevated shingly ridge to seaward of the small creek at the south end of the bivouac, and christened it Cornish-row.

On the 5th, the boiler of the steam-engine was towed up the river, the different vents having been first plugged, so as to make it float. On the beach a speculator from Sydney attempted to sell some goods by auction in the open air, and collected a goodly throng of gaping emigrants; but he wanted an advance of 50 per cent. on Sydney prices for bad Sydney things, and could find no buyers.

On the 6th, the *Aurora* sailed for Hokianga, to get a cargo of *kauri* spars. One of the colonists departed in her with a saw-mill, being led to believe that he should be able to work it there with more advantage than here. Vessels had been seen outside the harbour during the last two days, prevented from reaching the heads by calms and light land breezes.

About four in the afternoon of the 7th, Colonel Wakefield and I were sitting outside Mr. Moreing's tent, enjoying a cigar and the genial weather, when we made out three large vessels at once at the entrance of the harbour. I soon recognized the old *Tory* as one of them. Just as it fell dusk, they brought up a sudden storm of southerly wind, lightning, and rain, which made us retreat under the tent as the squadron emerged from behind Somes's Island under full sail. We had not been very long under shelter, when Dr. Evans, one of the earliest members of the Association of 1837, burst into the tent, soaked through, but apparently wild with excitement and pleasure at having at length landed on the shores of the country in which he had been so long interested. He told us that the three ships were, the *Adelaide*, in which his family and those of several other principal colonists were passengers; the *Glenbervie*, which bore the manager, clerks, and well-lined safe of a branch of the Union Bank of Australia, both from London; and the *Tory*, with which they had kept company from Port Hardy.

In the morning, a grand salute was fired by all the ships, which lay at anchor in an extended line between the beach and Somes's Island. The weather was delicious; and a large concourse of those on shore assembled to gaze on the imposing sight. Six large ships, decked with colours, above which the New Zealand flag floated supreme, were thundering away. The natives shared in the general excitement, and proposed to take Colonel Wakefield in their canoes round the fleet. No sooner said than done; and away they started in three large war-canoes, racing under the stern of each ship in succession, while the salute continued. In Te Puni's canoe, the place of honour near the stern was assigned to Colonel Wakefield; and the two other canoes were commanded by Wharepouri and Tuarau. They shouted their war-song most vigorously as they passed close to each astonished poop-load of passengers, and completed the circle of the vessels at full speed without a single pause. I was much amused by the grimaces of Moe, or 'Sleep', who plied his paddle at the bow of his brother Te Puni's canoe, which got back first to the beach. 'Sleep' grinned hideously over each bow alternately in unison with the wild canoe-song.

During the next few days, the passengers of the *Adelaide* made themselves acquainted with the respective merits of the two sites for the town, and gave their voices almost unanimously in favour of Thorndon. It was therefore decided to commence the survey of that district. This change of course caused some delay, as the time already spent in cutting lines and laying out the streets in the valley of the Hutt became almost useless. It was doubtless, however, a wise change.

The machinery of the provisional government being now complete, the ratification of the chiefs of Port Nicholson was obtained to its Constitution, and the Committee was approved and empowered by them as a 'Council'. Measures were put in readiness for all sorts of public works; the appointment of officers, the regulation of finances, and the selection of sites for a powder-magazine, infirmary, and other public institutions, were considered; and the note of organization and arrangement sounded busily in all quarters.

CHAPTER VII

Journeys to Wanganui

THINGS WERE in this state, when I determined to set off on a journey along the coast towards the Wanganui river.

I had been much confined hitherto by the pretty constant employment of writing, for I had acted as secretary to my uncle; but now that a regular clerk had arrived in one of the ships, I resolved to take an opportunity of seeing for myself some of the natives unvitiated by intercourse with savage white men, and unimproved by missionary labours. I proposed to proceed past Mount Egmont as far as Mokau, and then to return, or proceed still further, according to circumstances. A great advantage was held out to me by the arrival in Port Nicholson, on a visit to some friends, of Te Rangiwhakarurua, or 'the Calmed Sky', one of the chiefs of Wanganui who had received a gun in part payment for that district on board the *Tory* at Kapiti, in November, 1839. He promised me a body of slaves to carry my baggage as far as Waikanae; where he said he would join me, and make arrangements for passing me on in one of his canoes. I agreed to this rendezvous; and the old chief brought me, on the morning of the 13th March eight native lads, who were to carry my baggage.

On the morning of the 14th, my goods were packed up into *kawenga*, or 'loads', by the slaves. They consisted of blankets, shirts, tobacco, pipes, axes, powder and shot, fish-hooks, beads, two double-barrelled guns besides my own fowling-piece, a little biscuit, log-books, and pencils, etc., etc. The 'boys' were extremely handy in making up the bundles, which they strapped on to their backs by belts resembling braces in form, neatly plaited of flax.

The usual farewell was shouted by the assembled Petone natives; and I started up a steep footpath beyond the Korokoro, or 'Throat' stream.

The Maori farewell is simple and dignified in its expression. The traveller says to those he leaves—'E *noho!*' ('Sit down!' or 'remain!'), or '*E noho ki to koutou kainga!*' ('Stop in your place.'); and the stationary party answer, '*Haere ki tou kainga!*' ('Go to thy place!'). In this case they shouted '*Haere ki Wanganui.*'

We ascended a steep hill, through extensive potato-gardens belonging to Tuarau; and from thence had a noble view of the harbour and the infant settlement. After a tedious march of two or three hours over very undulating ground on the top of the range, along a track constantly obstructed by webs of the *kareao,* or supple-jack, we came to the brow of a descent, from which we had a view of a narrow wooded valley, and a peep of the sea in Cook's Strait over a low part of the further hills. On descending the hill, we found ourselves in a fine alluvial valley, through which a considerable stream brawled and cascaded. Noble forest-trees and plenteous underwood intercepted all view of anything but the beaten track along which we progressed. Just about dusk, we emerged from the forest into a jungle of flax, shrubs, and long reeds, at the spot where the stream discharges itself into an arm of the sea which forms part of the harbour of Porirua, or 'Dark pit'. Wooded hillocks of moderate height surrounded this arm, and gave it the appearance of a small inland lake, which trended away to the northward. I was very anxious to push on to the spot where 'Geordie Bolts' of Te Awaiti had his whaling-station, as a heavy rain made it desirable to seek some shelter for the night. On advancing about a mile along the flat muddy beach of the harbour, I came to a hut, where three Europeans were gathered round a fire. They told me that it was yet two or three miles to the station, and that the tide was now up to the foot of the wooded hills further along, leaving no dry path. I therefore accepted their offer of a part of their hut. It was a miserably-built affair, and let in plenty of rain; but I covered myself with two or three thick blankets, and they kept me warm, although wet through before morning.

The three men were exceedingly rough-looking fellows. I after-

wards heard that I had passed the night with three of the most
dangerous characters on the coast, all supposed to be escaped
convicts from New South Wales. They were the positive refuse
of the whaling-stations. They treated me, however, with kindness
and hospitality in their rough way.

At daylight a sawyer's boat, attached to the whaling-station,
came into a creek close to the hut; and I made a bargain with
him to convey me to Parramatta,* as the whaling-station had been
named, after a town in the environs of Sydney in New South
Wales. My native attendants had been but scantily supplied with
food, and started off along shore to a settlement near the mouth
of the harbour where they had some friends. As I proceeded in
the boat, I saw them wading along under the branches of the
trees, often immersed up to their waists in the high tide.

After a pull of about three miles, we arrived at Paremata. It is
situated on a low point of clear land, on the north side of a narrow
gut by which the waters of Porirua harbour communicate with a
deep bay, opening into the sea nearly opposite the island of Mana.
The harbour consists of two arms; along one of which I had come
in the boat this morning, while the other, of nearly equal extent,
runs in to the north-east. The gut which I have mentioned is not
more than two hundred yards wide at high water, and both the
ebb and the flood run through it with great rapidity.

Jim Cootes, one of the three ruffians in whose company I had
passed the night, very hospitably took me to a comfortable hovel
near the whaling-station in which he lived; for neither Toms nor
any one whom I knew were at his house at the station, this being
out of the busy season. Two or three houses, such as we had seen
at Te Awaiti, and a filthy pigsty-like *pa*, were situated close to
the sheers under which the whales are cut up.

I had not been long at Paremata, when one of my boys, a free
native from Paripari, or 'Cliff-cliff', a settlement between this and
Kapiti, came over in a canoe to tell me that the slaves refused
to go any further. They were anxious to return and finish a house
which they had commenced for the white people at Port Nicholson,
and fearful lest some other natives should complete the house and
carry off the payment for the whole work.

*Paremata. Wakefield's account of the origin of the name has been questioned.

I paid the repudiating boys some pipes and tobacco, and sent them back with many reproaches for breaking their agreement.

The free man, however, resolved to go on with me. He was a strong, tall, and good-humoured young man, and seemed to take a fancy to the journey. He was named Puketotara, or '*Totara* hill'. The *totara* is one of the finest trees of the forest; and is the principal wood used by the natives, whether for canoes, houses, or fencing. Another who stuck to his bargain was Konatu, or 'Stand there!' I procured one or two more boys at Waikawa, and, by increasing the weight of the loads, managed to distribute all my cargo among the diminished number.

It was only on the next day, about noon, that the weather would allow us to cross the bay, as a strong southerly gale caused a rippling sea in the entrance, which is nearly a mile wide. About the middle lies a reef of rocks; and vessels enter between this and the south head, over a bar which bears fifteen feet at high water spring-tides, the fall of tide being from six to seven feet.

We now ascended a wooded ridge, through forests of much smaller timber and less impeded by *kareao* than that between Petone and Porirua. Four or five miles of easy travelling brought us on to an extensive and somewhat tabular amphitheatre, cleared to the extent of two or three hundred acres for native potato-gardens; and whence we looked, through the naked trunks of the trees left standing in the clearing, upon the island of Kapiti, and a long reach of the sandy beach and level country opposite. Penetrating through the gardens to the edge of a steep declivity over-looking the beach of a semicircular bay, we saw, on a spur of the table-land separated by two deep gullies through which streams run to the sea, a native *pa* or fort. This, my guides told me, was Pukerua, or 'Two hills', the usual residence of 'the Wild Fellow', [Tungia] whose noisy acquaintance we had made at Kapiti. From the depressed end of this spur the cliffy edge of the amphitheatre rises on either hand to a great height. To the north, especially, the coast for four or five miles is backed by an almost perpendicular wall 300 feet in height, but completely covered with stunted verdure.

In crossing the gully to arrive at the *pa*, we were met and welcomed by a madman, the first I had seen among the natives.

He was fantastically dressed in a mixture of European and native clothing, and jabbered away on all subjects with great speed, to the unbounded amusement of the monkey-like children, who flocked around the *pakeha hou*, or 'new white man'. The madman was quite harmless, and led me very politely to the hut assigned for my residence.

I found that 'the Wild Fellow' was absent at Kapiti; but the few natives in the *pa* prepared to make me comfortable, and the women soon produced an ample meal of vegetables and birds for myself and my train. The madman fastened himself to one of the posts of the house with an iron hoop, and amused the natives by extravagant orations till a late hour.

In the morning, having given some tobacco to the owner of the hut, and to the women who cooked the food, I proceeded along the foot of the verdant wall of which I have spoken. The beach was shingly and studded with rocks. I picked up several pieces of sponge on my way. At one spot we passed through a natural arch in a spur of rock which jutted into the sea. I had to get on to Te Puke's shoulders; and he seized a favourable time to run through the passage, as the surf occasionally rolled breast-high into it. A little further on, some neat plantations of the *kumara*, or sweet potato, betrayed the neighbourhood of a settlement. They extended about thirty yards up the face of the hill, in terraces formed by logs of wood laid horizontally, and supported by large pegs. The terraces were covered with sand from off the beach, which the natives assured me was the best soil for the growth of the *kumara*. In storms, these plantations must be covered with salt spray, and swept by the north-west wind; but on this day a hot sun shone upon the bank, and I was told that such a position was esteemed highly productive.

We soon reached Paripari, Te Puke's residence; and he insisted on my remaining there till the next morning. The village is situated on a terrace of the hill, about fifty feet above the beach, and very neatly built. Below, two or three canoes were hauled up under some *karaka* trees, which formed a pleasant grove in a sort of recess from the beach. The old men of the *pa* were sitting beneath their shade, enjoying their pipes. They greeted me very cordially, and held out their hands to be shaken, having lately become *mihinare*.

Puke explained to me that they were all of the Ngatiawa tribe. Arrived at the house assigned for my sleeping-place, one of the numerous children who had eagerly followed me presented me with a water-melon, which the heat of the day made me enjoy very much. I gave him a fish-hook in return, which the rest of the audience no sooner saw, than a large proportion of them started for more melons, and before the evening I was abundantly supplied. The natives were rather annoying by their eagerness in crowding round me, especially when eating a melon, as they would scramble across me for each single seed. I at last declared that I would throw all the seeds away if they did not all sit at a convenient distance; but that if they did I would take care of the seeds, and return them to the person who had sold me the melon. There were about one hundred natives at this village, men, women, and children: at Pukerua I had seen only about twenty, but some others were said to be absent at Kapiti with their chief.

About half-a-mile beyond Paripari the hills recede from the coast, and the rocky shore is replaced by a shoal sandy beach backed by sand-hummocks. Along this we travelled the next day about eight miles to Waikanae. The day was again extremely hot, with scarcely a breath of wind stirring; and I repeatedly stopped to sit down and eat a water-melon. We crossed several small streams, at the mouth of which were fortified villages. These were Wainui or 'large river'; Whareroa, or 'long house'; and Whare Mauku, or 'Mauku house'. At each of these I was pressed by some of the inhabitants to '*haere ki uta*', or 'go inland', meaning me to accept of their hospitality; but I had determined to get to Waikanae, and so refused them all. I learned that all these villages were inhabited by Ngatiawa.

At Waikanae I was recognized by many of my old acquaintances. Some had met me in Queen Charlotte's Sound; some in Port Nicholson; and some showed their healed wounds, and reminded me of my visit to them with the surgeons. My name was well known, and shouts of 'Tiraweke, Tiraweke!' passed along the avenues and court-yards. They told me that a white missionary was now living here.

In the native villages there are always two kinds of houses. The *wharepuni*, or 'house of rest', I have already described at the village near Ship Cove. I had since seen many much larger and more commodious than those at that place. They are all, however, built on the same principle, of keeping in the animal heat; and are therefore most repulsive to a European. Some of them have their front wall removed back three feet from the front of the roof. In this case a nice airy veranda is formed, which makes a very good sleeping-place. The *whare umu*, or 'oven-houses', have open walls, built of upright sticks at intervals of an inch or two. They have thatched roofs to protect the cooks and the store of firewood, which is generally piled up inside in rainy weather. The open walls let out the smoke and let in the air, and these kitchens are therefore much more adapted than the others for the bedroom of a traveller. At this time, too, the natives, although most of them professing Christianity, had by no means divested themselves of many of their ancient superstitions; one of which was a positive interdiction against the very presence of food or drink in a *whare-puni*. To light a pipe from the fire inside was considered equally sacrilegious. In order to avoid the inconvenience of these restrictions, and yet refrain from offending against any of the customs which I found still revered by my kind hosts, I therefore found it much better to take up my abode in a *whareumu* or *wharekauta*, both which names apply to the kitchens. Here I had only to avoid one thing, namely, the hanging food overhead; for this also is a terror, and if done intentionally, a grievous offence to the Maori anywhere.

Old Te Rangiwhakarurua not having arrived from the south, I got a canoe manned, and went over to Kapiti. The mouth of the Waikanae is choked up with sand-banks, but at high-water a whale-boat can enter and ascend the river about six miles. The hills are about seven miles from the beach here; and the *tahatika*, or 'flat tract', seems to improve as it recedes from the sea. Groves of high timber extend outwards about two miles from the foot of the hills.

Kapiti is about four miles from Waikanae. I took up my residence on Hiko's Island, and saw several of the chiefs who had been parties to the sale. They had all become converts since I was here before, and on the 22nd I heard prayers read and a sermon preached by a native teacher. Rauparaha was absent at Otaki.

On the 23rd March, Konatu and two or three other boys came over in a canoe to tell me that Te Rangi had arrived. I therefore bade adieu to my friends at Kapiti, and returned to Waikanae.

In the morning I gave Te Rangi a pair of blankets and some other little presents in return for the loan of the canoe; and we poled out of the river, some delay being occasioned by the necessity for steering clear of the numerous sand-banks. While on the beach waiting for the rest of my party, Whiti, one of the principal parties to the sale in East Bay, Queen Charlotte's Sound, addressed me. He reproached me strongly with having bought Taranaki, which, he said, belonged to him and the other Ngatiawa at this village. I told him that they ought not to have run from it; and that we had paid the people who had maintained possession through great troubles and danger.

§

We at length hoisted our sail before a fresh southerly breeze, amidst the discharge of muskets and shouts of '*haere!*' ('go!') about an hour before noon. Our vessel was a strongly-built canoe, with more beam than they generally have, and an extra top-side plank to keep out the sea. Te Ao, or 'the air', a son of Te Rangi, and half-brother of Kurukanga, was in command of the craft. Besides him, six young men, among whom was Puke, worked their paddles; and Konatu steered with a paddle, whilst another man yawed the canoe about with a clumsy imitation of the steer-oar used in whale-boats. Te Ao's wife and child, with two slave women, and two wretched-looking curs, completed our muster-roll. Cold cooked potatoes and fish were stowed in the bottom of the canoe, with large baskets of the kernel of the *karaka* berry.

The *karaka* tree much resembles the laurel in its growth and foliage. It bears bright orange-coloured berries about the size and shape of damsons, growing in bunches. The fruit is sickly and dry; but the kernel forms an important article of native food. It is enclosed in a tough stringy husk. The natives gather the berries when ripe; and after separating the pulp of the fruit from the kernel by steaming them in large *umu*, or ovens, they collect the kernels in baskets and soak them in a pool, dammed up in a running stream. They are allowed to remain in soak until they ferment, when they are fit for use. As they require no cooking, the natives use them extensively in travelling. A cockle-shell is used to break the husk. Their odour is so offensive that I could never prevail on myself to eat them; but I have known many Englishmen who had acquired a taste for them, and described them as very good food.

In the large canoes, a wattled floor, made of *kareao*, is raised level with the junction of the body of the canoe and the topsides; and on this the passengers sit. A square hole amidships is left for the use of the *ta*, or baling-spoon. This is rather a graceful implement, being often handsomely carved. It somewhat resembles the small shovel used to take coals out of a scuttle, with the handle turned forward over its upper side. We were provided with a duck sail, which most of the canoes now possessed, the owners having bought them of the whalers in exchange for provisions. The former native sail was made of a fine grass, woven into very pretty patterns, with graceful open work in various parts.

The boys pointed out to me the mouth of a river called Ohau, about fifteen miles from Waikanae. As we ran along about two miles from the shore, I saw a remarkable grove of high pine-trees rising from behind the sand-hummocks. This was an hour before sundown; and they told me that it was near the mouth of a river called the Manawatu, or 'Hold-breath', which flows into the sea about twenty-five miles from Kapiti. The hills between this and Otaki turn in to the eastward, so that the country begins to form a plain of great breadth.

At sunset the wind died away, and the boys paddled hard to reach another river called Rangitikei; but we found a heavy surf at its entrance, and although the moon shone bright, and fires were made by the natives on shore, it was reckoned prudent to defer the landing till daylight. When we had made an offing of about a mile, the crew repeated a short prayer, and then composed themselves to sleep, except those who alternately watched against a change in the weather or the drifting of the canoe towards the shore. When I woke once or twice during the night, the canoe was lifting over the long swell, the moon and stars shining bright and clear, and a heavy dew falling on the sleepers coiled in their blankets, and the only sound to disturb the calm of the scene was the distant roar of the surf. At the break of day I found the natives engaged in a lively discussion; unable, from the monotonous appearance of the low sand-hummocks which form the coast, to determine our exact locality. After some vain pulling about, first north, then south, they at length made up their minds that Wanganui lay about twelve miles north of us, and pulled in that direction.

A very heavy surf hid the coast from us every now and then; and when they discovered signs of an immediate gale from the south-east, my crew held a long consultation. My advice was asked as to whether we should at once land through the surf, or run the chance of being caught by the gale in order to seek smoother water at the entrance of the Wanganui. I left it entirely to them, and they soon afterwards turned the head of the canoe towards the shore. Before entering the surf, they made all preparations for an accident. They shook off their mats and blankets, and made me strip to my shirt and trousers. The guns and other heavy articles were lashed to the thwarts of the canoe. I was placed in the bow, between two strong fellows, who were enjoined to have a particular regard for my safety.

All hands now took to the paddles; two at the bow and two at the stern assisting the manager of the steer-oar to keep her square before the sea.

A 'smooth' or favourable moment was seized, and we dashed along on the top of a foaming roller, with our liveliest stroke and a cheering song. '*Tena! tena!*' ('Hurrah! hurrah!') shouted the steersman. '*Kia tika!*' ('Keep her straight!'), yelled the others; and the roller broke on either side of us, and roared along towards the shore. As the surf extended nearly half-a-mile from the beach, this was repeated several times; and the operation of landing was very well performed, excepting the conflicting advice which was given by all hands at once in the shrillest tones every time a roller passed. The moment we touched the sand, my two supporters lifted me up with a jerk, and pitched me high and dry on to the beach. Before I had time to recover myself, they had all jumped out into the water, and hauled the canoe out of reach of the next wave.

We encamped on the barren sand-hills at the back of the beach, and proceeded to dry our clothes, which had all been well drenched.

I was sorry to find that one of my only pair of boots had been lost during the landing. Ten minutes after we were in safety, the predictions of the weather-wise among the natives were verified, and a fresh gale came up in a puff from the south. It was accompanied, however, by fine, clear weather; and thus proved rather agreeable than otherwise.

One of the lads was at once despatched to Wanganui to give news of our arrival, and to bring back Kurukanga to meet me. In the meanwhile I walked along the sand-hills to the south, to a small river called the Wangaehu. At its mouth it was not more than twenty yards broad, but seemed deep and rapid; inside, it expanded to the width of a quarter of a mile. I picked up, on its banks, lumps of scoriæ and pieces of stone containing petrified shells, of the same kinds, however, as those now existing. Quantities of pumice-stone also spoke of the volcano of Tongariro, from which the natives told me that this river, as well as the Wanganui and the Waikato, take their source. All the coasts of Cook's Strait, indeed, are sprinkled with the pumice which constantly floats down the first two of these rivers.

In the evening, Kuru and about a dozen of his attendants arrived, with some slaves bearing potatoes and *karaka* nuts for our party. I had been much attracted by the engaging disposition and manners of their young chief during the few days which he spent on board the *Tory;* and was delighted to renew our acquaintance. He also appeared much pleased, and greeted me most cordially.

The drift-wood, which abounded on the beach, served to maintain large fires, in the ashes of which the potatoes were roasted; and it also formed a shelter from the wind, no despicable precaution against the fine sand which otherwise penetrates everything. Two small court-yards were formed by placing logs upright close to each other; one for our party and one for our visitors. At dusk, prayers were said, all having become *mihinare;* and then we lay down inside our fences. The wind died away with the setting sun, and the same clear moon and stars and heavy dew presided over the night.

In the morning, the sun rose cheerfully into a sky of pure blue; and the surf being much abated, the young men launched the canoe and proceeded towards the mouth of the river. I preferred walking with Kuru along the beach. I was of course bare-footed, all attempts at finding my unfortunate boot having proved ineffectual. The survivor was borne as a melancholy memento by one of my attendants; who took great pride in explaining its details and the fate of its companion to the wondering strangers. At one or two spots we got a glimpse between the sand-hummocks of the snowy summit of Tongariro, a broad-topped mountain. Although at least seventy miles distant, it was perfectly clear and distinct.

After walking about eight miles along the beach, we struck off across the hummocks, and two miles more brought us to an elevation whence I discovered the first reach of the Wanganui river. We were close to its south bank, and the entrance appeared about two miles to the westward, leaving but a narrow tongue of sand between this reach and the sea. I at once recognized the low cliffs of sand on the north head, and perceived the snowy cone of Mount Egmont over the tapering point of land to the west. A large extent of flat open country stretched away to the north-west on the opposite side of the river, here about half a mile in width. Descending to the beach of the river, we soon reached an encampment at the foot of a high cliff, which formed a bluff point on the south bank. A tent had been made purposely for me of the mast, yard, and sail of a canoe; and food, cooks, and steaming-ovens met the eye on every side. Kuru gracefully waved me to the tent, and invited me to rest. He prevented the inquisitive crowd from entering its door, and sat outside himself until I asked him to come in. It was lined with clean mats, so as to form a comfortable covered couch.

Several large canoes arrived in the course of the day from the villages higher up; and there were soon about a hundred persons assembled near the tent. Many of the chiefs made formal speeches, to the effect that I was welcome to the place. They afterwards approached the tent, and Kuru told me their different names and relationship to himself. Immediately on my arrival, he had killed a pig for me; at that time an invariable custom of native politeness towards a guest. During the speeches, he took particular pains to explain to me whatever expressions I had not understood, and to impress me with a knowledge of the character and influence of each speaker. His attention, generally, was most pleasing, and perfectly dignified and free from obtrusiveness.

The cliff I found was called Wahipuna, or 'place of the spring', from a small rill which gurgled from half-way up its side. As the water of the river is almost always brackish here, this becomes a great place for the encampment of passing visitors.

About noon, Kuru took me in a canoe to the principal village on this part of the river, on the same side as our camp, and about a mile above it. The high land, of which the cliff forms one extremity, recedes from the river near the mouth of a small tributary, and another low range of table-land closes in upon the river about a mile above this. On the river bank, in the midst of the level between the two ridges, the *pa* named Putikiwharanui was situated. On landing, I found about thirty large canoes ranged along the shore, and 300 or 400 people assembled to receive me. Kuru introduced me in due form to the three principal chiefs of the Wanganui tribes. Each of them sat in his own court-yard, surrounded by his own immediate followers. The first was Turoa, or 'High-stand', an old chieftain of the tribes which had migrated hither from Lake Taupo. He was cased in a thick coat of red paint, made of ochre and shark's oil, which covered his very hair and clothes. He motioned me to a clean mat spread by his side, and spoke a few words of welcome with much dignity of manner. He said the land was for me; that his child, Kuru, had told them all to sell it to 'Wide-awake',* and that, as I was come, it was there for me. Like speeches were made to me by Rangitauwira, or 'Sky Marked with Lightning', a very venerable grey-haired chief, bent nearly double with years, and uncle to Kuru; and by Te Anaua, or 'the Rainy Cave', the head chief of the Ngatiruaka, or aboriginal tribes, whose sister was Turoa's principal wife.

Te Anaua handed me a strip of paper from a cloth in which it had been carefully wrapped. On perusing it, I found it to bear the following written statement: 'Wanganui, December 17th, 1839: This is to give notice, that this part of New Zealand has been purchased of the native chiefs residing here for the benefit of the Ngatiawa tribes, extending from Rangitikei to Patea, towards Taranaki, by Henry Williams.' I translated this to the large concourse of natives who were assembled on the spot, and asked them

* Colonel Wakefield.

if it was true. They assured me most fully and unanimously, that neither had any such agreement been mentioned to them, nor had a single fish-hook or piece of tobacco been paid to any one, except to the boys who carried Mr. Williams's things, or to those natives who became converts to the Christian religion. I then asked Te Anaua whether he had been aware of the contents of the paper. He answered that he had not; but he thought it was a certificate of good character and hospitality left him by the missionary.

I answered the speeches of the chiefs by telling them that I was not come to buy their land, but to look at the people and the country; and that they must apply to 'Wide-awake' for the completion of the purchase, as I intended to travel about the country for a month or two. I presented each of the three head chiefs with a red blanket, and distributed fish-hooks and tobacco among the inferior crowd. I also bought with some more of the same articles a large store of *paua*, or native fish-hooks. I have already described these hooks, which are used for the *kahawai* fishery, and take their name from the *haliotis*-shell, with pieces of which they are lined. I had a long conversation with Turoa and some other chiefs after the ceremonial visits were over. This old chief described, in a pithy way, the effect produced on the natives of this place by Mr. Williams's visit in December. It appeared that, after missing us in Cook's Strait, that gentleman had landed at Waikanae with Mr. Hadfield, the missionary whom I had heard of there, and had travelled on foot nearly as far as Ngamotu at Taranaki, and then returned, leaving his companion at Waikanae. On my asking Turoa what sort of a man Williams was, and how he behaved to the natives, the old man answered, 'He is a *tangata riri*, (angry man) who shuts his tent-door upon us, and does not sit by our sides and talk kindly to us, as you do: but he had the *Atua* (God) upon his lips, and we are afraid of his anger.'

At daybreak next morning a whole fleet of canoes went out to sea to fish. Together with Wide-awake's* party, there were at least fifty sail. At the flood, which was in the afternoon, they all entered the river, and proceeded to fish for the *kahawai*, large shoals of which had come in with the tide. As this fishery is always con-

* A Taranaki chief, then on his way to Waikanae with a large party, whose nickname had been transferred to Colonel Wakefield by the Maoris.

ducted at full speed, the sea-reach, about three miles long, presented a most lively scene. A light breeze favoured the sailing one way; so that half of the canoes were under sail, and the others pulling in the opposite direction. They continued thus to alternate for two or three hours, singing as they paddled, and yelling with delight whenever an unusually large fish was hauled in. I passed through the centre of this fishing fleet, on my way to a fishing village on the opposite side, about half a mile above Putikiwharanui. While I was here, talking to several of the chiefs, sunset approached. The canoes came dashing in from the fishery, and a sort of harvest-home took place. Each crew joined in a triumphant chorus as they neared the village, and the old women, perched in various attitudes on the large racks erected for drying the fish, yelled out their discordant welcome, attended with much hideous grimacing. The fishermen jumped out of their canoes, and prepared to attack huge meals which had been cooked in readiness for their arrival; and the women cleaned and opened the fish, and hung them up on the racks.

While here, I collected a considerable number of mats of all kinds, some of which were given to me by chiefs, and the others sold by inferior natives. The mats are generally of four kinds. The plainest and least valued is the *porera*. This is plaited very closely with unscraped flax, split into narrow bands, and is used as floor-cloth for a house or a couch. It has a glossy straw-like surface, and is very useful in keeping a bed from the damp ground. I bought some about seven feet square for a few heads of tobacco.

The next in value is the *korowai*. It is woven of *muka*, or scraped flax, and ornamented with bunches of twisted tags of the same, dyed black. The tags are, however, sometimes left white; at other times they are formed of strings scraped only at regular intervals, thus leaving the gold-coloured straw on the spaces not scraped. By thus dyeing or not dyeing, scraping or not scraping the tags, or by alternating dyed and scraped, undyed and unscraped tags, on the same mat, a great many varieties of the *korowai* are made; but the most general one is that with scraped and dyed tags. These mats, although often worn by men, are more commonly the dress of the women.

A third sort of mat is the *tiehe*, or rough outside covering. Its

E

outside is formed of the refuse from the operation of flax-scraping; but the inner surface is often woven very closely, and of the finest flax. The slaves generally wear very coarse mats of this kind, having no women who are allowed to bestow pains on mat-making for themselves and their relations. The *tiehe*, like the *korowai*, varies much in colour and quality. They are all perfectly waterproof, the leaves of the outside thatch overlapping each other like tiles.

But the most valued Maori mat is the *kaitaka* or *parawai*. This is woven of the very finest, silky, snow-white *muka*, and is unsullied by any tag or ornament except a border of a foot in width at the bottom, and six inches on the two sides. This border is dyed black, except where sets of parallel zigzag lines, and the lozenge-shaped spaces between them, are left white or stained chestnut-colour with another dye. Lately a very bad taste of introducing coloured worsted, taken from European clothing, has spoiled the chasteness of their execution; but an old *parawai*, with nothing but Maori materials and manufacture, is certainly a very handsome garment, and the border is really classical in design.

The two sexes have different ways of wearing the mat or blanket. The man wears it tied on his right shoulder like a Roman toga, so as to have his right arm free; the woman ties it over her breast, and holds the sides together with her hands. In carrying a child, the man dresses like a woman, as the child clings round the neck of the person who carries him, and is sustained by the blanket, grasped tight round both their bodies.

On the afternoon of the 29th March, I told the assembled chiefs that I could not accede to their request to buy their land at once, but should proceed on the next day to the northward. They then determined that Kuru should accompany the Ngatiawa fleet to the south, and urge upon Colonel Wakefield the completion of his bargain. He, Turoa, and Wide-awake, took me up to the top of the cliff, from which a wide view of the country on the west bank was obtained, as well as of the valley in which Putikiwaranui is situated, of two or three miles of the river's course above that spot, and of the distant mountains of Tongariro and Taranaki. On the summit a carved and half-burnt post marked the site of an ancient *pa*, whence the assembled tribes of this district had

KAURI FOREST ON THE WAIROA RIVER, KAIPARA, NORTH AUCKLAND

Colonel W. Wakefield is at the steer oar of the boat

MAORI PROVISION HOUSE, OTUMATUA *PA*

formerly resisted the passage of the Ngatiawa across the mouth of the river. The three chiefs begged me to carve the name of my *matua*, or 'parent', as they called Colonel Wakefield, on this post; in order that his name might keep the land for him, as his child refused to do so. They said they wanted to prove to Mr. Williams, should he return to buy the land, to whom they had really promised it. I did as they requested me; and then passed over in a canoe, with all my goods, chattels, and retinue, to the opposite shore, where some of the boys had already pitched the tent.

In the morning I made agreements with a body of carriers, including one or two of those who had accompanied me from Port Nicholson; and started over the sand-hills to the beach about two miles beyond the river's mouth. We walked for about fourteen miles along a hard sandy beach, at the foot of cliffs varying in height from one to two hundred feet, broken in two or three places by the gullies through which streams descend from the table-land on the top. Coming to a point, where the sea dashed against the cliff, we ascended a beaten path in one of the natural breaks, and got on to the top. Plains of barren sand, only varied by occasional hummocks and stunted shrubs, extended four or five miles into the interior. Groves of trees, however, peered over the glowing horizon, and spoke of fertile land in the interior. Five miles across this desert, by a half-beaten track, brought us to the top of a sand-hill, whence we got a delicious peep into the valley of the Waitotara, or '*Totara* river'. The valley seemed about a mile and a half in width, and the opposite side was clothed with timber. Close to the further bank of the river, which wound through the vale, was a sort of Acropolis, on which stood the village to which we were bound. Except on the very top, the houses were shaded by a luxuriant grove of *karaka* trees, which encircled the base and feathered up the sides of the fortified hill. The village was called Te Ihupuku.

I was much struck by the want of cordiality shown by the inhabitants. As I ascended the steep hill with my train, scarcely any greeting was addressed to me, no shouts of '*Haere mai*', so universal a welcome to the stranger, were to be heard; and the few inquisitive natives that ran out to look at the arrival, sat in silence, or slowly retreated to their huts. On reaching the summit, we found two or three natives awaiting us; and I was about to ask for the chief, when Konatu, whose advice I had always found it prudent to follow, whispered me to sit down in silence like the rest of my train; and explained that there was no chief of consequence among this tribe.

After some little consultation among the inhabitants, whose number continued gradually to increase, and much whispering and mystery, we were shown into a large building used as a chapel by the natives, who had been all converted very recently. A large fire was lighted in the centre of the house, so as to illumine every part of it; and while we partook of some food which was placed before us, the whole population of the village, amounting to perhaps 100 of all ages and sexes, walked in and took their places. A native teacher performed prayers as soon as our food-baskets were removed; and then entered upon a long Philippic against me and mine.

I began now to understand the unusual distrust and want of friendliness shown by the inhabitants of this village. The preacher, for he remained in the wooden pulpit from which he had read prayers while delivering his oration, spoke for an hour in the most cruel way of me, of Colonel Wakefield, and of the intentions of the white settlers who had followed us. He insisted upon the old story, so widely spread about to our damage, that we were come to buy all their land and drive them to the mountains.

After breakfast, for which I took care to pay liberally, I left the inhospitable Christian village, and proceeded along the north bank of the river, through fern and grass, to the sea-side. About two miles north of the river's mouth we again came to cliffs, and were obliged by the high tide to travel along their summit. This was very tedious work, up and down sand-hummocks and through heavy hot sand for about ten miles. Descending to the beach as the tide ebbed, we passed along the foot of the cliffs, which diminished in height for about two miles, and then gave way to low sand-hummocks, like those south of Wanganui. Turning a point in the sandy beach, we discovered a bay bounded on the north by two or three high bluffs, and proceeded for about a mile to the mouth of a small river flowing out of its bight. Two villages, built on either side of the river, poured out their inhabitants upon the beach to greet us. They 'had cooked food for the white man,' they said, 'as soon as they saw him come round the point.' This village was called Te O, and consisted of about a dozen houses.

I was shown into a *whareumu*, which had been carefully carpeted with fresh fern; my boys deposited their loads inside; and the gaping crowd gathered round the narrow door. A chief kept them from pressing too close, and occasionally reproved them for attempt-to crowd in. The Maori expression for 'Get out of the way!' is simply '*Pouri!*' ('It is dark!'), thus answering somewhat to the Irishman's 'Stand out o' my daylight!'

In travelling among strange natives, there is nothing more disagreeable than their habit of crowding round a stranger. In these cases, a good-humoured joke has often more effect in repressing the nuisance than passionate or testy behaviour. I soon learnt numerous expressions which served to make them ashamed of their pertinacious staring. '*He pura ahau?*' (Am I one-eyed?') '*Tokohia nga ngarara ki taku moko?*' ('How many lizards are there on my face?') were among the most efficacious. If eating, I would ask them if they were looking for my *kai*, or food; and the old men would then reprove the crowd, and tell them that they were annoying the guest. A large audience assembled to see me wash in the river at daybreak. Roars of laughter and screams of astonishment resounded from every quarter when I proceeded to brush my teeth.

Crossing the river in a canoe, I climbed up a steep ascent to the main *pa*. The cliff is nearly precipitous on all sides, except where a narrow neck joins it with the mainland. This neck, however, slopes upwards to the *pa*, and is defended by native fences and trenches of the strongest kind. A double row of stockades is filled in with earth to the height of a man, leaving small holes level with the ground. A trench inside the stockade is dug to the depth of a man's body; and spears and muskets are thrust by the defenders through the small holes. A second bank is raised inside the trench, from behind which a second row could ply their weapons against the stormers of the palisades; and high fighting stages, protected by fences stuffed with turf, also afford commanding stations for defenders to fire over the outer fence. The entrance, through which only one man can pass at once, is so twisted as to be exposed to the enfilading fire of the whole line of defenders.

There were signs, outside the stockade, of two outer rows of defences in former times; as artificial banks reached from cliff to cliff across the neck. Thus three strong stockades, one commanding the other, must have made this side impregnable to Maori warfare; and an assault, except by stealth, on the other faces, would have been sheer madness. It was here that Rauparaha paused for some months during his invasion of Cook's Strait. The security of the position had been well appreciated by that clever general.

Descending on the other side of the *pa*, we passed round the foot of one of the bluffs which we had seen the day before, and found ourselves at the mouth of another and larger river, called the Patea, which takes its source in the eastern side of Mount Egmont. About a mile up the south bank, a *pa*, called Haere hau, was perched on a cliff. I was persuaded to go there and stop another night.

[*From this point Wakefield returned to Wellington, travelling by land to the Wangaehu, thence with a fleet of Maori canoes to Otaki, and thence by whale-boat to Petone, which he reached on 29th April 1840.*]

§

I was welcomed by Colonel Wakefield into the house which I had seen building for him when I was here before. It was very neatly constructed of wooden uprights, ridge-pole, and rafters, all bound together by flax-bands, and covered with a thick coating of leaves of the *nikau* (a kind of palm) and tufts of grass. It afforded a good shelter from the rain, but allowed the wind to circulate with perfect freedom. A planked floor and partitions, and English-made doors and windows, with brick chimneys, gave it a comfortable appearance. It had the advantage of being on a dry bed of shingle, and was protected from the weather by a wooden railing filled in with bunches of the *manuka*. This is a shrub very abundant in some parts. The plant resembles the tea-plant in leaves and flower, and is often used green by the whalers and traders for the same purpose. If made strong, however, the beverage had a nauseous bitter taste resembling that of hore-hound. It sometimes grows into large trees, and the timber is then hard and close-grained.

It is the most valued for firewood of any of the New Zealand woods; and is used by the natives for clubs and spears, on account of its hard, heavy, and tough qualities.

I was soon informed by Colonel Wakefield of the principal events which had happened during my absence. Several vessels had arrived from Sydney, Port Philip, and Hobart Town, with a stock of cattle and sheep for the young colony. This had been placed on the fern-covered land at the south end of the harbour. Among the importers of stock was Mr. James Watt, from New South Wales. He brought with him two horses; one of which was a young thorough-bred 'Figaro', which afterwards became the sire of many New Zealand-born steeds.

A trading-vessel from the Bay of Islands had brought the news of the arrival of Captain Hobson there, and a copy of his proclamation assuming the office of Lieutenant-Governor, under the Governor of New South Wales, 'in and over any territory which was or might be acquired in sovereignty by her Majesty, her heirs, or successors, in New Zealand'.

The Council, authorized by the chiefs of the district, had met weekly; and had proceeded to take measures for the administration of the provisional government. After appointing officers, including a magistrate and constables, they had prepared an address to the colonists, which was printed in the first number of a newspaper on the 18th of April.

The apparatus of a newspaper had been obtained by subscription among the principal colonists, and the management of it undertaken by Mr. Samuel Revans, who arrived in the *Adelaide* [which also brought the printing press]. The first number had been published in London, in September 1839, under the title of the *New Zealand Gazette*.

Various appointments under the Company had also been made. Captain Chaffers was harbour-master; 'Worser', pilot, living near the heads with a whale-boat and crew; Doddrey, superintendent of works; and Barrett, agent for natives and interpreter.

The infant government had worked smoothly enough. A few lawless wanderers from other parts and still fewer quarrelsome emigrants had been checked in their disorderly outbreaks by the police. The utmost cordiality between the natives and the whites had continued to exist, almost without a blemish. The first serious interruption to the working of the young institution had been caused by a stranger. A dispute had arisen between Captain Pearson, the master of the barque *Integrity*, and Mr. Wade, who had chartered her from Hobart Town. The charterer had applied for the interference of the authorities, and the captain had been arrested, on the 14th, by warrant and brought before the Police Magistrate. He had refused to recognize the court, and had escaped on board his ship, and defied our puny constabulary force.

On the 19th April, the Rev. Henry Williams had arrived from the Bay of Islands, in the *Ariel* schooner.

It appeared that one of the first measures of Captain Hobson, after his arrival in January, had been to acquire some territory over which he might extend his dominion. He had accordingly assembled some two hundred natives living at or near the Bay, and about one hundred Europeans, including missionaries and officers of his suite; and had proceeded to ask the chiefs, through Mr. Williams as interpreter, to give the Queen the power to protect and restrain them. And a document had been read and interpreted to them; which, after a good deal of hesitation and opposition, thirty or forty chiefs had signed on the next day. We understood that by this document the chiefs had ceded their sovereignty to the Queen of England; but we remained in ignorance of any of its other provisions.*

Now it just oozed out, that Mr. Williams was charged to procure the assent of the chiefs in Cook's Strait to a similar cession of their sovereignty, in order to make the document a secure foundation on which to build the assumption of the sovereignty by the English Crown. Although Mr. Williams's negotiations with the chiefs of Port Nicholson for this purpose were conducted with great privacy and mystery, of course they had constantly reported the proceedings to Colonel Wakefield; who had yet been, for a long time, unable to discover what they were required to sign.

On the 21st April, another ship, the *Bolton*, had arrived from England; bearing, among other passengers, the Rev. J. F. Churton, and the Rev. J. G. Butler. The arrival of these two gentlemen with their families had been hailed with much pleasure by the

* This was the Treaty of Waitangi.

members of the Church of England. Previous to this time, the religious duties had been performed by the Rev. John Macfarlane, a minister of the Kirk of Scotland, who had accompanied the colonists from the Clyde in the *Bengal Merchant*.

On visiting my friends up the Hutt, I found the same cheerfulness, activity, and sanguine hope of success prevailing. Nice gardens were well cleared, neatly fenced and cultivated, and fresh with young vegetables and plants; every one was loud in praise of the fertile soil. Boats and barges were being built; and the little children were learning to paddle a light canoe in the river. Sawyers were located among the abundant timber; the sounds of the axe and saw as they cut the noble pine-trees into useful proportions, and of the hammer nailing some useful building, rang through the air; and a general appearance of progress and satisfaction pervaded the place.

Kuru, who accompanied me on these excursions, could not refrain from expressing his unfeigned pleasure at the sight, and would tell me, with tears starting from his eyes, that he hoped the same would soon be at Wanganui.

At Thorndon, the bustle of settlement was also apparent.* Numerous houses had been built by the natives, and occupied by some of the colonists. Some few wooden houses brought from England were also in process of erection. Dicky Barrett had returned from Queen Charlotte's Sound in the *Cuba*, with his whole establishment and property, and had installed himself in a clay-walled house at Thorndon, in exactly the same manner as at Te Awaiti. The house was always half full of hungry natives, and idle white men who had wandered from the whaling-stations, and the large iron pots and spacious table constantly extended his too undistinguishing hospitality to all applicants. He was quite proud of the change which he had aided to produce in the appearance of the place and the prospects of his friends the natives, and used to spend his time in watching the proceedings of the newcomers; sometimes mystifying a whole audience of gaping immigrants by a high-flown relation of a whaling adventure, or of some part of his Maori campaigns.

---

* Wakefield's diary states that there were 900 settled at the Hutt and 400 at Thorndon at this time.

§

On the 14th May, I started for Wanganui in a schooner of thirty tons. She belonged to a man named Macgregor, who had been living by sealing and other pursuits for some years in the neighbourhood of Foveaux's Straits. With the assistance of some other men, he had built this boat; and, having got on board some natives connected with Wanganui, he had come up in search of that place in order to land them and obtain payment for their passage in pigs and potatoes, which he meant to sell to the whaling-ships on the coast to the southward. To escape some rough weather, he had run in here one night, seeing an appearance of shelter, and had been highly astonished in the morning to find himself in the midst of an active European settlement of more than a thousand persons, where he had thought to find an uninhabited country, or at any rate only natives. He had consequently named his vessel the *Surprise.*

Colonel Wakefield chartered the craft by the month, and caused to be put on board a large quantity of goods, approved by Kuru, and considered by him sufficient for the purchase of the Wanganui district. He then requested me to proceed to Wanganui in the vessel, and act as agent for the Company in procuring the confirmation of the resident chiefs to the deed executed by Kuru, his father, and another chief, at Kapiti, in November 1839. I readily acceded. The third chief, Te Kirikaramu, was also at Port Nicholson, and had already entered into some negotiations with Macgregor; and I soon found that some jealousy existed as to which chief should have the honour of taking the first vessel into the Wanganui river. These scruples were easily adjusted, as I said both should go, and I would claim the envied distinction. Several other natives of Wanganui were allowed a passage on board, and Captain Chaffers was instructed to accompany me in order to make a survey of the entrance and bar of the river.

Our craft was no crack sailer, but she was safely and strongly built, round as a Dutch-dogger, under-rigged, and as comfortable below as could be expected for her size. After weathering Cape Terawhiti, we were detained between Mana and Kapiti for some days by foul winds; and again, after anchoring under Rauparaha's island, in a strong south-east gale and pitch-dark night.

On the 19th May, we at length entered the Wanganui river, passing through heavy breakers on the bar caused by two days' continued westerly gale. The soundings on the bar were twelve feet at nearly high-water. Whilst in the most dangerous part of the entrance, Kuru, who was perched on the top of the foremast to pilot us in, could not restrain his exultation at bringing a vessel into his river. He let go his hold, balanced himself on the cross-trees on his feet only while the vessel lifted and drove on the high rollers, and shouted out an impromptu song in celebration of the event, flourishing his hands and arms with the usual quivering motion. When he had brought his '*Io triumphe*' to the concluding yell, we were sailing up the river in smooth water.

We saw but few natives at the villages near the sea; and Kuru started off up the river in order to gather them to the sale, telling me that he should be several days away. We had anchored about a mile above Putikiwharanui, opposite the mouth of a creek called Purua, where Turoa had lately built a few huts and established himself.* The river was very deep here, our anchor being down in seven fathoms not twenty yards from the shore.

While I was waiting for the return of Kuru and the gathering of the clans, Messrs. Williams and Hadfield arrived by land. They held no communication with me; but I heard from the natives, and also from Macgregor, the skipper, who called upon them in their tent, what had been their proceedings. Turoa ard Te Anaua, with several other of the chiefs who had held communication with them, told me that Mr. Williams had asked them to sign a paper,† and promised them a present of a blanket from the Queen. They had answered at first by requesting him to show the paper to the other white people then on the spot, in order that the transaction should be a public one; which he had refused to do. He then asked them who the white people in the ship were; and upon their

* Purua Creek is near Shakespeare Cliff.

† As the 'paper' was a copy of the Treaty of Waitangi, Wakefield's first impressions are worth recording. Under the date May 23rd, 1840, his diary gives a different version: 'Brooks heard from Turoa that he and Te Anaua had each received a blanket from Williams, but had neither signed nor consented to have their names put to any paper. They said he put their names to his paper without asking them, and said the Queen had sent the blankets out to be given to the natives. . . . I suppose he reckons the sovereignty a very light thing, as he gives a single blanket for it, and does not think it necessary for the Chiefs to put their hands to the pen. They do not understand the meaning of it. God knows how many names he has *put down* to his paper, or what that paper is."

informing him, he had urged them not to sell their land, saying that 'all the goods in the vessel were light, and might be lifted with the hand, but that the *oneone,* or "land", could not.' They took care to assure me, however, that this *hangareka* or 'joke' of Williams, as they termed it, had not shaken their resolution of abiding by their bargain.

In the evening of the day after Mr. Williams's arrival, they came on board, and told me that Turoa and Te Anaua had received a blanket each on signing, and that Williams had departed to the southward. I could not ascertain whether any other chiefs had signed or not. I gathered from Macgregor that the paper was one ceding the sovereignty to the Queen, similar to that to which the adhesion of the Port Nicholson chiefs had been obtained; and was rather surprised that Mr. Williams had not taken pains to acquire the assent of more of the chiefs, or of any of those towards Patea and the country to the north.

On inquiring of Turoa whether he understood what he had signed, he repeated to me, that my Queen had sent him a blanket, and that he had been told to make a mark in order to show that he had got it. When I explained to him that my Queen had become his also, and that she and her Governor were now chiefs over him as well as over me, he became very agitated, and repeatedly spoke of following Williams in order to return the blanket and upbraid him for the deception. He finally determined, however, that he must have got to Wangaehu by that time, and that he could not catch him. 'But,' said he, 'a blanket is no payment for my name. I am still a chief.'

About a week after Kuru's departure, large bodies of natives began to arrive in canoes down the river. As they rounded the low point above and came in sight of the ship, they would often fire guns, which were returned from Purua. On the ninth day, some men in a canoe in advance told me of the near approach of Kuru with his *nuinga,* or 'host', from the Wahipari, or 'Place of Cliffs'. Soon after this announcement, twenty or thirty crowded canoes, closely touching each other, glided in silence round the point; and as they came full in sight, discharged their fire-arms in a grand volley, which was answered from the schooner and the shore. They continued to advance in this formal manner until near the vessel, when Kuru's canoe came alongside, and the others pulled to the north bank, where they soon formed a temporary encampment on the fern-covered level.* There were now about seven hundred natives assembled in the immediate neighbourhood; and Kuru told me that all were here who could possibly be collected, and that we might proceed to business.

After several discussions at the different villages and on board the schooner, at which I explained, through the interpreter, the whole force and meaning of the transaction† which was about to be made, I invited Kuru to assemble them all at one place. This was done at the fishing-village at which I had formerly seen the people from Wahipari. On a bright sunny day, I landed there from the schooner, and found a truly imposing audience assembled. In a small court-yard of the village all the superior chiefs, to the number of 20 or 30, were sitting on the ground dressed in their best mats and feathers, with all their green-stone clubs and *taiaha* shown off to the best advantage. The roofs of the adjoining huts, the fences, the fish-racks, were bending under the weight of crowds of inferior natives, who sought for a peep at the conference. The rest of the assembled hundreds were contented to sit or stand so as to hear the expected speeches. Among the assembly were some of the wildest natives I had yet seen. Most of them were stout and muscular, more than half of them nearly naked, and plentifully bedaubed with red paint and charcoal; all constantly carried some weapon, as though by instinct and the habit of danger.

Captain Chaffers, John Brooks the interpreter, Macgregor, and some of his crew, accompanied me to a *porera* which had been spread in a place kept clear for me.

Perfect silence reigned throughout the multitude while speeches were made; and every word must have been heard by every member of the assembly. I began by asking the chiefs if they had finally made up their minds to complete the sale. Five or six of them immediately answered, that they had had many moons (months) to do that in, and that all that they wanted was for me to bring the paper that they might sign, and the goods that they might carry them away. Several chiefs then rose in succession,

* This is at the present Moutoa Gardens.
† i.e., the purchase of land at Wanganui.

and fully described the country sold, tracing all the rivers up to Tongariro, and saying '*tou kainga!*' (thy place), after the name of each.

Rangitauwira, the old chief nearly bent double with age, arrogated, without exciting a murmur of dissent, the right to be called the *take* or 'root' of the tribes. 'I am so old,' said he, 'that you can all remember from tradition better than I can tell you, whether this is not true. This is my white man; the land is for him!'

Kuru still remained by me, explaining the full meaning of the expressions used.

Though I had not shown the natives the goods intended as payment, I had repeatedly read to them the list; and on this occasion the head chiefs shortly answered to my inquiries whether they were satisfied with the quantity: 'Kuru has seen them—it is good!' It was then agreed that the chiefs should come on board the schooner and sign the deed, and that several large canoes should be brought alongside under the direction of Kuru, to receive the goods, and land them at the spot where this concluding conference had taken place. It was also agreed that this chief should distribute the goods, as I hoped, from his great influence and connexion with all the different branches of the Wanganui tribes then assembled, that he might accomplish this in peace. The general assent to this arrangement seemed to confirm my view.

Twenty-seven head chiefs signed the deed on the deck of the schooner, after it had been read and interpreted, with full explanations, to them, and to a large audience which surrounded us, either floating about in numerous canoes or clustered on the bank at Purua. The goods were then handed into the canoes by men appointed by Kuru. No attempt at pilfering took place; and all the things were carried in order and quiet to the shore. The spectators proceeded gradually to the scene of distribution; and when I landed, some time after the last canoe had gone away, with all the white men except one to keep the vessel, the distribution was going on.

On an extensive level at the back of the little village, a piece of land a hundred yards long and twenty broad had been cleared of the fern. About twenty-four heaps of goods were ranged along this space; and Kuru, with his elder brother, a chief of no great note, were adding gradually to each heap, and explaining their proceedings in a loud voice. We took our seats on the roof of a hut, from whence we could survey the whole proceeding. The different tribes were gathered in groups at short distances from the row of heaps each under their respective leaders; and watched the process with the most eager anxiety. Now and then a little knot might be seen encroaching on the space, and creeping, without rising, nearer to some tempting heap. Then a chief of another tribe would rise, and, although scarcely able to restrain his own followers or perhaps himself from imitating their example, would rebuke them for their dishonest intentions. Then Kuru would flourish his bright tomahawk high in the air, and fly along each side of the line of goods, anger and menace in every gesture, and determination in his features; and the boldest retired to their former stations. But while he was busy unpacking a bale, or making his calculations as to the fairest way of sharing out the contents, the almost invisible encroachments and the loud rebukes became more frequent and daring, the offenders became less willing to hear reason, and the others more prone to share in the offence. At length neither Kuru's eloquent appeals to the dignity of the chiefs, nor his terrific threats against the multitude, could produce their intended effect: little children were first sent to pilfer a pipe or a looking-glass, and though they were seen no one would touch them; then the parents, watching, rebuking, envying, and seeking to overreach each other, were closing in on all sides. A crisis was evidently at hand.

Kuru threw down what he had in his hand, and walked slowly and moodily to a seat by my side. This seemed to create a pause for a few minutes, as though the covetous crowds were uncertain of his intentions. 'Go on board ship,' said he to me, 'with all your white men. I cannot get them to do it quietly, and we shall come to a fight. You might get hurt if you remained; and, moreover, I am ashamed that you should see us fight madly for these things when I have engaged to do my best to count them out quietly. But such is their custom, and they will have a scramble. Go!' I immediately acceded to his request.* We had hardly got on

* Possibly Kuru engineered the 'riot', and outwitted Wakefield as well as Turoa and Te Anaua. He is said to have given his followers a signal in 'pakeha words' for the 'scramble'.

board ship before we saw and heard a truly wild scene. We were about a quarter of a mile from the spot, and on the opposite side of the river.

Seven hundred naked savages were twisted and entangled in one mass, like a swarm of bees, over the line of goods; and their cries of encouragement, anger, disappointment, vengeance, pain, or triumph, were blended in one ferocious growl. With a telescope could be distinguished brandished weapons, clenched fists, torn blankets, uplifted boxes, and occasionally a man's body as he leaped or was borne against his will over the heads of the throng; and the faint breath of the sea-breeze, as it died away with the setting sun, brought an occasional shrill yell or the scream of a woman in louder tones than the general buzz. I much feared that some loss of life would ensue.

Shortly after, Turoa and Te Anaua came alongside in two canoes, tolerably laden with spoil, and exclaimed against the smallness of their share, saying that Kuru had got all for himself and his people. They wanted to return the goods to me; but I steadily refused, and told them that the bargain was concluded, and they must now arrange the division in their own way. They then went to their settlements with the goods. Te Anaua appeared to have been wounded, having a bandage round his head.

After the riot had subsided, Kuru himself came on board. He was very excited and angry.

In the morning, things were much more quiet. Many of the wildest natives had departed with what they had been able to secure; and Kuru distributed some of the other things.

I was now taken ashore to see a present, or *homai mo homai*, literally a 'gift for a gift', which had been prepared for me. It consisted of thirty pigs and about ten tons of potatoes, ranged in a row along the line which had been occupied two days before by the goods. Having counted them and got them on board, I gave Kuru a blanket each for the pigs, and a pipe or a head of tobacco for every two baskets of potatoes. The baskets being small, this was reckoned a very liberal rate of payment. The chief divided it at once among the owners of the provisions, who were almost entirely his own people.

I accepted and paid for this gift as a private speculation on my part. I have been thus particular in detailing this private pig-dealing adventure, because I was long afterwards accused by some 'repudiating' natives and some of their white protectors of having received the cargo of provisions as payment for the goods belonging to the Company (worth about £700) which I had paid for the land.*

Having bidden farewell to Kuru and the other natives, after promising to return soon and trade with them, and begging them to build houses about this part of the river, for which the white people would be glad to pay them, I weighed anchor and got safe out. On the 2nd of June we got back to Port Nicholson. In beating up to Petone, we fell in with a whale-boat, which used to ply daily with passengers between Thorndon and Petone, at the fare of half-a-crown. It was started by a man named Wright, who had been one of Barrett's companions in the Taranaki wars, and a whaling headsman at Te Awaiti.

§

I must now again look back to the leading events which had occurred since my departure.

The name of 'Britannia' had been determined on for the town. Many people had moved over to Thorndon, where it was to be founded, and a brisk traffic was carried on between the two places. Merchants and retail dealers were beginning to show a little order in their arrangements; and two or three rough attempts at shops were to be seen up the Hutt, at Petone, and at Thorndon. The newspaper was published regularly once a week, proposals had been made for the establishment of a local bank, two or three taverns of respectable appearance were organized, and a school-master was busy showing his testimonials and craving support. A schooner had come from the Bay of Islands, and brought a cargo of pigs which she picked up on the east coast. The *Jewess*, as she was named, had been bought by two or three mercantile colonists, and was the first decked vessel belonging to Port Nicholson. She had arrived on the 17th of May, bringing news of the recovery of Governor Hobson's health from a severe attack of paralysis, and of the arrival of 150 soldiers at the Bay of Islands. His Excellency

* It is possible that the Maoris quite honestly took this view of the transaction.

was still there, and still undetermined as to the site of his future capital. The Port Nicholson people had, therefore, great hopes that he might arrive here within a short time, at least to judge of the fitness of this place.

Brick-making had been commenced by two enterprising colonists, one of whom was Mr. Dudley Sinclair. The bricks brought out from England were so dear that there seemed every chance of success for these beginners. Firewood was abundant and close to the kiln, which was on the beach, under a cliff said to consist of excellent clay for the purpose.

On the night of the 25th of May, the line of cottages which I have formerly described as 'Cornish Row' had been burnt down; the inflammable nature of the roofs and walls having overcome all the efforts of the settlers of all classes, who had hurried from their beds to the scene of the first alarm. No lives, however, were lost. The houseless families were received, some by their neighbours, some in the Company's emigrants' houses; and a ready subscription had replaced the burnt clothes and other things belonging to some of the labourers, who, being poor, could ill afford even so small a loss.

The blaze had hardly subsided, when the sleepers were again aroused by the shock of an earthquake. This had been but slight, and had done no damage. I was much amused by the description of the alarm produced upon some settlers, who ran out in very light clothing and fired their muskets and pistols, under the idea that a troop of natives were trying to pull the hut down. The natives, especially, related with great glee the want of presence of mind displayed by some of the more timid whites. It was now remembered that Captain Cook had mentioned his feeling the slight shock of an earthquake in Ship Cove seventy years before, and that a shake had been felt at Te Awaiti whilst we were up the Pelorus river with Jacky Guard. The effect seemed to have been only partial, for no one at Wanganui had experienced the slightest vibration.

On June 2nd, a boat from Thorndon brought the news to Petone at night, that the *Integrity* had returned, bearing Lieutenant Shortland (the Colonial Secretary), a detachment of thirty soldiers, and some supernumeraries, consisting of 'mounted police' without their horses, constables, etc. It was rumoured that Captain Pearson had

S. C. Brees. Engraving

THOMS'S WHALING STATION, PORIRUA HARBOUR, about 1843

NGAHAURANGA *PA* AND STREAM. Women foot-passengers on the road to Petone were carried across the stream by Maoris for a fee of sixpence

reported us at the Bay of Islands as 'a turbulent set of rebels, who were establishing a republic at Port Nicholson', and that the thirty soldiers had been sent to quell the rebellion! It was added, that the invading force had held no communication with the shore, the prudent Colonial Secretary having probably deemed it advisable to reconnoitre before landing on the insurgent shore.

Merry and loud were the jokes that rang through the tents up the Hutt, whither I carried the news. Bombastes Furioso, Tom Thumb, and Jack the Giant-killer, were quoted and parodied, and some hours' amusement was derived from this ludicrous mistake of the Government as to our hostility, and the overwhelming force which they had sent to exterminate us.

The first measure of the Royalist forces was to send a man on shore the next morning to pull down all the New Zealand flags which he might find hoisted. This was probably an experimental measure only; as a single constable performed the task very early, almost before anybody was up. The man who performed this bold deed at Petone assumed, while he did it, the most ridiculous appearance of authority. He had been one of our early immigrants, brought out, I think, in the *Aurora*. He was usually styled 'Captain' Cole. He had succeeded in getting appointed Chief Constable for Port Nicholson, and had accompanied Lieutenant Shortland, not a little elated with his official dignity. Although I have often since observed the remarkable pomposity which a Government official of every class assumes in a colony, I never saw a more complete instance than Constable Cole.

As he strode up to the flag-staff near Colonel Wakefield's house, on which a rather ragged New Zealand flag was hung, he threw disdainful and yet cautious glances around him. When he saw that there were only two or three people in their night-caps peeping from their doors and windows to know who had been boating so early on such a cold morning, he plucked up spirits, and seemed to reflect that he had to represent the dignity of the British Crown. His funny little head arranged itself quite straight in a most appropriate military stock; his ungainly figure and gait became almost martial; he frowned sternly, as though to awe the rebels; and advanced straight upon the flag-staff with as much resolution as though he had been taking Ciudad Rodrigo by storm. He had some little trouble in undoing the string, and it would not run very freely through the hole at the top of the staff; but at length he accomplished his gallant undertaking, and proceeded with a flourish to extend the sovereignty of England over the flags which adorned the snoring grog-shops along the beach.

It was not till the 4th of June that Lieutenant Shortland disembarked at Thorndon, to hoist the Union Jack and read the proclamations of the sovereignty of the Queen of England over New Zealand. A large assemblage of the colonists, including Colonel Wakefield and most of the members of the much-dreaded Council, joined in the proceedings in the most loyal manner, and expressed to Lieutenant Shortland their pleasure at the event. The soldiers landed, and encamped in tents at one end of Thorndon; and Lieutenant Shortland, with his suite, ensconced themselves in some half-finished houses at that place.

A little dissatisfaction was now to be found among some of the settlers at Port Nicholson, owing to the delay which had appeared to exist in the survey. These early grumblers, however, had hardly made allowances for the obstacles presented by the hilly and densely wooded country in which part of the town had to be laid out, or for the time occupied by the first mistake of surveying a site in the valley of the Hutt. The survey was now progressing fast; and Captain Smith confidently promised that the map of the town should be ready for inspection about the middle of July.

I had now become so interested in the progress of the colony—especially since the establishment of British government—that instead of seeking for a passage towards home by one of the emigrant ships going to India or China for a cargo, I postponed my return to England indefinitely. I determined to see a little of the first formation of a town and of the first agricultural operations. As the town-sections were not to be chosen for a month at least, I set off to spend this interval at Kapiti, having conceived a great desire to observe the proceedings of the whalers, then in full work.

CHAPTER VIII

Life on a Whaling Station

MACGREGOR WAS just about to return to Wanganui, having turned the dollars which he received for his charter into goods fit for bartering with the natives. I took a passage in the *Surprise* to Kapiti, and we sailed on the 17th of June. Having to deliver some casks at Porirua, where two of our colonists had hired Tom's fishery at Paremata for the season, we entered that harbour, and anchored close to the sheers in twelve fathoms. A whale was being cut-in under them, and we took swarms of fish, which had been attracted by the carcass. Lieutenant Joseph Thomas, one of the lessees of the fishery, received me very hospitably in his hut, and described himself as highly amused in his new pursuit. He was an old traveller, and had seen many countries and people; but he was most pleased with the eccentricities of the 'whaling mob' which he had to rule, and which he ruled very well. He got on very well with the natives too, having been recommended to the especial protection of Rangihaeata by his landlord Toms.

In two or three days, the *Surprise* having completed her discharging, we sailed for Kapiti with a light north-east breeze. While I remained there, I was most kindly and hospitably treated by all the whalers, as well as the natives. I soon became as it were free of the place, and could reckon on being a welcome guest in any house. I was much interested in observing the life of these rough men, and in finding that many generous and noble qualities redeemed their general inclination to vice and lawlessness.

The whalers who established themselves on the coasts of New Zealand were composed of sailors, who had committed no crime, but were tempted, by the facility of living in comfort on shore there, to leave their ships; and of runaway convicts from the neighbouring penal settlements in New South Wales and Van Diemen's Land. Some few, born in those colonies, were probably descended from members of one or the other of these two classes. These 'currency lads', as they are called, are distinguished for great physical strength and beauty; and have probably been indebted to their early acquaintance with the hardy life of a stock-keeper or shepherd, and their consequent experience of the inter-course between the white man and the savage, for that moral ascendancy which they generally acquire over their classmates in New Zealand.

From the varied nature of these ingredients arises the contra-diction of character for which the whalers are so remarkable. The frankness and manly courage of the sailor mingle with the cunning and reckless daring of the convict, or 'lag', in no common manner. Though prone to drunkenness and its attendant evils, the whaler is hospitable in the extreme, and his rough-built house is a model of cleanliness and order. His unbounded generosity would soon have encouraged the covetousness of the natives to grasping and bullying, had he not gained universal respect among them for undoubted courage, and openly expressed his hatred and contempt for such as distinguished themselves by those bad qualities. His want of book-learning is counteracted by a considerable knowledge of the world; the consequence of which is a remarkable power of discrimination between quackery and real ability, between hypo-crisy and sincerity, in those with whom he meets. Thus, since the first days of regular colonization, no man better than a whaler can distinguish between a charlatan doctor, or a low-minded, hypocritical missionary, and a doctor who knows his business, or a worthy minister of the Gospel. He is the first to expose and ridicule the faults of one class, while he yields a willing respect to the virtues and knowledge of the other.

It is difficult to learn how soon this rough class of pioneers first established themselves in New Zealand. As early as 1793, the whaling-ships of different nations began to touch on the coast. Their intercourse with the natives was marked by great cruelty and injustice on one part, great treachery and dishonesty on the other, and revolting blood-thirstiness and a strong spirit of revenge on both sides. The lives of many innocent persons, both native and European, were sacrificed to the feelings excited by former oppression and murders. It was during some part of the period between this date and 1807, that George Bruce, an English sailor, accompanied a chief named Te Pehi ashore, in the north of the islands, married his daughter, and became, under the chief's protection, a *tattooed* chieftain himself. It appears that this was the earliest time at which a European ever resided in [northern]· New Zealand.

It is more difficult to ascertain the date at which sealers began to establish themselves on the southern coasts. Even in the end of the last century, certainly, parties were left with provisions and ammunition to collect seal-skins for colonial vessels on those coasts. There being but few natives in that part, it was probably some time before the two races came into collision.

The foundation of the whaling settlements on shore seems to have been laid about 1827, when the same men who had for years pursued the arduous life of a sealer along the coasts of the Middle Island and Foveaux's Strait were encouraged to engage in the pursuit of the whale, and to form establishments for that purpose in the neighbourhood of Queen Charlotte's Sound, Kapiti, and Cloudy Bay. The two latter places were for many years great rendezvous for whaling-ships, and some of their crews also formed stations on the land.

At this period the native wars were raging in all their fury. Rauparaha had not yet succeeded in totally expelling 'Bloody Jack' and the Ngaitahu tribe from their original dwelling-place, and the European protégés, for they were at first no more, had to share in the hardships and losses of the invading tribe with whom they had fraternized. More than once their dwellings were burnt and their little all plundered, in a successful foray of the expelled inhabitants.

The white men, however, increased in number, while they rebuilt their establishments, and by communication with Sydney acquired property, by which they became the protectors of the natives.

In 1839, when we arrived in Cook's Strait, the whalers' relations with Sydney were upon a regular footing, and they had been for several years uninterrupted by hostile inroads from pursuing their occupation. The whaling-town of 'Tarwhite' (Te Awaiti) I have already partly described, as well as the numerous stations at Kapiti and Cloudy Bay.

In the first beginning, these men associated together in small parties, and agreed upon one more skilful than the rest to direct the boat and take the principal part in killing the whale; but his authority probably extended no further. As these establishments became more numerous, and were regularly fitted out and maintained by merchants in Sydney, not only were the members of a 'party' enrolled under articles to serve for the season, but the head man of each obtained a species of despotic authority, maintained both on shore and in the boats by the exertion of a strong will. The result was a discipline almost as good as that of a man-of-war, which could not fail to excite admiration.

It is very remarkable that there exists among the whalers a certain code of laws, handed down by tradition, and almost universally adhered to, relating to adverse claims to a whale. Each whaling-bay has its own law or custom; but they are generally very similar. It is recognized, for instance, that he who has once made fast has a right to the whale, even should he be obliged to cut his line, so long as his harpoon remains in her; and each harpooner knows his own weapon by some private mark. The boat making fast to the calf has a right to the cow, because she will never desert her young. A boat demanding assistance from the boat of a rival party shares equally with its assistant on receiving the required help. These and many other regulations are never written down, but are so well-known that a dispute rarely arises, and if so, is settled according to precedent by the oldest 'headsmen'. The only instance I ever knew of going to law on the subject occurred in 1843, when a boat had seized a whale that drifted from her anchorage, and returned the harpoon remaining in her to its owner. The whale was nearly ten miles from the place where she was killed; but universal indignation was expressed against the man who insisted on appealing to a court of justice against the 'laws of the bay'.

The season for which the men engage themselves begins with

the month of May, and lasts till the beginning of October, thus extending over five months which include the winter. It is during this season that the female or cow whales resort to the coasts of New Zealand with their young calves; and this in such numbers during some years, that whaling-ships were accustomed to anchor at Kapiti, Port Underwood, and the ports in Banks Peninsula, and thus to carry on a fishery subject to less hardship than in the open seas.

The men are enrolled under three denominations—'headsman', 'boat-steerer', and common man. The headsman is, as his name implies, the commander of a boat; and his place is at the helm except during the moment of killing the whale, which task falls to his lot. The boat-steerer pulls the oar nearest the bow of the boat, fastens to the whale with the harpoon, and takes his name from having to steer the boat under the headsman's directions, while the latter kills the whale. The common men have nothing to do but to ply their oars according to orders; except one, called the 'tub oarsman', who sits next to the tub containing the whale-line, and has to see that no entanglement takes place. The wages are shares of the profits of the fishery, apportioned to the men according to their rank—the headsman getting more shares than the boat-steerer, and the boat-steerer than the common man. The leader of the 'party' commands one of the boats, is called the 'chief headsman', and is said to 'head' the party, as each headsman is said to 'head' his own boat. The boat-steerer or harpooner is likewise said to 'steer' the boat to which he belongs, or, more frequently, its headsman. Thus, on meeting two whalers, and asking them what is their situation, one might answer, 'I heads the *Kangaroo*', while the other would say, 'and I steers *Big George*'.

Their whole language in fact is an *argot*, or slang, almost unintelligible to a stranger. All their principal characters enjoy distinctive appellations, like the heroes of the Iliad. Thus I know one of the chief headsmen who was never called anything but 'the old man'. Another was called 'Long Bob'; a third 'Butcher Nott'; and a fourth, an American, 'Horse Lewis', to distinguish him from his two brothers of the same name. I have already said that Joseph Toms, of Te Awaiti and Porirua, never went by any other name than 'Geordie Bolts'. Another was only known as 'Bill the Steward'.

'Flash Bill', 'Gipsy Smith', and 'Fat Jackson', 'French Jim', 'Bill the Cooper', and 'Black Peter', may be allowed to conclude our selection from the titles of the whaling peerage. Then every article of trade with the natives has its slang term—in order that they may converse with each other respecting a purchase without initiating the native into their calculations. Thus pigs and potatoes were respectively represented by 'grunters' and 'spuds'; guns, powder, blankets, pipes, and tobacco, by 'shooting-sticks, dust, spreaders, steamers', and 'weed'. A chief was called a 'nob'; a slave, a 'doctor'; a woman, a 'heifer'; a girl, a 'titter'; and a child, a 'squeaker'. Then for the different native chiefs they had also private names—such as 'Satan', 'the Old Sarpent', 'the Bully', 'the Badger', 'the Sneak', 'the Greybeard', 'the Murderer', 'the Wild Fellow', and 'the Long-un'.

The parties enrolled in Sydney received an advance and spent it there; a brig or schooner then carried the whole 'mob', as the party was sometimes called, to their station in New Zealand, with new boats, tackle, provisions, spirits, goods with which to barter for firewood and fresh food from the natives, clothing, tobacco, and various other necessaries, which were placed under the care of the chief headsman, and charged to him at an immense profit by the owner of the party in Sydney, as an advance on the produce of the season. Arrived in New Zealand, the party was joined by such members as had considered it convenient or agreeable to spend their summer there, and soon stood on a complete footing.

The boats, which are now painted and fitted up, deserve a particular description. The whale-boat is a long clinker-built boat, sharp at both ends, and higher out of water at the head and stern than amidships, about twenty to thirty feet long, and varying in breadth according to the make. At the stern, a planking even with the gunwales reaches five or six feet forward, and is perforated perpendicularly by the 'loggerhead', a cylindrical piece of wood about six inches in diameter, which is used for checking the whale-line by taking a turn or two round it. On this, too, it is customary to cut a notch for every whale killed by the boat. The old-fashioned boats were generally made to pull five oars, the rowers of which were called respectively, beginning from the bow, the boat-steerer, bow-oarsman, midship-oarsman, tub-oarsman, and after-oarsman.

Boats are now built, however, for the shore-parties, to pull six, seven, and even eight oars. I believe an uneven number is the best, as in that case there remains an equal force on each side of the boat when the boat-steerer, who is also harpooner, stands up to do his work. The boat is steered by means of a long and ponderous oar, called the steer-oar, which leans on a piece of wood fixed to the stern-post, and is confined to its place by a strap reaching from the top of the stern-post to the end of the support. The oar, however, moves freely in this loop, and is generally covered with leather for eighteen inches of its length to protect it from wear and tear. Close to the handle is a transverse iron peg, which is held with the right hand, and serves to turn the oar.

The headsman stands up to steer in the stern-sheets, and exhibits great skill in the management of the steer-oar, which is twenty-seven feet long in large boats. In a rough sea, an inexperienced person would not fail to be thrown overboard by it, but a whaler manages it with great ease and grace. The oars pull between thole-pins, which always have a small thole-mat and spare pin attached, and are also protected by leather. On the opposite side of the boat to the tholes, below the level of the thwarts, a piece of wood with a small niche is strongly fixed to the side of the boat. This is for 'peaking the oars', or placing the handles into, without taking the oar out of the thole, so the the blade of the oar remains out of reach of the water, whether sailing or running when fast to a whale. A boat in the act of peaking her oars to stop, is said to 'heave up'. The mast and large lug-sail are stowed, while rowing, under the after-thwart with the other end projecting on the starboard hand of the helmsman, who can thus stow or unstow it himself. A whiff, or light flag-staff with fancy colours attached, is stowed with the mast and sail. The mast is shipped in the bow or second thwart, and the halyards are made fast to the midship-thwart. These boats are very fast under sail, and will bear a great press of canvas. In the bow of the boat a planking, similar to that in the stern, reaches some three or four feet aft, and has at its after end a notch large enough to admit a man's leg. This is to steady the harpooner while striking the whale. One of the forward thole-pins is called the 'crutch', from having branches on it which support the harpoons ready for use.

The harpoon is an iron weapon, shaped like the top of a fleur-de-lis, and barbed so as not to draw out. It is placed on an ashen handle, five feet long, and its point is covered by a small wooden case. The line is already fast to them, and communicates with two tubs in the middle of the boat, in which two hundred fathoms of whale-line are neatly coiled. Spare harpoons, and lances with oval steel-pointed heads, all covered at the points, are ranged under the thwarts; a light kedge is in the head-sheets, a water-keg and a bottle of grog are placed in the stern-sheets, with the pea-coats of the crew, and a box of biscuit if they expect to remain out late. Sometimes a 'spade' is added to the armoury of the boat; this is a sharp iron weapon, like a small baker's shovel, on a long handle. It is used by some of the boldest whalers to cut about the whale's tail and render her less dangerous after she has been struck.

The boats are fancifully painted by their headsmen with mouldings of different colours, and a 'nose' different from the body. In the nose is generally painted some fanciful design, as a star, a crescent, a ball, or an eye. The name, too, frequently figures along the outside of the stern-sheets.

The words of command are, as they need be, short and clear: one side is called the 'two-side', where the two oars are in the five-oared boat, and the other the 'three-side'; but in giving directions, the headsman only say, 'pull two, back three', or vice versâ. The other terms of 'head all', 'starn all', 'peak', 'heave up', etc., require no explanation. These boats are remarkably lively in a sea-way, will run very long before a gale of wind with safety, and will land safely through a very high surf. They often run on when they are obliged to reef the sail by fastening the weather yard-arm to the gunwale; and are believed capable of standing any weather, if hove-to with the steer-oar peaked, under the lee of a raft formed of the oars, mast, and sail. Some years ago, two whale-boats reached Guam in safety from Drummond's reef near the Equator, where their vessel had been wrecked. During heavy weather, they had frequent recourse to this plan, in the course of their perilous voyage of two thousand miles.

The 'try-works', or large iron vats for boiling out the oil, are also cleaned, repaired, or renewed as circumstances may require; the ways for launching the boats are strengthened and repaired;

the 'sheers' and scaffolding with their tackle, the windlass, and planked way, used for cutting the blubber off the whale, are looked to, and made fit for use; the boat-sheds, dwelling-house, cook-house, and cooperage are made weather-tight against the winter; and the provisions and other 'property' are stowed away. The proper officers have been selected—such as cooper, carpenter, steward, cooks, painter, and 'tonguer'. The last-mentioned digni-tary takes his name from having an exclusive right to the oil obtained from the tongue and other interior parts of the whale, in payment of his duty of 'cutting-in', or dissecting, the whale. To a large party there was generally attached a clerk, who kept the accounts of each man at the store; that is to say, that the men were all allowed to run into debt at the beginning of the season, receiving clothing, tobacco, and spirits at most exorbitant prices, so that the balance, if any, to be paid them in money at the end of the season might be as small as possible. Then the station was provisioned with potatoes and firewood bought from the natives; pigs bought, killed, and salted down, and every preparation made.

A very important one was the providing the whole party with native wives for the season. Those men who had remained during the summer were generally provided with a permanent companion, among whose relations they had been living, either in perfect idleness, or employed in cultivating a small patch of land, or in buying pork and potatoes from the natives and selling them again for goods to the ships which touched on the coast. But the men who returned regularly with the oil to Sydney, or were then entering on their first season, went with such of their comrades as were well known by the natives to the different villages in the neighbourhood, for the purpose of procuring a helpmate during the season. Regular bargains were struck between the experienced headsman or boat-steerer and the relations of the girls selected and in most cases the bargains were punctually adhered to. In cases where the wife was negligent or slow to learn her duties of cooking, clothes-mending, and washing, the uncle or father would often take away the delinquent and bring another more fitted to perform his part of the bargain. The whaler's part consisted in a payment made on the completion of the bargain, and in a certain degree of indulgence to the begging visits of his new relations during the season. This provision appears to be looked upon as a necessary one by the headsmen; and doubtless contributes much to the cleanliness, steadiness, and good order of the men.

The duty of the *wahine* is to get up an hour before daybreak; cook the breakfast and arrange what her lord means to take in the boat, which ought to start before the day; wash and mend his clothes; keep the house in order; and prepare his supper for his return. Then upon her reposes the task of granting hospitality to the traveller while the master of the house is away. And to these she often adds the voluntary one of exposing herself to the brutality of the latter and his companions, excited by her attempts to dissuade him from the drunken orgies and wild scenes of combat which frequently succeed the return from the chase. These whalers' wives are generally distinguished by a strong affection for their companion; are very quick in acquiring habits of order and cleanliness; facilitate the intercourse between the whalers and their own countrymen; and often manage to obtain a strong influence over the wild passions of the former. Wives in everything but the ceremony, many of them become so formally on the arrival of an English clergyman in the neighbourhood. They form a very pleasing part of the picture, assisting in the civilization of their own countrymen by showing their esteem for the estimable qualities of the half-civilized man, while they partly succeed in softening and destroying those blamable features in his rough character which nature teaches them to pity rather than to despise.

The preliminary orgies are nearly over; the clerk stops the advances until something has been earned; the headsmen administer a severe personal castigation to some few notorious characters who grumble at this curtailment of their ease; the boats are practised every day in pulling and sailing; when at length, one morning early in May, a whale is signalled from a hill near the bay, where a look-out is constantly kept.

Three or four boats are quickly launched, and leave the ways at a racing-pace; the boats of the rival stations are seen gathering towards the same point; and the occasional spout of the whale, looking like a small column of smoke on the horizon, indicates the direction to be taken. A great deal of stratagem and generalship is now shown by the different headsmen in their manœuvres to be first 'alongside'. The whale may probably go for two or three miles in one direction, and then, after the various speed of the boats has placed them in a long file, tailing one after the other, suddenly reverse the position by appearing close to the last boat. The six-oared and seven-oared boats have greatly the advantage while the chase continues in a straight line; but the short, old-fashioned five has the best of it if the fish makes many turns and doubles. It is very common for some of the boats to dog the motions of that of a rival party commanded by a headsman of known experience; and thus two boats may sometimes be seen starting suddenly in a direction totally opposed to that taken by the others, and a race shortly begins between these two, the rest having no chance. The 'old file' in one of these two has guessed from some circumstance in the tide, wind or weather or from some symptom noticed in the last spout, that the fish would alter its course a point or two; and another headsman, who has been attentively watching his movements, at last declares that '*George* is off', and, with a fresh word of encouragement to his crew, follows swiftly in his wake.

The chase now becomes animating: this last manœuvre has cut off a considerable angle described by the whale; her course and that of the boats almost cross each other; and the crisis seems approaching. The headsman urges his rowers to exertion by encouraging description of the animal's appearance. 'There she breaches!'* shouts he; 'and there goes the calf!' 'Give way, my lads; sharp and strong's the word!—there she spouts again!—give way in the lull—make her spin through it! *George* a'n't two boats' lengths a-head of us. Hurrah! Now she feels it—pull while the squall lasts! Pull!—go along, my boys!' All this time he is helping the after-oarsman by propelling his oar with the left hand while he steers with the right. This is technically called 'backing-up'. Each oar bends in a curve; the foam flies from her bows as a tide-ripple is passed; and both boats gain perceptibly on the whale. 'And there goes flukes!' continues the headsman, as the huge animal makes a bound half out of water, and shows its broad tail as it plunges again head-first into the sea. 'Send us alongside, my lads—now give way!—hurrah, my bonnies—hearty and strong!—

---

* Leaps out of the water, or breaks the surface.

hurrah! I'll wager a pint (there goes the calf again!)—I'll wager she tries out eight tun if she makes. a gallon—hurrah! hurrah! hurrah then!—three or four strokes more and she'll come up under our nose. Stand up, Bill!' The boat-steerer peaks his oar, places one leg in the round notch in the front of the boat, and poises the harpoon, with line attached, over his head.

A new hand, pulling one of the oars, begins to look frightened, and flags at his work, looking occasionally over his shoulder; a volley of oaths from the headsman accompanies a threat to 'break every bone in his skin if he funks now'; and, beginning to fear the man more than the fish, he hardens his heart and pulls steadily on.

A momentary pause is occasioned by the disappearance of the whale, which at last rises close to the rival boat. Their boat-steerer, a young hand lately promoted, misses the whale with his harpoon, and is instantly knocked down by a water-keg flung full in his face by his enraged headsman, who spares no 'bad French' in explaining his motives. Our original friend then manœuvres his boat steadily to the place where the whale will probably appear next. 'Pull two, back three!' shouts he, following a sudden turn in the whale's wake; and, as she rises a few yards in front of the boat, he cries in rapid succession, 'Look out!—all clear?—give it her!' and the harpoon flies true and straight into the black mass. This is called 'making fast'. 'Peak your oars', says the headsman; the line whistles over the bow; a turn is taken round the loggerhead to check the rapidity with which the line runs out, and the boat flies positively *through* the water, forming ridges of foam high above her sides. The men sit still with folded arms by their peaked oars, the boat-steerer with a small hatchet in his hand to cut the line should any entanglement occur; and the after-oarsman occasionally pours water on the loggerhead, which smokes furiously. Now is shown the skill of the headsman in steering the boat at this tremendous speed, and in watching every motion of the frightened whale. Now he gives directions to 'haul in', when the line slackens; now says 'veer away again', as the fish takes a new start; and ever and anon terrifies the new hand, who can't tell what's going to happen, into a sort of resignation. The others seem to think the 'running' rather a relief from work than anything else; they positively look as if they would smoke their pipes, were it not against all rule.

The whale rapidly takes the line—and the 200 fathoms in the boat are nearly exhausted by its sudden determination to try the depth of water, technically called 'sounding'—but another boat of the same party, which had 'hove up', or peaked her oars, when the chase was resigned to the two, comes up in answer to a whiff hoisted by our boat, and fixes a new harpoon in the whale as she rises to take breath. She soon becomes exhausted with her efforts, runs less rapidly, and rises more frequently to the surface; and the headsman at last foresees the lucky moment.

'Come aft!' he cries; and he and the boat-steerer change places. The boat ceases her progress as the whale stops to rest. 'Down oars—give way!' are the orders given in sharp, clear tones; and the crew, at least the old hands, know that he is nerved for his work by the decision apparent in his voice, and the way in which he balances the sharp, bright, oval-pointed lance.

The whale seems to sleep on the surface; but she is slowly preparing for a move as the boat comes up.

He follows her every movement. 'A steady pull! Row dry, boys!—lay on! Pull two, back three!—Lay on! head of all! lay me alongside!' and, as the whale slowly rolls one fin out of water, the lance flies a good foot into the spot below where the 'life' is said to be. The quick obedience to his instant order of 'starn all—lay off!' saves the boat from annihilation, as the whale swings round its huge tail out of water, and brings it down with a tremendous report. She then 'breaches', or leaps, and plunges in every direction; the headsman continues to direct his crew and boat-steerer, while he poises a new lance, and keeps just out of the vortex formed by her evolutions; the assistant boat and a third one have come up, and, being all of one party, watch outside the splashing for the best chance. One goes in, and having fixed a lance, receives a blow which smashes the boat and two men's legs; the third boat picks up the men; our first man at last gets steered into the vortex, gives a well-aimed lance in the life, and retreats from the foam, which receives a roseate hue. The monster leaps out of the sea, flourishing her tail and fins, and strikes the water with a noise as loud as cannon. She wriggles, and plunges, and twists, more furiously than ever, and splashes blood over the boat's crew, who still restrain their excitement and remain collected in

F

all that they do. She in now in her 'flurry'—she is said to 'spout thick blood'; and is a sure prize. The boat, by great good management, escapes all accident; and the headsman chuckles as he cuts a notch on the loggerhead, and gives the crew a 'tot all round', promising the novice that he will have to treat the party to a gallon to-night, in order to pay his footing on killing his first fish.

If the tide is favourable, all the boats of the party assemble, and tow the whale home; if unfavourable, she is anchored for the night; and the boats reach the ways at dusk. A drunken rejoicing lasts till the middle of the night; the headsmen meet in the principal *whare* at supper, and spin long yarns about their old whaling feats, the speed of their new boats, the strength of their crews, and the likelihood of a good season; the doctor, generally the runaway surgeon of a whaling-ship, who gets fed and clothed by all the neighbouring stations, attends to the broken limbs; and the little town gradually subsides into silence, now and then interrupted by the barking of a bull-dog from one of the huts, or the jibbering of a night-bird (called the *titi porangi*) as it flies across the bay. So passes the season; except that while a whale is trying out, the operation goes on night and day; alternate gangs, still commanded by their headsmen, being 'on watch' at the try-works. This has been already described at Te Awaiti.

Should a stranger visit the settlement on his travels, he is met by a hearty welcome. The best of eating and drinking is placed before him; the steward and the women are ordered to attend to him while the boats are away; and the best bunk is prepared for him at night. For the information of those who do not know what a bunk is, I must explain that it is a bed-place built against the wall of a house or ship. They are commonly ranged in double tier, like those in the saloon of a Channel steamer.

A whaler's house is generally built by the natives. It is either entirely composed of reeds and rushes woven over a wooden frame —or else the walls consist of a wattled hurdle made of supple-jack (*kareao*) covered inside and out with clay, and the roof is thatched. A huge chimney nearly fills one end of the house—and generally swarms with natives, iron pots and kettles, favourite dogs, and joints of the whale's backbone, which serve as stools. A view of some fine hams, bacon, and fish, repays the exertion of peering through the wood-smoke up the chimney. Bunks with neat curtains line the greater part of the sides of the house. A large deal table and two long benches stand in the middle of the hard earthen floor. The rafters support spare coils of rope, oars, masts and sails, lances, spades and harpoons, and a tin oil-lamp carefully burnished. Two square holes in the wall serve as windows, with wooden shutters for the night. The harness-cask (for salt meat), flour-keg, and water-butt, stand on one side, and a neat dresser, shining with bright tin dishes and a few glasses and articles of crockery, on the other side of the door. On the threshold an old mongrel pig-dog, scarred all over the head and neck by repeated battles, lies repelling the advances of a tame sow, and those of some begging natives, who have an equal desire to be allowed the opportunity of picking up anything which may have been left about inside. Two or three of the Maoris are asleep, rolled in their blankets against the sunny wall; and a few half-caste children are playing with the goats or hallooing at the fowls and pigeons on the oily beach before the house. The great cleanliness and neatness which prevail in the house, and in the dress of the native women and their children, reminds one of a Dutch coaster; this is evidently a point on which the whaler is exceedingly particular.

Should a vessel heave in sight, boats will pull out a long distance to meet her, and pilot her in. This arises partly from a wish to hear news, and partly from the proverbial readiness of the sailor to assist his fellow. When the *Tory* was lying at Kapiti in October 1839, a brig was seen to the southward, making vain attempts to reach the anchorage against a strong north-west gale. Ignorant of the locality, and weak-handed, the captain was exposing himself to the unfavourable tide, and losing ground. Tommy Evans, the 'old man' who headed the principal station, started in the worst of the gale to get on board. The vessel was badly managed, and, by wearing instead of tacking, missed the boat, which was thus left about three miles from the station, in the midst of a heavy tide-rip, to struggle back against a spring-tide and gale of wind. For two hours the boat remained pulling in the same spot, unable to advance. At length the tide slackened, and we saw the tired crew haul up the boat on the ways. The brig was by this time ten miles off, and the gale more violent than ever. One of the men muttered as he walked to his house that 'he had not signed to pull after Sydney brigs'. The 'old man' turned round and said with a string of oaths, 'You grumble, do you? I shall pull out to her again—Launch my boat!' and it was with great difficulty that he was dissuaded from the enterprise, which would probably have been his last. This man's station on Tokomapuna, or Evans's Island, was always a model of discipline. His boat might have been taken for a fancy gig from a man-of-war or yacht. She was painted flesh-colour, with a red nose bearing the Prince of Wales's feathers; and her name, the *Saucy Jack*, was painted near the stern. The crew were generally in a sort of uniform—red or blue worsted shirts, with white binding on the seams—white trousers, and sou'-westers. A mat was in the stern sheets; the tholes were carefully covered with matting; the harpoons, lances, mast and sail, and the very whiff, were protected by covers of canvas painted green. When she dashed alongside a vessel at anchor, the oars were shipped, and the steer-oar was drawn in and received by the after-oarsman as the headsman left the boat. She was then shoved off, with a line from her bow thwart to the vessel, each man remaining at his place, in regular man-o'-war style. The same order and discipline is preserved at the different look-outs where the men land, while waiting till whales appear. If there is deep water, the boat is moored off the beach, with a shore-line; if it is on a shallow coast, as between Waikanae Point and Otaki, the boat is hauled up out of the tide and supported by chocks, and a boat-keeper constantly attends to her. Two fires are lighted for each crew; at one are the headsman and boat-steerer, the rest of the men at the other.

They have sometimes very hard work: in seasons when the whales are scarce, I have seen boats from Kapiti at Horowhenua, a distance of fifteen miles to windward, half an hour after daylight. And the whole distance is rowed without a rest; it is not until arrived on the ground selected for the day that the headsman allows them to peak their oars and light a pipe.

They seemed to dare the elements on almost all occasions. During the season of 1843, a whale pursued by several rival boats fled into the surf which breaks a quarter of a mile from the shore off Otaki in or after heavy weather. Most of the boats 'hove-up' outside the surf; and I believe none of the headsmen would have engaged even to land that day without capsizing. But 'Bill the Steward', who was luckily heading a short, handy boat, went boldly in after the fish, fastened, ran, and killed her, all in the surf.

In some of the stations, the common men are all native lads— and those who have employed them speak well of the experiment. It may be supposed that, in consequence of this custom, and that of having native wives, the whalers had effected a considerable change among the natives before the arrival of the *Tory*. We found many who dressed constantly in European clothes, and spoke a good deal of English—some few had acquired a considerable knowledge of carpentering; the canoes were most of them sailed with duck sails instead of flax ones, and steered with a steer-oar, in imitation of the boats. Two boats were fitted out from the native village of Wekanui, close to Te Awaiti, entirely by natives; who, though they never succeeded in killing a whale, often made fast, and received £20 for each one from the boat which profited by their exertions.

But the bad points of the whaler's character have also passed, with the very worst effect, into the disposition of some of the natives. They have acquired, in some few cases, the habits of drinking; in many, boastful and insolent behaviour, and callousness to feeling. The old chiefs have become accustomed to be bribed and flattered into good-humour in the early days when the whalers were not numerous enough to defend themselves, and also in the summer when they are dispersed about. In consequence, these chiefs have acquired an overbearing, grasping, and bullying demeanour; which, though laughed at by the whalers when assembled, falls with redoubled force on new-comers unused to deal with them, or on scattered settlers.

The whalers had thus, before our arrival, braved the first dangers of the intercourse between the savage and the civilized man— they had explored the coast and seaboard country, and had introduced new wants as well as new vices, and a considerable degree of respect for the physical qualities of the *pakeha* among the aboriginal population. With the exception of the expedition made by Marsden in 1814, I believe that in every instance these rough pioneers had smoothed the way for a more valuable civilization; and that the missionaries, or the settlers, followed on their traces.

I mention this with no wish to detract from the credit due to that system which first proposed to seek the benefit of the natives alone, and to obtain a deserved moral influence over them; but I state as a curious fact, that, whether as whalers and sealers in the south, or sawyers and flax or provision traders in the north, the first rough and unconscious pioneers of civilization were those who experienced the greatest hardships; and that they preserved their station among the natives by the display of their physical force.

In his dealings with the European settlements, the whaler very much resembles a sailor off a cruise. After the men have been paid the balance due to them at the end of the season, they go to Wellington or Nelson to spend it. The trade of supplying them and buying their oil has naturally fallen out of the hands of the Sydney merchants, into those of persons at Wellington, who pay them better, and send the oil direct to England. During six weeks or two months, Wellington becomes a Portsmouth in miniature. Every public-house has its fiddle and hornpipe going; a little theatre fills once a week; and the weak constabulary force of Wellington suffers from various practical jokes. Boat-races, on which heavy bets sometimes depend, come off, and an occasional fight, arising from the profound contempt which the whaler expresses for the 'lubber of a *jimmy-grant*', as he calls the emigrant, completes the programme of the amusements during the period. Should the whaling-trade increase and prosper, the quiet people will soon be forced to reside in villas out of town, and resign Wellington to its business as a sea-port. When the money is spent, most of the men seek for employment in the settlements.

Some join with the sawyers, a class of men who are composed of nearly the same materials, and whose character is somewhat congenial to that of the whaler, as they live a wild life in the forest on the outskirts of the settlements, love drink, and have known many of the same places and people. The sawyer's habits, however, do not encourage the same hardy daring, or an equal degree of order and cleanliness. The sawyer proper is decidedly an inferior grade of the whaler.

Others trade with the natives for pigs and potatoes, which they bring to market in the settlements. The mere trader, also, is naturally a degree below the whaler. in order to make a profit, he must take pains to fawn and flatter the natives, without making any unnecessary presents; a task very difficult, and debasing in its moral effects. The best man is the one who retires, after his 'spree', to the village where the tribe of his native woman reside, and spends the summer in cultivating a bit of land given to him by the natives. Some few of these are in constant doubt between the quiet pleasures of agriculture and a domestic life, and the wild excitement of the whale-chase. I have heard more than one declare, as he showed me his neat patch of wheat, or promising fruit-trees, that 'he had had enough of whaling', he should 'let those fag that would next year'; but the 1st of May saw him again at his steer-oar, eagerly backing up, and shouting, 'There she spouts!'

The lumberers and sawyers of the *kauri* districts, the pork and flax traders who catered for the Sydney coasters for many years in the Northern Island, at Kawhia, Taranaki, the Bay of Plenty, and Poverty Bay, and Rotorua and the other neighbouring inland districts, were all of the same class, and have often displayed the same reckless courage while taking a part in the native wars. The sealers of the south were as nearly as possible the same men, and were distinguished for the same qualities.

The whaling stations dependent on Wellington in the season 1844 were as follows:

On the North Island there were—

2 boats at Mana;
7   ,,   Kapiti;
11   ,,   Hawke's Bay;
3   ,,   Palliser Bay;
2   ,,   Taranaki;

and on the Middle Island there were—

2 boats at Te Awaiti;
7   ,,   Port Underwood;
8   ,,   Kaikoura, south of Cape Campbell;
4 boats near Port Cooper;
9   ,,   on the south side of Banks's Peninsula;
2   ,,   at Waikouaiti, between that and Otago; and
11   ,,   at stations further south.

These sixty-eight boats employed in their own management and that of the small craft attending on them about 650 men.

In the last season they procured 1215 tons of oil, and 49 tons of whalebone; worth altogether about £50,000 in the London market.

The success of the fishery varies, of course, every season; but there is every reason to think that it is on the decline. The whales are, doubtless, unnecessarily thinned by the practice of killing the cows, and even the young calves, who do not survive the practice of making fast to them in order to catch their mother.

The shoals seem to set in from the southward late in April or in the beginning of May and are seen first in Cook's Strait at Palliser Bay and Port Underwood. They then proceed up the Strait, preferring the north shore, which is generally shoal, and thus passing close to Mana and Kapiti. They fill the shoal 'Motherly' bay extending along nearly 150 miles of coast, between Kapiti and Cape Egmont, and are also seen for some distance north of the Sugar-loaf islands. In the 'Motherly' bay, as it is called, because they resort to it for calving, they have never yet been disturbed; and I have seen them in great numbers, basking outside the surf, from the coast between Manawatu and Patea. I cordially join with those who consider that all shore-whaling should be forbidden, as I am convinced that a much greater advantage would result to those who profit by the trade, were ships fitted out from our Australasian colonies, and the fish allowed to visit, unmolested, the calving-bays to which they resort during the period of gestation.

I am bound to say that I owe the whalers personally many obligations. Although they have a dark side to their character, they claim gratitude for their frankness and hospitality, and admiration for their extraordinary intrepidity, their unbounded resolution, their great power of enduring hardships, and their perseverance in overcoming practical difficulties.

When I was tired of catching fish and seeing others catch whales, I got a cast over to Waikanae in one of the boats, and walked to Petone, resting one night at Captain Thomas's hospitable *whare*. I reached Port Nicholson about the 14th of July.

CHAPTER IX

Sundry Expeditions: Some Wellington Gossip

O N THE 20th June, her Majesty's ship *Herald* had visited Port Nicholson. Major Bunbury had been instructed to proceed in that frigate to extend the sovereignty of the Queen of England over the Middle and Stewart's Islands. He had visited various ports in both those places, and obtained the signatures of Tuhawaiki or 'Bloody Jack', and of several other chiefs, to a copy of the agreement signed at the Bay of Islands. He had declared the sovereignty of her Majesty by formal proclamation, and taken possession of both islands; at Southern Port, in Stewart's Island, on the 5th of June; and at Port Underwood, in Cloudy Bay, on the 17th of the same month. In the latter case alone the proclamation based the assumption of sovereignty on its cession by the native chiefs.

He had then visited Kapiti, and meeting Rauparaha in his canoe, had taken that chief down to Mana, in order to obtain the signatures of Rangihaeata and Te Hiko. The latter was absent on the mainland; but Rangihaeata and Rauparaha had both signed on board the *Herald* on the 19th of June. Rauparaha thus signed twice, for his signature had been previously obtained by the Rev. Henry Williams.

On the 20th, the *Herald* had anchored in the entrance of Port Nicholson, and Major Bunbury had communicated with the Colonial Secretary. On the 21st, the frigate sailed all about the harbour, and Major Bunbury had landed and been introduced to some of the settlers at Captain Smith's house.

A public meeting of the colonists had been held on the 1st of

July, for the purpose of voting an address to Lieutenant-Governor Hobson. Colonel Wakefield had presided at this meeting, and had been unanimously called upon to proceed to the Bay of Islands for the purpose of presenting the address to his Excellency. The utmost loyalty and good feeling had reigned over the assembly.

The *Brougham*, which had arrived from England while I was with the whalers, was preparing to convey Colonel Wakefield on this mission when I arrived, and he sailed on the 19th of July, after appointing Mr. Hanson as acting Agent of the Company in his absence.

The *Platina*, which had brought Governor Hobson's wooden house, and some more provisions and stores for the Company, had arrived on the 6th. Colonel Wakefield had therefore to obtain the instructions of the Lieutenant-Governor as to the destination of his residence. It was sanguinely hoped that, in answer to the concluding paragraph of the address, his Excellency would send back word to have it erected here, in readiness for his arrival amongst us.

The *Platina* brought news of the assemblage of some thousands of emigrants in England, in readiness to embark as soon as they should hear the first accounts of the arrival and proceedings of the *Tory*; of the change of the name of the Company, now styled the New Zealand Company; of the formation of another company at Plymouth, who were to be in connexion with the main Company, but to have a town and district for their colonists distinct from that of the first settlers; and of the publication of a newspaper in England especially devoted to news relating to this colony, and called the *New Zealand Journal*.

On the 13th July, the *Cuba* returned from the Chatham Islands. Mr. Hanson, the Company's agent, had succeeded in purchasing the whole of the group. These islands have been so fully described by Messrs. Dieffenbach and Heaphy,* who formed part of the expedition, that I refrain from following in their track by repeating what I collected from them.

On the 28th July, the selection of the town-lands commenced. The meeting for this purpose took place in a large unfinished

* *Narrative of a Residence in various Parts of New Zealand*, by Charles Heaphy, 1842. *Travels in New Zealand*, by Ernst Dieffenbach, 1843.

wooden building, which Dr. Evans had brought out with him, and which Dicky Barrett had bought and erected on the beach for a hotel.* A table was placed on that part of the ground-floor which was floored, to support the map of the town and the books of the principal selectors. The most interested or most querulous settlers were gathered round Mr. Hanson, Captain Smith and his assistants; asking questions, raising difficulties or meeting them, and keeping an eye to some desired section; while those who had but late choices, or others who were mere spectators, stood talking in the windows of the long room, or explored the skeleton upper story of the embryo hotel. On the 31st, some mistake was discovered in the plan; and the further selection was consequently postponed to the 10th of August, and was not completed until the 14th.

Ample reserves for public purposes appeared on the plan; one acre was reserved for the Company, as a site for the immigration buildings, and the Native Reserves, consisting of one hundred sections of one acre each, were judiciously selected by Captain Smith. Among others, the section on which the hotel was building, which is of as great value as any in the town, fell to the lot of the natives.

Two acres adjoining each other, and possessed of some of the best water-frontage, were also excluded from the general choice, in accordance with the arrangement made between the Rev. Henry Williams and Colonel Wakefield.

On the 4th of August, intelligence was received from Sydney, which produced great agitation among the settlers at Port Nicholson. The views of Sir George Gipps, the Governor of New South Wales, with regard to claims to land in this country, had been embodied in a measure called the New Zealand Land Bill, and this, we heard, had passed the Legislative Council.

The Bill declared any title to lands in New Zealand not derived from the Crown null and void†. All claims to such lands were to be addressed within six months to the Colonial Secretary of New South Wales, in order that he might refer them to a Board of

---

* This was on the site of the present Hotel Cecil, opposite Parliament Buildings.

† On this point the Bill embodied the policy concerning titles to land already announced in the House of Lords on 25 June 1839, in Governor Gipps's proclamation of 14 January 1840, and in Captain Hobson's proclamation of 30 January 1840.

Commissioners; for whose appointment, operations, and remuneration, the Bill also provided.

But the most remarkable feature of the new law was a most stringent provision, which forbade the Commissioners from recommending favourably to the Governor any grant of land 'exceeding in extent 2,560 acres, or comprehending any headland, promontory, bay, or island that might hereafter be required for the purposes of defence or for the site of any town, nor any land situate on the sea-shore within a certain number of yards of high-water mark, or any other land situate within so many miles of the mouth of any river navigable for vessels of more than fifty tons burthen'.

The panic which seized the great body of colonists on the receipt of this intelligence is hardly to be conceived. The measure promised to deprive them of the very site of a town under their feet, which was at that moment being distributed to them for occupation and improvement. Moreover, it seemed uncertain whether any country lands at all would be shared among them; as the Company, like any other claimant, might be restricted to the maximum allowance of four square miles of land.

The Port Nicholson settlers had reason to cry out against the injustice of this sweeping measure; and they moreover felt that they had deserved some better reward for the courage with which they had extended British occupation over this part of the islands, and the loyalty with which they had hailed and assisted the establishment of British allegiance. Various were the projects suggested by the panic-struck adventurers, each according to his disposition.

§

This agitation was at its height when, early in August, I proceeded to explore the lower part of the Manawatu river. I had joined with a merchant of Port Nicholson in supplying Captain Lewis of Kapiti with some of the goods necessary for building his schooner, and he was to pay for them either in pigs and potatoes or in a share of the vessel; so that I went to see what facilities the river might afford for trading. I proceeded by land to Waikanae, crossed in a canoe to Kapiti, and there engaged Geordie Young's half-decked boat for the trip. Starting with the end of the breeze, we soon reached the mouth of the Manawatu river; and landed through the surf on the beach to the north, the bar looking dangerous. At midnight, the tide being more favourable, we threw out our ballast, and poled our boat, through the inner rollers on the north sand-spit, into the river. About a mile along the north bank, we found a small deserted *pa*, where we put up for the night. At daylight, we proceeded about fifteen miles up the river, to the spot where the vessel was building. The river was deep but narrow, and the land on both sides level, and apparently very fertile; but the waters of extensive swamps drained sluggishly over the low banks in many places. Until near Captain Lewis's huts, the country was nearly clear of timber; and we enjoyed an uninterrupted view of the north-western face of the Tararua range over the high flax and reeds on the south bank. To the north the horizon seemed unbounded. Near the small dock-yard, forests of large timber began to line the banks; and in one of the finest groves we perceived the skeleton of a small vessel on the stocks, two reed-huts, a pig-sty, and a saw-pit. Captain Lewis and his brother, now looking more like Yankee backwoodsmen than whalers, a sawyer, a carpenter, and their native wives and relations, greeted our arrival.

After inspecting the little clipper, which was about thirty tons burthen, we sat down to the usual meal of pork and potatoes, and spun yarns till bed-time. The night was warm and calm, and I spread my blankets outside the huts, as our party was rather numerous.

The next day, I returned to the *pa* at the mouth of the river, accompanied by young Lewis, who was to fetch some pigs from Rangitikei. Geordie Young and I borrowed the whale-boat of an English trader, who arrived from an expedition up the river soon after us, and proceeded to sound the entrance. The day being fine, the cone of Mount Egmont appeared exactly between the two sand spits at the mouth. Over the level tract of country nearly due north appeared Tongariro; and the top of a range of distant mountains tipped with snow, called Ruahine by the natives, bounded the horizon between that and the east. In that direction a gorge exists, between the southern end of the Ruahine and the low north-eastern extremity of the Tararua range, which I imagined to communicate with the country towards Hawke's Bay.

This conjecture was confirmed by the narrative which Jack Duff, the trader, gave us of his journey. He had ascended the river as far as a whale-boat could go (about fifty miles, according to his calculation, from the mouth), through country of the same level and fertile character, and abounding with the finest timber. Having obtained a canoe and native guides, he proceeded two or three days' journey higher up, over numerous rapids and shallows, and through a gorge where the river formed a cataract between the cliffy extremities of the two mountain ranges. He described the country as again opening out beyond this gorge, and related that the natives of the furthest settlement to which he attained spoke a somewhat different dialect from the Ngatiraukawa, and called it only two days' walk to the 'East Cape'. As I had found this name applied by the Cook's Strait natives to the eastern coast generally, I concluded that his informants probably referred to some part of Hawke's Bay. He described a numerous population as dwelling below the gorge, and complained much of their rude and savage manners. He even attributed his safety from plunder or outrage to the company of his native woman, who was related in some distant way to the tribe.

The next morning, Lewis having returned with a dozen fine hogs for me, we left the river, Duff showing us a tolerable boat-passage through the breakers about the middle of the south spit. We stopped a night at Kapiti, where I picked up two sawyers who begged for a passage; and a few hours at Mana. Rangihaeata was also there, and, hearing that I had been looking at Manawatu, took occasion to tell me that it belonged to him and Rauparaha. We then sailed with a squally breeze from north-west round Cape Terawhiti, beat into the harbour during the night, and landed at daybreak on Petone beach.

I found that the choice of the town sections had been concluded on the 14th, to the ultimate satisfaction of all the squabbling agents and proprietors.

The panic caused by Sir George Gipps's New Zealand Land Bill had increased to a very high pitch; and I heard that a set of the colonists had seriously proposed a general re-migration to Chile.

On the 16th of August, the return of the *Brougham* with Colonel Wakefield from the Bay of Islands restored general confidence.

On the 19th, a public meeting was held in the unfinished hotel, to receive the answer of Captain Hobson to the address of the colonists. Colonel Wakefield stated the results of his mission— that he had been received by the Lieutenant-Governor in the most courteous manner; and that he was assured that the feelings of Captain Hobson to the settlers at Port Nicholson under the auspices of the Company were of the most friendly nature. He then read the answers to the address and to the offers of support from the Company and the settlers.

The first letter graciously acknowledged the loyalty of the inhabitants of the district of Port Nicholson. The second letter quietly declined the invitation to his Excellency to reside in this part of the country. He acknowledged that this was at the sacrifice of his own ease; but he said that a sense of public duty induced him to select 'a more *centrical* position, and one more adapted for internal communication'.

[*Wakefield next speaks of the work done by the Wellington magistrates in maintaining order. They had been particularly remarkable for their infliction of large fines—£5 for drunkenness or breach of the peace.*

Sam Phelps, a drunken, foul-mouthed bullock-driver, was a frequent contributor to the public revenue. He was an excellent hand at his profession, which is a very flourishing one in all new settlements, and his pockets were always well lined with money. If he made it like a good bullock-driver, however, it was his pride that he spent it in the same way, in drinking large doses of ardent spirits. The Magistrates and constables of course interfered with this predilection. Sam took his own means of revenging himself.

His team of bullocks were soon christened 'Shortland', 'Smart', 'Best', and 'Cole';* and he used to apply the coarsest epithets to them as he flogged them along. One day the Colonial Secretary, stately and pompous as usual, happened to pass the dray which they were dragging over the beach. Brutal threats to 'cut Shortland's tail off if he didn't move on'; to 'break his heart', to 'cut his liver in two', or to 'whip his skin off', startled him in his promenade; and on turning suddenly round he beheld old Sam 'whacking' his team.

* Shortland, the Colonial Secretary and Chief Magistrate; Cole, the Chief Constable; and Lieutenant Best, the military commander.

To the surprise of the spectators, the Chief Magistrate asked the bullock-driver whether 'he applied those expressions to him?'

Sam answered, with an innocent grin, 'I wasn't a speakin' to you; I'm a driving my bullocks; that's my business'; and the Colonial Secretary retreated from the scene, amidst a loud repetition of the most frightful imprecations, threats, and mockery of the bullocks by the bullock-driver, who triumphed over his superior. A crowd of the lower classes roared with laughter during the whole scene.

Sam Phelps was quite a character, only to be seen in new colonies. He had been exercising his trade in the recent settlements in Australia, where he had no doubt witnessed and appreciated on many occasions the pride of tyro Government officers. After this scene, he completely gained his point in holding up the early Magistracy to ridicule; and a crowd of idlers would always collect at the door of each public-house to see Sam pass, and hear him address his titled team. As long as he remained in this settlement, his habits were precisely the same, and he only changed the names of his bullocks according to those of the magistrates who fined him. 'Colonel', 'Murphy', 'Halswell', etc., were subsequently substituted for the first offenders, as fresh Magistrates sat on the bench. But he was naturally attracted to new settlements, where money was plenty, and good labour, like his, scarce; and he successively visited the later settlements of New Plymouth and Nelson in their first days.

An event had occurred at Petone in August which serves to show how affectionately the natives of that village still regarded us. A boat from Thorndon, overladen with passengers, and steered by an inexperienced hand, had been suddenly capsized in the surf which was rolling on to the beach before a strong southerly gale, and the whole crew and passengers were immersed in the breakers. The Petone natives, men and women, headed by Te Puni and his wife, dashed into the surf, and used their utmost efforts to rescue the drowning men. They succeeded in saving two or three, but nine men were brought dead upon the beach. The scene was most impressive. Natives and colonists of every class were employed in bearing the bodies under shelter, and using the means at hand for attempting to revive them. The relations of those who were expected from Thorndon that night were rushing wildly from group to group, the venerable clergyman entreating them to hope and resignation, and comforting the distressed women in the midst of the howling storm; while the natives, wet and shivering from their generous exertions, wailed in their customary way on the out-skirts of the crowd. Every now and then one of them would rush to me, and asking whether 'Wide-awake' was in the boat, plunge again into the rollers, and dive in different directions till he was tired. I had been very anxious about my uncle, as he had been over at Thorndon, watching the progress of the settlers there, and it was reported that he had been one of the party. Under this impression, the natives never ceased their laborious search until I ascertained from the master of the boat, who was one of those fortunately saved, that Colonel Wakefield had not been one of his passengers.

An opinion seemed to be prevalent at this time that the whole country was as mountainous as the district in the immediate neighbourhood of Port Nicholson. Colonel Wakefield therefore determined to despatch a party of surveyors by land to Taranaki, in order that their official report of the quantity and quality of land observed by them between the two places might dissipate this unfounded conjecture. The party was to consist of Mr. Robert Park and Mr. Robert Stokes, two of the Company's Assistant Surveyors; and Mr. Charles Heaphy, the draughtsman. Mr. Deans,* an enterprising young Scotch settler, who had already been employed in superintending a party of labourers while cutting surveyor's lines through the valley of the Hutt, volunteered to accompany the expedition; and I also offered my services as far as Wanganui, whither I was desirous of returning. Six labourers were selected from the surveying-staff to carry the requisite supply of instruments, blankets, and provisions; and I engaged a native lad to carry my *kawenga*, or load, as far as Waikanae.

We started from Petone amid the affectionate farewells of Te Puni and his followers, on the morning of the 27th August, and slept that night at Paremata whaling-station, in Lieut. Thomas's new house, the floor of which was well strewn with clean fern. The second night we reached Paripari, and early the next afternoon

*William Deans. With his brother John Deans, in 1843, he pioneered the settlement of the Canterbury plains.

we arrived at Waikanae, well drenched by a heavy shower of rain. We were most hospitably received by old Rangiwhakarurua.

Mr. Stokes called on the Rev. Mr. Hadfield, who resided in the midst of the principal *pa*, and was received very kindly by him. He insisted on our making use of a new house built for him at Otaki, and gave Mr. Stokes a letter to one of his native teachers, who had charge of the key. Mr. Hadfield had not yet succeeded in effecting a complete reconciliation between the two tribes, [the Ngatiawa and the Ngatiraukawa], and I could not at first engage any native to carry my burden through the hostile country. Old Rangi, however, ordered Heuheu, a lad of thirteen, who was a slave to his son Kuru, to proceed as my servant, and we started along the unknown coast the next morning.

[*After minor adventures on the coastal route, Wakefield reached the Turakina river, fording it waist-deep.*]

After another mile of sand-hills, we reached the banks of the Wangaehu. The fording of this river was more difficult, the current being extremely rapid, and the bed of the stream a shifting quicksand which seemed to move along with the water, and varied in consistency, so that at one step your ankles were hardly immersed and at the next you stand up to your arm-pits. The river is here about two hundred yards in breadth, and the water was painfully cold. After warming our limbs and drying our clothes at a large fire, we pushed along the beach, and at length reached the hill near Wahipuna, overlooking the valley of the Wanganui. A glowing sunset warmed the features of this lovely scene, and we sat for some time enjoying the view. The *Surprise* schooner was lying at Purua; we could distinguish numerous large houses on either bank of the river, especially two or three apparently inhabited near the large *pa*; and we could see the hospitable smoke, and hear the hum of people from the native villages. After our long dreary journey, and breaking suddenly from barren sand-hills upon this pleasant scene, we all felt lively and good-humoured; and, after firing our guns as a signal, raced and skipped and shouted like children down the sand-hill to the river's beach, notwithstanding our sore feet and hunger.

On reaching Putikiwharanui, I was loudly greeted by many of

my old friends, and Kuru soon dashed on to the beach in a boat manned by natives, and gave me his usual dignified but most hearty welcome. We got into the boat, and landed at the spot where the scramble for the goods had taken place. Kuru signed to me to follow him, and led the way to a very large *whare*, about twenty yards from the bank. 'This house is yours,' said he; 'tell your white men to go in.' On entering, I found it indeed a noble present. The house was fifty feet long and twenty-eight feet broad. Slabs of *totara* wood, two feet broad, neatly smoothed with the adze, and placed at regular intervals of five feet, formed the framework of the walls; and these, nine feet high and six inches thick, were composed of neatly packed bundles of *raupo* or bulrushes, lined inside with the glazed reeds of the *toetoe*, and outside with the *wiwi*, or fine grass. The reeds are as thick as a finger, of a golden yellow colour, and stand horizontally between the slabs, bound in their place by flaxen ties, which are noosed round each separate reed, and cross horizontally from slab to slab at distances of a foot. The roof, also six inches thick, was composed of four layers: the innermost, *toetoe* reeds, like the walls; the second, bark of the *totara*; the third, *raupo*; and the outside one, tufts of fine grass, put on like shingles, with the roots downwards. The roof was supported by one post in the centre of the house, a foot in diameter, which upheld a huge slab as a ridge-pole; and four large corner rafters, and several smaller ones, all neatly adzed out of solid trees, sloped down to the four walls. Two tie-beams, six inches each in diameter, supported the inward pressure of the walls, directly under each end of the ridge-pole, to which they were attached by perpendiculars.

A splendid hog was brought alive as the customary present; and one of the surveying-men, a butcher by trade, proceeded to show his science. A store of potatoes, pumpkins, *kumaras*, and shallots, was piled up in one corner of the house, and a fire was lit near the middle, on the hard earthen floor; and a numerous troop of Kuru's followers and relations busied themselves in helping the butcher and the cook, fetching water, peeling potatoes, or strewing one end of the house with clean fern for our sleeping-place.

Little Heuheu was as busy as the rest, and chattered a lively description of all our proceedings. I remember being struck by

the kind greeting which Kuru gave him, almost as though he had
been his own son. He kindly dwelt on his courage in coming,
and his endurance in carrying my heavy load, and evidently felt
sincere pleasure when I loudly praised the boy's services. By this
sort of treatment, Kuru had secured the perfect devotion of his
slaves. Except in cases of misconduct, I never heard him use a
threat or a harsh word towards them. They were treated exactly
as members of the family, and allowed to take part in the amusements as well as the labour of the tribe. They were always as
well clothed and fed and supplied with tobacco as himself. By his
own example, and by frequently holding them up to the emulation
or ridicule of the rest, according to their merits, he had succeeded
in raising them to great perfection in all the parts of a native's
education, and to a very complete discipline: they were confessedly
the best paddlers and polers and pig-hunters, the most expert
house-builders and woodsmen on the river; and under so good and
noble a master they gloried in the title of slave. I have frequently
been told by some among them that they would far rather remain
his slaves than return freed to their own tribe and country.

The condition of a New Zealand slave is indeed rarely very
painful or oppressed. *Mokai*, the word for 'slave' most used in
the native language, is the same which they apply to favourite
birds, dogs, or pigs, and is fairly represented by the English word
'pet'.* To be sure, they hold their life at the mercy of their lord,
and obey his orders under penalty of death; but they rarely do
harder work than the other members of the tribe, and are not
separated from the society and conversation of their masters, except
the latter be of remarkably tyrannical or avaricious disposition,
and thus inclined to make them endure his caprice, or work hard
in order to gain for him large payment. The following are a few
examples of the latter class of masters. Rauparaha wantonly killed
one of his slaves who brought him tribute at the Mana feast, in
1839, in order to serve a dainty dish to his Ngatiraukawa allies.
Rangihaeata once took a young slave-child by the heels and dashed
its brains out against a post, in Otaki *pa*, for breaking his pipe

---

* The more offensive and insulting term, *taurekareka*, is less frequently used, and is applied
rather to captives newly taken in war, and while the passions of the master are hot. A
third word, *ponanga*, answers rather to our 'servant': and the fourth, *kuki*, is probably only
a corruption from the 'cook' on board ships [Wakefield's footnote].

while lighting it. A chief at Taupo in the interior threw his slave into one of the boiling ponds there for stealing a few potatoes.

After a solid meal, we began to exchange our news. Kuru told me that two white missionaries had arrived;* one of whom lived in the houses near Putikiwharanui, while the other inhabited a house at the point about 400 yards above this spot. He told me that a great many houses had been built by the natives in readiness for the white settlers, and that the clearings for potato-gardens had been increased and extended, in order to insure an ample supply of provisions for them.

A trading-boat from Port Nicholson, the very one built by Joe Robinson, (i.e., the *Venture*) had been brought hither by one of the settlers from England. He had ascended the river seventy miles in a canoe, reaching a large and populous *pa* called Pukehika;† and had gone away again with his boat well loaded.

Mr. Matthews, the missionary whom Kuru had described as living on this side of the river, was very kind in his offers of hospitality to our party, and sent us sugar, wine, and several other acceptable supplies. He also gave us an interesting account of a battle which had taken place between two tribes of the natives, at Waitotara, very lately.

Macgregor, the owner of the *Surprise*, had made a trip to his old abode in the South of the islands since I last saw him. He had brought back with him several of his fellow-settlers; and these had been located by Kuru about five miles up the river, near a grove of pine-trees, from which they were cutting the timber for a small vessel. Macgregor had, in accordance with his intentions formerly agreed to by me, established a trading station at Turoa's village of Purua. I accompanied the surveying party as far as the north head of the river, and wished them a prosperous voyage to Taranaki.

Having engaged a passage in the *Surprise*, which was well laden with live hogs, I bade farewell to Kuru; promising to return soon in order to establish a trading station, and to hasten the arrival of surveyors and settlers to inhabit the numerous houses which had been built for them.

* Messrs. J. Mason and R. Matthews.
† Pukehika was across the river from the present Jerusalem.

I landed at Kapiti, and in a day or two after crossed over to the main, and walked to Port Nicholson. In the course of this walk I was benighted on the hills between Porirua and Petone, having mistaken the time of the rising of the moon. As it was too dark to proceed along the tortuous path beneath the thick foliage, I lay down to sleep for a few hours among the moss and forest-fern beside the path. It is worthy of remark, that although everything was so damp that I could not light a fire, and I had no blanket or any other clothes but those in which I walked, to shield me from the wet, I suffered no inconvenience from cold, and rose fresh and vigorous at the first dawn of day. A bull-dog, presented to me by a whaler at Kapiti, kept watch on the path while I slept, and scoured the bushes all round whenever an owl or other night-bird disturbed the sylvan silence. On reaching the hill above Petone, just as the sun rose over the eastern range, I felt as if returning home, and gazed with pleasure on the majestic harbour and sleeping settlement. The day was calm, and the sky unclouded. This was the 27th of September.

§

I must now retrace the events which had occurred at Port Nicholson during my absence.

The *Coromandel* had arrived from London, *viâ* Sydney, with a heterogeneous cargo of passengers, and a large stock of sheep, horses, and cattle. Several ships from Sydney had also arrived during this period, laden with stock and other articles suited to the new market. Among the arrivals in the port had also been her Majesty's brig *Britomart*, which had conveyed a Magistrate to Akaroa, in anticipation of the arrival of the French colony. Mr. Michael Murphy, formerly Clerk of the Bench at Parramatta in New South Wales, had arrived in this vessel to take his place as Police Magistrate for the district of Port Nicholson, and Mr. Shortland had returned to the court at Russell.

Dr. Dieffenbach had returned from a trip to explore the valley of the Hutt, which produced no great result. He had traced it nearly to its source, and ascended to a spot on the Tararua range, from which he obtained a view of Kapiti and the adjacent part of the Strait. It was proved, however, beyond a doubt, that no extension of this valley led to the plains North of the range; and also, that the valley contained a considerable quantity of very rich alluvial land and luxuriant timber.

The colonists had been busily engaged in removing to Thorndon and the flat near Te Aro *pa*, where substantial wooden buildings were fast assuming the appearance of a town. General consent had established its future name as 'Britannia'; and the newspaper, which had stopped its weekly issue once in order to effect a removal, now sprang from a neat wooden printing office under the additional title of the *Britannia Spectator*.

The Company's barque *Brougham* had been employed in transporting the more bulky articles across the harbour. Among these was the iron safe of the bank, which had arrived in the *Glenbervie*, containing the specie and notes which were to form the currency of the settlement. Mr. John Smith, the manager, showed great anxiety during the transit of the safe, and having been observed by the natives sitting upon its summit as it lay on the deck, acquired from them the title of 'Jacky Box', by which he was ever afterwards known among all shades of colonists.

Colonel Wakefield was busy, like the rest, getting up a town residence.* A swampy clay mound of some six acres in extent had been reserved for public purposes near Barrett's hotel; and on a spot near the summit of this some labourers were busy digging the holes for the foundation-piles. He had bought a house brought from England in frame from a colonist who hesitated about setting it up for himself; and proposed, by the addition of a veranda and kitchen, to make it a tolerably comfortable dwelling. The holes filled with water as fast as they were dug; and I remember ridiculing the idea of the location ever becoming tenable. Te Puni, too, who had once tried a crop of potatoes on the very spot, declared that it was good for nothing. A person who should now walk up the hard drive, and inspect the lawn of rye-grass and clover, or the fertile garden near the house, with its geraniums grown into hedges, could form no idea of what the place was before it was drained by careful cultivation.

* This was on the site of the old portion of the present Parliament Buildings.

The state of the community was at this time exceedingly cheerful. All the labour of the settlement was absorbed at high wages in the work of building, gardening, and fencing; and everybody was well and pleasantly employed either in working or superintending his workmen.

It was at this time that a club was formed, called the Wakefield Club in honour of Colonel Wakefield. The original members were about twenty; and a small house was bought. Visitors and travellers were allowed to become honorary members for three months —and at a house-dinner held every Saturday a stranger was sure of meeting some of the principal colonists; for the subscription and entrance-money had been purposely fixed at a high sum. A remarkable *esprit de corps* prevailed in this little select society ever since, and Saturday soon became for most of the members a *tapu* day, on which no invitation was accepted.

On the 5th of October, a selection took place of such of the country lands as were already surveyed. These included thirty sections, of 100 acres each, in the lower part of the Hutt valley, twenty-five of which were chosen; and ten between the town and the sea-coast to the south, of which four were chosen.

Mr. Molesworth, who had long had an eye to a beautiful tract of land about two miles up the east bank of the river, secured two sections with some early choices; and proceeded immediately to clear a few acres for cultivation. Several other persons followed his example; and the sound of the axe rang merrily through the lower part of the valley.

Mr. John Carne Bidwill, a gentleman engaged in mercantile pursuits in New South Wales, but who added a great knowledge of natural history and shrewd powers of observation to that enterprising spirit and love of adventure which combine to make a good colonist, was at this time visiting our settlements, and I was fortunate enough to be introduced to his acquaintance. Mr. Bidwill had on a former occasion visited the Bay of Islands, the Frith and valley of the Thames, and the districts of Taupo and Waikato. During that journey, he had ascended the volcano of Tongariro, and his narratives of this and other adventures were most interesting.*

I was just now about to proceed to Wanganui by sea, having

* *Rambles in New Zealand,* by J. C. Bidwill 1841.

chartered a decked schooner of twelve tons burthen for the purpose of keeping my engagement with Kuru. Some idea may be formed of the demand which was now existing for small craft to manage the coast-trade and supply the settlement with pigs and potatoes, from the fact that I agreed to pay £100 for three months' use of this little boat, the owner paying the wages of the skipper only; and these wages were £6 per month, besides food and grog. The two other men's wages were £4 per month each.

Mr. Bidwill and Mr. Dudley Sinclair, wishing to see something of the other parts of Cook's Strait, accompanied me in the trip.

On my arrival at Wanganui [having previously called at Port Underwood and Kapiti] I presented some goods to Kuru, to be distributed among the builders of my house; landed a large stock of goods for barter; and embarked a cargo of pigs which had been collected in readiness for my arrival. I had established, through the authority and with the co-operation of their own head chief, an amicable intercourse with a large number of natives. They were dependent on me to a certain degree for the supplies of European articles which they required, and I on them for a cargo. And this commerce being carried on entirely by myself and the upright chief in mutual presents, a friendship more lasting than that of mere customers was soon engendered.

The natives at Turoa's village and at Putikiwharanui were by no means to be traded with on the same terms. They had already acquired in great measure the cunning habits of low traders from Macgregor and his crew; who, although constantly trying to over-reach the natives, profited no more than if they had treated them with constant openness and generosity.

We here met several natives from Taupo who remembered Mr. Bidwill's ascent of Tongariro; and he was soon known among them by no other name than that of the mountain.

The weather during our stay was very wet, and the river much swollen by floods. I returned by way of Kapiti, and arrived in Port Nicholson on the 19th of November; having left a person in charge of my house, who was commissioned to carry on the trade and get a cargo ready by my return.

A schooner had arrived, soon after we left Port Nicholson in October, from the Bay of Islands, and the Thames. The report was, that the Lieutenant-Governor intended shortly to visit the future site of his Capital, an uninhabited place called Waitemata in the Frith of the Thames, in her Majesty's ship *Favourite,* then lying at the Bay; and that he would afterwards come on from 'Auckland', as he had christened it, to us.* But on the 5th of November, the *Favourite* arrived in the harbour, having been eleven days from Auckland, without his Excellency, who had remained there with his suite and hangers-on, who now swelled the total population of his metropolis to the number of 150. It was added that Captain Hobson expressed no intention of coming hither for the present.

An American brig, which had called at the Bay of Islands, had brought a file of newspapers from the Bay. These contained a ridiculous account of the taking formal possession and foundation of Auckland by the Government Surveyor-General, Mr. Felton Mathew on the 18th of September, 1840. Formal possession was taken in the name of the Queen, and her health was drunk at the foot of a flag-staff. Salutes were fired from the two vessels which had brought the party there three days before, the boats ran races, and a lunch on board ship was honoured, we were told, by the presence of the following Government officers—the Police Magistrate, the Colonial Surgeon, the Harbourmaster, the Superintendent of works, the Sub-Protector of Aborigines, the Surveyor-General and his lady! This brilliant staff assembled on the uninhabited shores of a harbour in which their own two vessels lay, contrasted singularly with that provided for the large and stirring population of Britannia, to wit, a Police Magistrate and an Assistant Postmaster. The grand show thus made at Auckland before nobody by Mr. Felton Mathew and his brother officials, without even waiting for the arrival of the founder, was strikingly characteristic of the man and the class. Mr. Mathew had been promoted to the situation of Surveyor-General of New Zealand from that of Town-Surveyor of Sydney.

The surveying expedition had returned from Taranaki; and the report of Mr. Stokes to the Chief Surveyor had satisfied every one that a very large and available district of land must finally become dependent upon Port Nicholson for the outlet of its produce.

* At this point in his narrative, Wakefield begins to reveal both his personal detestation of Hobson, and his local, Wellingtonian contempt for Auckland.

The Directors of the Company signified to their principal agent their earnest wish that the town founded on the shores of Lambton Harbour might be named after the Duke of Wellington, in order to commemorate the important support which his Grace had lent to the cause of colonization in general, and more particularly to those principles of colonization by which these settlements were guided. The settlers took up the view of the directors with great cordiality, and the new name was at once adopted. The newspaper now took the final title of the *New Zealand Gazette and Wellington Spectator*.

On the 27th of November I made another trip to Wanganui in the schooner, and returned on the 14th of December.

The main feature in the affairs of Port Nicholson during this interval had been the return of the deputation from Sydney [concerning the validity of the land purchases]. The local Government engaged not to disturb the settlers at Port Nicholson, but to endeavour to procure for them a confirmation of their titles to 110,000 acres of land, and to their town, on certain conditions.

The *Cuba* had put in at the Bay of Islands, in order that Captain Hobson might be informed of the result of the deputation. His Excellency had appeared to be disappointed at the important concession made in favour of the Port Nicholson settlers by Sir George Gipps, and had remarked ill-humouredly, in the presence of the deputies, when they presented him with his superior's dispatch informing him of the arrangement, 'What does Sir George Gipps mean by this? He might as well have given up the government of New Zealand to the Company!'

On the 12th of December, the ship *London* had arrived from England with 250 emigrants and passengers. Among the latter was Mr. Frederick Alonzo Carrington, who held the appointment of Chief Surveyor to the Plymouth Company before mentioned. This body had bargained to receive from the parent society a district of 50,000 acres, including a site for a town to be called 'New Plymouth', and to be distributed in the same way as the preliminary settlement at Port Nicholson. Mr. Carrington was deputed to confer with Colonel Wakefield on the subject of selecting the next most eligible site within the territory claimed by the Company on either side of Cook's Strait.

Various associations were in course of formation at this time, for purposes calculated to advance the prosperity of the settlement —such as the importation of cattle on a large scale from the neighbouring colonies; the encouragement of inventions for the preparation of the *phormium tenax* or indigenous flax-plant; and the establishment of an Exchange and Public Library. The making of bricks was now first successfully carried on; and a large kiln was in active operation at Kaiwharawhara, a mile from the town.

§

On December 24th I again sailed for Wanganui, taking with me Mr. W. Carrington, one of the assistant-surveyors, and five or six of the Company's labourers, with their goods and chattels. Colonel Wakefield had decided upon having a district surveyed at that place.

At Wanganui, Mr. W. Carrington established himself in a house near the *pa* at Putikiwharanui, and commenced the survey on both sides of the river by cutting the necessary lines through the high fern along the banks.

Soon after this, the *Jewess* schooner entered the river, and anchored at Purua. There were several passengers on board, who had come to inspect the proposed district. As I intended to travel up the river to Kuru, who had gone to collect pigs at the inland settlements, I offered places in my canoe to three or four of them; and we thus formed a merry party.

The canoe was roomy and safe, fitted with a mast and sail, and manned by four or five strong rowers, selected from the train always attendant upon 'Whare Wikitoria', or 'Victoria house', as Kuru had christened my establishment.

The *kareao* platform was covered with clean native mats, and abundance of food and bottled beer was stowed away in the bottom of the canoe. The weather was uniform, sunny, and exhilarating because not oppressively hot; and thus we were rather on a party of pleasure than an exploring expedition.

We slept the first night at a village opposite Te Kauarapawa, that place being deserted by the inhabitants, who were busy gathering their crops; and pushed on the next day. We found the scenery improving in magnificence as we proceeded. Occasionally we passed picturesque little settlements hung midway down the partly cleared acclivities, or laid out on small flats bounded by the mountains and a bend of the river. Long reaches walled in by steeps that were mantled with noble forest or high fern, and dotted here and there with stern crags, stretched between the bends; and at each bend the river generally foamed over a rapid of greater or less ascent. After passing several of these by poling, and ascending the current about ten miles from our sleeping-place, we gave the natives a rest at mid-day on a shingly beach at the foot of a rapid which shot down with more than usual force. The river above it turned sharp to the right, and facing us was a steep wall of verdure rising to the height of some hundred feet.

My boys had told me that Kuru was entertaining a large party of visitors from Waikato, and that we might expect to meet him before we reached his settlement. We had not long disembarked before the regular song of the war-canoe rang from the woods opposite; and, as we rose to look about us, a large fleet came round the point and shot the rapid at full speed. Kuru was in one of the last canoes, and beckoned those who had passed to turn in to our encampment. Here the whole party rested for an hour. The chief introduced me to the principal men among his visitors, who already knew me by name as 'the white man who had paid for Wanganui'; and he reminded me of several old acquaintances among his relations, who were also in the train. He then invited me to travel in his canoe, where the stern-sheets were covered with fine mats; and we returned towards the sea, reaching my house about mid-night.

Several persons travelled by land from Wellington at this time to make themselves acquainted with the Wanganui country. I now made my house a caravanserai for all travellers, inviting them to accept of its shelter until they had agreed for the purchase of some of those built by the natives.

I had divided the great barn into three parts with rude reed partitions: one for the sleeping-room, where people might spread their blankets on the floor; one for goods and provisions; and the large space in the middle as a sort of public hall, where natives, sawyers, travellers of the lower class, my crew, or any one else, might sit round the fire and partake of whatever *kai*, or food, was going on. I continued this system as long as I kept the house; and even after the two wings were furnished with wooden floors, walls, and ceilings, and civilized doors and windows, the centre remained an open hall where all but known bad characters of either race might assemble and be welcome round the ample chimney-corner. But the separated rooms were kept strictly *tapu*, and not even the chief himself ever ventured into them without my permission. In the absence of established laws and usages, I found this sort of feudal system very effectual. I had always a crowd of attendants ready to perform any task; the natives who partook of the shelter and hospitality of the house would have felt ashamed if they had not kept it constantly well supplied with food; and it soon became a word of reproach among the natives to any man, that he had been refused permission to enter the outer door.*

Having loaded a cargo of potatoes in bulk, I started for Port Nicholson towards the end of January, with several passengers who were returning, and who spread their blankets on the top of the potatoes. We made a prosperous run to Kapiti; and, after remaining there one day, and taking two natives as passengers, started early in the morning with a freshening breeze from north-west.

When we rounded Cape Terawhiti an hour before dark, the breeze had increased into a gale; and we flew along before the squalls which dashed down the gullies of the high land, and raised the spray in whirling columns high over our little masts. Hugging the shore in order to avoid being driven to sea, we rounded Sinclair Head in safety; but the night came on pitchy dark, and the gale increased in fury, so that we could not see our way to an anchorage in which I had before taken refuge under the eastern head; and I was obliged to heave-to and drift till the morning, after passing within half the craft's length of one of the reefs. The gale was so violent that the sea was white with foam and almost smooth, for some miles from the shore; but when we were well out, and exposed

---

* The Rev. Taylor, missionary at Putiki *pa* in 1843, has this description of Wakefield's 'Whare Wikitoria': 'They had a large raupo building near the Commercial Inn, with a large table down the centre and a cask of rum at one end for each to help himself from— a rude representation of a baronial hall, of which Jerningham was the chief, wearing a native mat like a toga, and a large manila hat with an ostrich feather in it.'

to the steady blow through the Strait, a heavy and dangerous sea knocked us about like a nut-shell. The only sail we could carry was a balance-reefed mizzen, about the size of a large pocket handker-chief; but under this the boat rode it out gallantly, and caught the seas on her well-rounded bow. I slept soundly during the heaviest part of the gale; but the skipper told me when I looked up, that during two hours he had never expected to see daylight again. At break of day we found ourselves in the latitude, but well to the eastward, of Cape Campbell, the wind being less strong, but a heavy sea running. My passengers had been much frightened and inconvenienced by the water, which leaked in at the topsides and reached up to them in the rolls of the boat. About eight o'clock we were able to make a little sail, hoping to fetch under the lee of Cape Palliser, and to find a temporary anchorage there. In the evening we had reached within a few miles of it, but the baffling willies of wind off the land and the set of the tide round the Cape prevented us from nearing the shore. In the morning it had fallen calm, but we had drifted ten or twelve miles to the north, along the eastern coast. The wind had been gradually drawing round to the south-west, and the clouds were gathering over the high peaks of the Middle Island. By night it was blowing as hard as ever from that quarter, and the sea, sweeping uninterrupted from the south, was as high as at the Cape of Good Hope. We were again under our pocket handkerchief, standing off and on near the coast, for two days and two nights. I had hoped to find some bay or cove large enough to afford us shelter; but when we examined the coast, we could see nothing but terrific surf, tumbling upon sandy beaches or flying in jets of spray from the faces of high cliffs. When the weather moderated, we were off Cape Turnagain; and we did not reach Port Nicholson until the 30th of January, very nearly out of water, firewood, and provisions.

Monseigneur Pompallier, the Roman Catholic Bishop of New Zealand, had visited Wellington during my absence, on his return from the French settlement at Akaroa to his head-quarters at the Bay of Islands. The gentlemen of the Club, and others who had enjoyed his acquaintance, spoke highly of his urbane manners and his philanthropic views with regard to the welfare of the natives.

'A merry Christmas and a happy New Year' had been celebrated in old English style. Fat bullocks had been slaughtered and dressed with evergreens, and the New Year, 1841, saluted with ringing of bells, firing of cannon, and hoisting of flags.

Two days afterwards, a vessel had arrived from Greenock with 200 emigrants; and these I found located in some houses which had been built on speculation by old 'Dog's-ear' and his tribe at Kaiwharawhara. He told me, in his usual comical way, that he thought 'Wide-awake' had slighted him by sending such poor people to his settlement; for he could not understand the bare feet of the Scotch lassies.

It was determined towards the end of the year, to celebrate the first arrival of the settlers, on the 22nd of January, by an Anniversary fête.

So favourable was the state of things in the settlement, and so bright were the prospects for the future, that everybody joined heartily in this idea.

The harvest was in progress in the valley of the Hutt. Consisting chiefly of potatoes, as a good cleaning crop for the newly-cleared land, it had surpassed the most sanguine expectations. The samples of wheat and barley produced in some small patches promised an equally good return under a grain-crop. The rapid improvement of the condition of sheep and cattle, on the natural pasturage of the hills south and south-east of the town, was no less remarkable. The fern, through which we used to ride up to the knees of the horses, had been trodden down in many places, and grasses had sprung up in its room.

Greater confidence was also felt as to the quantity of available land easily accessible in all directions from the site of the town. The first explorers in all directions had been followed by many others, and every one encouraged his neighbours by the accounts which he brought home. Port Nicholson was no longer looked upon as hemmed in by mountainous country and possessed of no rural district but the Hutt, but as the door of a large, fertile, and very available district, both east and west, and as the central harbour of a coast-line reaching from the East Cape to Kawhia. It began to be felt, in fact, that in spite of difficulties and obstacles, the colony had fairly 'taken root', and only wanted being left without interference to prosper by means of its own natural capabilities.

During the year, 119 vessels had entered, and 112 vessels had left the port. The white population already amounted to 2,500 men, women, and children; and there were nearly 200 houses erected in a town of which the inhabitants had been in possession but four months.

The prosperous state of the working-classes did not fail to show itself by their very obstinate, but inoffensive, determination to have a share in the arrangement of the forthcoming festival. The democracy and aristocracy of the place could not manage to agree about the persons to be appointed as a Committee of Management. A man or a measure proposed by one of the employing class was sneered at or joked down by the carpenters and tailors; a proposition from a mechanic or labourer was objected to or cavilled at by a *rangatira;* and no union could be formed. In vain middle-men tried to reconcile the merry disputants; in vain the leaders of the two jesting parties yielded here or condescended there; no lasting peace could be concluded: and after many days' good-humoured dispute, it was determined to satisfy all parties by holding two festivals on different days, to be called the 'Popular' and the 'Select' fête.

The 'Select' people gave a subscription ball at Barrett's hotel on the night of the 22nd; the stormy weather having prevented any out-door amusements. On Saturday the 23rd, a rowing-match took place in the harbour under their auspices: but a proposed sailing-match was put off, in consequence of an accident having happened to one of the boats.

On Monday, the 'Populars' presented a much more extensive bill of fare. The weather having declared fine by ten o'clock, flags waved over many of the houses and the masts of the shipping, and a spirited race between four whale-boats round the vessels at anchor started the proceedings.

Then came a hurdle-race by four horses, over some level ground at the back of Te Aro *pa,* for a purse of fifteen guineas: and the name of 'Calmuck Tartar', ridden by Mr. Henry Petre, deserves to be recorded as the winner of the first race in New Zealand.

A sailing-match followed; ten riflemen next contended for a prize of five pounds and entrances; and the minor sports of jumping in sacks, climbing a greasy pole, and wheeling barrows blindfolded, finished the fun of the day in a right merry manner.

G

A 'Popular' ball, joined by most of the male aristocrats, was given in the evening at one of the large wooden stores erecting on Te Aro beach.

The natives had not been forgotten. An ample feast of rice and sugar, which is a dainty dish with them, had been provided; and a prize in money was held out as an inducement to a canoe-race.

On the 24th January, Mr. F. A. Carrington, who had been despatched by Colonel Wakefield in the *Brougham* to seek a site for the New Plymouth colony, returned, after a partial examination of Blind Bay and a visit to the Sugar-loaf Islands. He had decided on choosing the latter and the neighbouring country for his operations.

On the 8th of February, the *Brougham* sailed finally for Taranaki, with sixty persons for the new settlement, including Dicky Barrett and all his train. He had long pined for his ancient residence in that part of the country; and was delighted to carry thither with him, as a boon to his native friends, the *avantgarde* of a large European population and market for their produce. The vessel was a perfect Noah's ark, bearing the germ of a colony; her decks were completely heaped up with furniture, animals, plants, and children.

S. C. Brees. Engraving

THE TOWN OF PETRE (NOW WANGANUI)

S. C. Brees. *Engraving*

THE WELLINGTON-PETONE ROAD

CHAPTER X

A Canoe Voyage on the Wanganui River

O N THE evening of the 5th of March, I sailed again for Wanganui, in the *Sandfly*, a schooner of ten tons which had been built on the banks of the Hutt, and which I had chartered for three months for the Wanganui trade. I was accompanied by Mr. Wicksteed, who, as land-agent for the Church Society* wished to examine the district of Wanganui, the Company having granted that society a land-order entitling them to 4000 acres of land.

Of course the white population of the place was much increased since my last visit; they now mustered fifty or sixty. Nearly all the houses built by the natives had been bought or bargained for by the new-comers; and a large number of Maori found ample and well-paid employment in erecting fences, assisting to land goods, and other initiatory measures of the settlers. Two or three gentlemen with their families were among the number; and I was delighted to see this settlement, which I almost considered identified with myself and Kuru, in such active progress. Several people had travelled hither by land, in readiness for the first selection of lands advertised by the Surveyor-General, on the 18th of March. But the Assistant-Surveyor was not yet ready for such a proceeding, and several walked back as they had come. Others, liking the place, and finding living very cheap from the abundant supply of food by the natives, determined to remain here until the land should be distributed. Some engaged in the trade with the natives; others wasted their money and their time at two grog-shops set up by Macgregor and another on either side of the river.

* This society was formed in England to negotiate for the appointment of a separate bishop for New Zealand and for the endowment of churches and clergymen.

[*A war-party of the Ngatipehi, led by Te Heuheu of Taupo on an avenging expedition to Waitotara, had come down to the banks of the Wanganui river. The missionary Maoris were preparing to go up to Pukehika (Pipiriki) for a conference with the invaders, and Wakefield determined to go also.*]

So I rigged a new canoe for my trip. She was a very graceful, light-looking vessel, without topsides, but with tapering head and stern well peaked up at either end; about thirty feet long, broad in the beam, quick and handy to paddle, and adapted for six people. She was painted a bright red with *kokowai*, or baked ochre, and from a long staff on the stern I hung an English red ensign. I gave a passage to a trader named Yankee Smith, who was bound to Pukehika with a boxful of goods, and four of my 'boys' completed the muster-roll.

Recommending the settlers not to be alarmed till I should return with a report of what was to be expected, I started a day after the missionaries and the body of natives, who were sure from their numbers to travel slowly. The first night we encamped close to Te Kauarapawa, after some trouble in finding a house free from fleas. In villages which have been the longest deserted, these annoying insects always abound most; and the only way to prove the houses is to make one of the native boys put his leg inside the door. In many cases he draws it back perfectly covered. Another canoe, bound to the *puni*, or camp, of the *taua* joined us here.

A small drizzling rain prevented us from starting till about ten o'clock the next morning; but the rest of the day was calm, warm, and cloudless. I shall not attempt to dilate upon the scenery, which was of the same lovely kind as that which I have described during a former excursion here. The whole way up, it was the same. The river winds, or glides, or rushes through a mountainous but fertile country, of which the luxuriant monotony is relieved by cunningly-placed native fortifications, or isolated huts among rich gardens. Canoes, laden with the various kinds of native produce for the sea, met us occasionally on our way; the occupants generally allowing their bark to drift listlessly with the current, except where a rapid required skilful pilotage. They basked idly in the sun, or ate, or smoked, or played with the pet parrots which are generally perched on a pliant stick overhanging the water, swinging themselves up and down, flapping their wings, and screaming in shrill discord. The kind greeting was never omitted; I was now generally known among all the denizens of the river; and the '*nau mai*' (come hither), or '*tena koutou*' (hail to ye all), was often accompanied by the present of a cooked pigeon or parrot, or a basket of *kumara*, or a melon.

About noon we overtook the fleet of the *mihinare* natives, lying at the foot of a moss-covered cliff, which was crowned with the stockades of a moderate-sized *pa*. On the top of a wooded mountain about a mile inland of this, another stockade surrounded the last refuge of the inhabitants in case of assault. I ascended to the village, where a large assemblage were busily engaged in doing justice to a feast prepared for them. Te Anaua, Mawai, and several other chiefs of Putikiwharanui, were among the throng. A basket of food was placed before me on my arrival; and I ate some, and took the rest into the canoe with me, according to etiquette. We now proceeded in company, and the scene became most enlivening. There were about twenty canoes, varying in size from the stately war-canoe in gala dress of clean feathers and oiled carving with its crew of forty warriors, to the low shell in which five little naked urchins pushed along, screaming and yelling with delight whenever the *pakeha* admired their efforts, and laughing at the upsets which attended them at nearly every rapid. Good-humour prevailed among the throng; merry jokes and jeers passed from canoe to canoe; and the thoughts of all seemed to be brightened by the delicious weather, which continued sunny and fine, without any great heat.

Nothing more pleasant than such a journey. Reclining on a platform covered with soft mats just forward of my steersman, under the shade of a broad-brimmed Panama hat, now smoking, now sketching, now noting some name, or legend, or genealogy of a tribe as related by Konatu, who always held the steering-paddle; now handing my pipe to be filled by one of the other boys, and then seizing a paddle or a pole and raising a canoe-song to encourage my crew, as some old acquaintance came up alongside and challanged me for a race, I entered heartily into the spirit of our expedition. The Maori himself is all excitement when in action, and enjoys nothing better than to see a *pakeha* in the same high spirits as himself. On such occasions, the loudest laugh, the sharpest repartee, the wildest cheer, the most skilful use of the paddle, may be said to win their hearts; and accordingly, whenever my canoe got puzzled by a severe rapid, a dozen of those who had passed it would leave theirs above, and jump screaming into the water to lend a hand. The old chiefs even, however calm and dignified at a *korero*, or discussion, make it a point to relax during a journey.

The only chill cast on the innocent gaiety of the throng was the cold and untimely gravity of Mr. Mason, the head missionary, whose large canoe kept up with the rest. I was surprised to see him maintain a face of which not a feature moved, a posture in which not a muscle changed, for miles and miles together. And his dress and attitude made me feel quite uncomfortable, from my certainty that it was all forced and annoying to himself. The black tail-coat, trousers strapped down, waistcoat and stiff cravat, black beaver hat and rusty kid gloves, could not possibly be agreeable in this weather; for I was quite warm enough in my shirt-sleeves, white duck trousers, and open collar. Then he sat on one of the thwarts of the canoe, not above three inches in breadth, perfectly upright, looking straight ahead, with his two hands leaning on a cane well before him. He seemed to keep his crew at a distance. No one sat or stood within a yard of him, and he hardly ever spoke. A bare 'good morning' was the only answer to my greeting the first time we passed; and during the whole of this, to me, highly exciting journey, neither jokes, laughter, nor songs, neither the scenery nor the weather, not even the nervous passage of some of the dangerous rapids, which made me look about for a place to swim to in case of upsetting, had the least effect upon Mr. Mason's automaton stillness. I could not help thinking how much more permanent an effect might attend the teaching of a man of education and discernment, who would have joined to a certain degree, on such an occasion, in the playful humour of these grown-up children.

The passage up the rapids, some of them having a fall of six feet in a short space, excited my admiration as soon as I had got over the nervousness. It was a good instance of the excellent time which the natives keep in their songs and dances, although perfectly ignorant of and unable to appreciate music.

On reaching the foot of a rapid the crew abandon the paddles, stand up in the canoe, and handle long poles made of *manuka, toatoa,* or other hard wood, and charred at the lower end. They now push against the bed of the river in perfect unison, the poles plunging and lifting, while the canoe foams ahead, as though by clock-work. The helmsman also steers with a pole, balancing himself in the high peaked stern, and guiding the canoe by polling under or away from it. The silence is only interrupted by the grating of the poles against the sides of the canoe and the foaming of the water, or by an occasional brief word of direction from the man in the bow, '*ki uta!*' (towards shore) or '*ki waho!*' (outwards). The canoes follow each other in single file, with scarcely two feet between the stern of one and the bow of the next; and though a collision would in most cases render the capsizing of both inevitable, such is the skill of the natives, that an accident rarely occurs in going up the rapids. The natives of Wanganui have a known reputation for this peculiar exercise; and men of other tribes poling on this river are much laughed at for their awkwardness and the numerous duckings they get in consequence. A crew of experienced Wanganui natives poling up a strong rapid is a very pretty sight. As it is hard work, they generally strip, leaving only a shirt or mat round the waist, and the exercise throws them into the most graceful attitudes and develops their muscular energy. A byword, much used all over the islands, alludes to the known practice in poling, while it mimics the uncouth dialect of this tribe. After I became as it were identified with them, it was often shouted after me by the Kapiti or Ngatiawa natives—'*Ira! ira! e weke, e toko ki uta!*' (Hallo! hallo! old man, pole away inland!).

We stopped for the night at a settlement called Oawitu; where we overtook many of Turoa's followers, who own extensive cultivations hereabouts. Towards dark the weather got cloudy and threatening, and I was busy making a tent on the bank of two blankets, when a small canoe came dashing down the river; and I soon recognized Kuru's manly voice in the loud chorus which accompanied the sharp stroke of the paddles. He had come to meet me, in order to *kawe* or 'escort' me to the conference. One of his brothers and half a dozen of his young men accompanied him.

I found that he still kept a strict neutrality. He told me that he should take no part in the conference, but would recommend me to the friendship of his *hungawai*, or 'relations by marriage', among the Ngatipehi. He assured me that Te Heuheu was a very noble-minded chieftain, and advised me to ask him frankly about his intentions to the white people, as he was known for a strict adherence to his word.

Fortunately, the night proved fine; and the next morning we started at peep of day. About twelve miles brought us to a *pa* called Operiki, consisting of two fortified villages, one on each bank of the gully, from which a stream falls about thirty feet into the river. The land on either side of the gully runs level, at an elevation of sixty or seventy feet above the river, for a considerable distance in all directions, and the level is covered with luxuriant crops. On a shingly beach opposite the *pa* we all stopped to break- fast, and two messengers from the Taupo party came down to meet us. They said little about the intentions of their comrades, but seemed to look about them well, and form a good estimate of our numbers and arms, while manifesting great indifference to the peaceful exhortations of the missionaries. Both White and Brown began now to fear that our journey would end in a rupture of some sort; for Kuru sent a canoe back to my house, and asked me to send a note for all my guns, flints, bullet-moulds, lead, and powder. A canoe containing one or two white traders joined us here from the settlement.

We now proceeded to Hikurangi, a *pa* about six miles further on, where it seemed resolved that we should all wait until more news was heard from the *puni* or resting-place of the Ngatipehi. Accord- ingly, all the canoes were hauled up, and tents built, on an island facing the *pa*. The Patutokoto people, whom we had passed at their resting-place last night, also arrived and took up their quarters on the island. It was altogether an animated scene. In the midst of lofty mountains, whose sides are diversified by wood, planta- tions, tracts of fern land, and cliffs peeping out here and there, on a level point which slopes gradually down to a sudden bend in the river, is situated the *pa* with its double fence and fighting- stages towards the river, and a perpendicular descent towards that reach of it in which the island lies, formed by a rapid foaming on each side. Between the island and the *pa*, all the canoes were either hauled up or moored to poles. A fishing-weir is built in the midst of this rapid, and the little children were swimming and splashing in the most dangerous part of it. The natives belonging to the *pa* were sitting outside their fence on the top of the cliff, watching the people on the island, which was quite gay with the little flags and banners of different colours that most of the canoes had hoisted in imitation of mine. Two canoes went up to the *taua*, and returned again this afternoon. Kuru, who went in one of them, told me he had not landed, being afraid that the Ngatipehi might owe him a grudge. Two or three of the Ngatipehi people came down in one of the canoes to see their friends among the Patutokoto; and a *tangi*, or crying-match, and speeches from both parties, lasted till I was asleep.

Starting again at break of day, we ascended about six miles, when a cry was raised to keep the canoes close together; and in this order, with perhaps fifty canoes and three hundred people of all ages and both sexes, we doubled a point, and came in full view of the Ngatipehi encampment. From the edge of a bank, rising very steep for forty feet from the eastern shore, the ground was cleared of wood, and rose gradually in the form of an amphitheatre, backed by a forest. Five hundred warriors were disposed in rows about this clear space, according to their tribes and families, each with his musket or two-barrelled fowling-piece. After a few shots had been fired from our flotilla, by way of greeting, I saw a chief running up and down haranguing the others; and immediately they answered by a regular discharge of musketry, backwards and forwards, along each row, which lasted for nearly five minutes. I was much surprised to find them so well armed; each man had a musket, and some two, and slaves to carry them. Our party all encamped in silence. Some of the Ngatiraukawa canoes pushed on to Pukehika, which is but a few miles further up. In the course of an hour, during which I was much amused by the perseverance of a Taupo dog, who earned presents of tobacco for his master by swimming across the river and back, the chiefs of the Patutokoto tribes, attended by all their people, pushed across to see their relations. They had dressed themselves out in what they considered 'full fig'. Many of the men were dressed *à l' Européenne*, with the exception of shoes and stockings; several of the women wore caps or bonnets, adorned with gaudy ribbons and albatross feathers; and those that had neither gown nor other European luxury to show, of which there were but few, donned their cleanest blankets or mats. The missionaries and I also went over. A *tangi* by all hands lasted nearly an hour, during which I walked about the encampment, and could not help admiring the well-formed limbs and clean skins of these natives, compared to most of those whom I had before seen. Quite free from the cutaneous disease which prevails to so great an extent among the inhabitants of Cook Strait, they were moreover the strongest and best-built natives that I had yet met with. I was told that this was owing to their constant bathing in the *puia*, or 'hot springs', near their settlements; from which they have earned the sobriquet of the Waikoropupu, or 'boiling water' tribes.

To the *tangi* succeeded speeches, many of them energetic and well-worded, by both parties, in purport as follows.

An orator spoke from either party alternately, and every speech began with nearly these words—'Come hither, come hither, my relations; come hither, my fathers, my brothers, my sisters, and my children; welcome!' The speakers on the Taupo side seemed to wish to sound the feeling of the others towards them; and urged their friends to send them canoes to descend the river, and also to join them in obtaining a revenge which both must desire over their mutual enemies at Waitotara. The answers of the Patutokoto were to urge them to return quietly, for various reasons: some said that they had no canoes to spare; that the Ngatipehi had lost all their young men, and that old men and women and children would be all slaughtered at Waitotara; others, again, said that they had turned *mihinare*, and could not join them, and urged the anger of *Ihu Karaiti** as a reason why they should give up the idea of fighting, and that the white *mihinare* said the *pukapuka* or book, would be strong against the heathen. But the tone of irony in which some of these reasons were stated, particularly by Turoa, who had never ceased to be a warm and zealous ally of the Ngatipehi, was highly amusing, and showed plainly that none of the Patutokoto had any idea of stating their real feelings in open assem-

* Maori for 'Jesus Christ'.

bly. Old Turoa, who alone of all his tribe appeared in a ragged mat, which, together with every part of his body, was well encrusted with *kokowai*, or red ochre, and a night-cap which partook of the same rusty hue, began with the usual plaintive greeting, comprehending, however, his grandchildren also in the list. 'You ask for canoes,' said he; 'how can I give them to you? You see I have but one, full of women, and boys, and children. How can you think that I have come to join you? Besides,' he added, looking with a most comic grin at Messrs. Mason and Matthews, 'I am just becoming a missionary; I have the book in one hand, and a cap on my head, which I never wore before; and the anger of *Ihu Karaiti* will come upon me if I go to fight.' He ended by urging them to return in peace. Some of the Taupo chiefs expressed their determination to go on, whether assisted or not; and after a Wanganui man had asked them to go across the country, in order to spare the Wanganui plantations, old Te Heuheu* concluded the conference.

Above six feet in stature, but so Herculean in limb as to disguise his height, he rose proudly from a spot of elevated ground where he had been sitting among a knot of his wives and children, shook his mats from his right arm, and began his speech with slow and distinct articulation. The most perfect silence prevailed among the hundreds assembled. Children who had been playing on the edge of the crowd; young men and women who had been renewing old acquaintances and exchanging the latest gossip; warriors who had been examining each other's arms *en connoisseur* while the great number of chiefs spoke; all were now hushed and still. Stragglers might be seen pressing close to the scene of conference; whispers might be heard that 'the *kaumatua*, (patriarch) was going to speak'; and then the whole audience held its breath. This was evidently the great speech—the lion of the day.

Like the others, he began by hailing his relations; and then proceeded with an oration full of majesty, terseness, and emphasis. His words must have been heard across the river by the men of Putikiwharanui, Kuru, and others who had not crossed over. 'You have all been speaking crooked,' said he, 'and hiding your words in lies. Listen to me! I am going to speak straight. I go to Wai-

* This is Te Heuheu II (Mananui) of Ngati Tuwharetoa.

totara, to avenge the death of my people, and to bring their bones home. I have not come to beg canoes, or food, or assistance. If you lend me no canoes, I can walk along the banks with my children; and we will cross at a ford when a cliff is in our path: we shall find our way to the sea. I can help myself to food; my children see the plantations, and they gather with a gun in one hand and a basket in the other. I want no help but that of my own *mere pounamu*, which my arm knows how to shake.' And he lifted it high over his head and brandished it haughtily before them.

'As to the missionary words,' he continued, 'who cares for them? What is the anger of *Ihu Karaiti* to us? Were they missionaries who shook hands and gave the *hongi* (salute) to my people, and then put them to death? Why, I am a missionary at that rate; but my creed is my *mere*. Will that not be stronger than your *pukapuka tapu*?'* He then blamed the missionaries and all white people for being the cause of much disagreement among the Maori, and severely censured those chiefs who had signed away their power to King George. 'You are all slaves now,' he said, 'and your dignity and power is gone. But mine is not—just as there is one man in Europe, King George, so do I stand alone in New Zealand, the chief over all others, the only free one left—look at me, for I do not hide while I say so; I am Te Heuheu, and rule over you all, just as my ancestor Tongariro, the mountain of snow, stands above all this land!'

He wound up by a spirited address to the Patutokoto, which brought tears to many an eye; and I could see the young warriors clutching their weapons tightly while every muscle quivered with excitement, when he shouted, in the wild yell to which he had gradually increased the tone of his voice, 'Where is Tauteka? Where are all your parents and brothers? Their bones are at Waitotara. Will you not join us in gaining possession of the bones of our ancestors? Will you not release your sisters from being slaves? A fight for your fathers' bones! Be brave! be brave! be brave! There has been enough of talk.' And he sat down, while the assembly dispersed.

In the course of the afternoon I brought some tobacco over as a present to the old chief, and gave him some more to distribute among his people, who had scarcely any. I then asked him whether

* Sacred book

he intended any harm to the *pakeha;* promising their friendship should he behave well, but assuring him that we were fully prepared and determined to resist any attack on our houses and goods on the sea-side. He answered, that he had seen white people in his part of the country too; and that he knew what great advantages he should lose by quarrelling with them: for instance, he said, he should not get tobacco, as he had just now, blankets, or powder, or any of those things which the Maori got by letting the white man live quietly among them. He assured me that no harm was intended to the white man, and that all his party were bound on no other purpose than revenge for their *tupapaku,* or dead; I felt now convinced that there was nothing to fear; although the missionaries persisted in assuring me that there was no trusting these natives, and that they knew no such feeling as gratitude, and had the worst reputation of any natives in the islands.

We remained two or three days in our encampment opposite to theirs, frequent visits being paid on both sides. During this time the old chief showed the most violent feeling of enmity towards the doctrine of the missionaries. Whenever he heard their followers sing one of their discordant hymns on our side, he would come out of his hut and muster one or two hundred to drown the sound by a native song. When they visited his camp, he pursued the same plan to drown their exhortations, though he treated them in other respects with dignified politeness.

I visited the *pa* at Pukehika, about six miles above the encampment. It is a very extensive *pa,* or rather a collection of seven or eight detached ones, on a hill at a bend of the river to the westward. It is about seventy miles from the sea, and well chosen as a mustering-place for the Wanganui tribes living within that distance from the coast, in case of attack from Waikato, Taupo, or the Strait. I found nearly all the missionary population gathered here, apparently to consult over Te Heuheu's avowed determination. Messrs Mason and Matthews had pitched their tent in the middle of the court-yard in the principal village. I returned to my encampment after a short look round. Here I found that the war-party had been supplied by their relations with an ample fleet of canoes, and that they would proceed the next day, by easy stages, towards the settlement. Kuru and I preceded them in my canoe.

On arriving at the settlement, I reported my opinion that no danger was to be feared, and advised the colonists to receive the travellers kindly and hospitably. One or two were nevertheless persuaded by the missionaries when they came, to carry their valuable goods over to the *pa* at Putikiwharanui, and leave them in charge of the chiefs; the *pa* having been newly fortified for fear of an assault.

The *taua*, to the number of five hundred, arrived some days afterwards, and built their huts close to the houses of the settlers. But during the period of their stay, not a single instance occurred, to our knowledge, of misconduct on their part. On the contrary, their presence had the effect of overawing many troublesome fellows among the missionary natives. The most perfect discipline reigned in the camp, and the chief evidently prided himself on the strict fulfilment of his promise.

One night, when he felt suspicious of a small body of Rotorua allies in his train, who were really of doubtful reputation, and who were said to have plotted a night-attack on our houses, he placed guards of his own followers at every house along the beach. On that night, twelve stout warriors lay round the fire in the midst of my house, with their arms in their hands, ready for any emergency. We were also on the alert; and I had arranged signals by bells and gongs so that we could all assemble at short notice in one spot. These precautions doubtless awed the conspirators, and no alarm was given. After remaining among us four days, during which they made themselves very useful in assisting the settlers for small payment, they had a grand war-dance and some more speeches, and then started off along the beach, joined by many Wanganui natives, and among others by Kuru, who had ended by deciding finally for his Taupo allies.

§

A few days after the departure of Te Heuheu, I went on board the *Sandfly*, which had made a trip in my absence, and arrived at Wellington on the 19th of April.

Great and good was the news which had arrived from England while I was away. New Zealand had been proclaimed as an independent colony, and Captain Hobson as Governor.

Two other ships had arrived from England. One, bearing the Agent of the Plymouth Company and the first batch of settlers for New Plymouth, had anchored in Cloudy Bay. This body of West of England settlers had started under the auspices of a very distinguished festival at Plymouth, at which the first announcement had been made of the happy termination of the negotiations with the Government. Bearers of good news, they had met bright hopes on their arrival; for each new account from the surveying-party and travellers spoke more highly of the great capabilities of the Taranaki district, and confirmed the reputation which had long earned for it among the natives the title of the 'Garden of the Land'.

Another vessel had brought nearly two hundred and fifty more immigrants and passengers to Wellington. Among the passengers was Mr. Edmund Halswell, who had been appointed by the Company Commissioner for the management of the Native Reserves.

I must add, that in the six weeks during which I had been absent, a road long in progress round the west side of the harbour had been completed by the Company's labourers; and Sam Phelps had been the first to drive his bullock-dray over it to Petone. A bridle-road from Kaiwharawhara to Porirua was also in progress, as well as one from the town into an elevated valley of some extent, called Karori, situated a mile to the south-west. A wooden building of some pretensions in point of architecture had been erected as a Public Exchange at Te Aro, and a wharf had been run out into the harbour near the same spot by Captain Rhodes. New stores, houses, and fences, had sprung up in every direction; and the clinking of the hammer and sudden apparition of new habitations still went on, day after day, with unceasing activity.

On the 21st April, a very severe gale from the north-west was experienced. No damage occurred to the vessels in our excellent harbour; but we were sorry to hear that the *Jewess* schooner, on her way to Wanganui, full of settlers and goods, had been driven away from her anchorage at Kapiti, and totally wrecked on the beach near Paripari.

Some chance arrivals from Auckland and the Bay of Islands about this time furnished a doleful account of the stagnation and despondency produced there by the various experiments in founding and governing cities. The people of Auckland, consisting of a few mere land-sharks or hangers-on, attracted from Sydney and the Bay of Islands by the expenditure of the Governor and his suite, and the approaching land-sale, vented their ill-temper at the disappointment of their hopes, by the expression of undisguised hostility and vulgar jealousy towards the thriving settlers of Wellington. The news concluded, as usual, with a report that Captain Hobson was about to visit us.

This last piece of intelligence, however, was already becoming too worn-out to attract much attention. It was a byword and a joke at all the hotels, at the Club, the Exchange, and other places of assemblage where the gossip of the day was discussed. To the question, 'what news from the north?' the invariable answer was 'Hobson's coming!' and it became the custom to say of a waiter, a ship, or anything else proverbially dilatory, but which was 'coming', instead of 'so's Christmas', 'so's Hobson!' This was in fact a better figure of speech, for Captain Hobson, unlike Christmas, had been 'coming' for more than a year.

I spent a month at Wellington very pleasantly. Horses were now plentiful, and the new roads afforded delicious rides; a curious contrast being presented by the neat macadamized causeway, and the groups of workmen and wheelbarrows, among the primæval forest and wild scenery which they penetrated. At the Hutt, the cultivations and clearings looked cheerful and promising. From sixty to a hundred families were now permanently settled in that district; neat cottages and luxuriant gardens appeared along the banks; the rich crop had induced many a doubting settler to clear some land this year; and the axe-men had begun to be a large and important class. Groups of smiling children bobbed and pulled their fore-locks to 'gentlemen from town' as they rode up the river-bank; and new fields were to be noticed at every successive visit.

Cattle-driving, too, on the pasture hills, afforded exercise and excitement. Following the system pursued in New South Wales, owners of cattle brand their herd and let them run loose over the hills, and then drive them at a gallop into the stock-yard when they are wanted. The cattle get exceedingly wild and fast; so that it requires bold and hard riding in some instances to head them. The gentlemen and the stock-keepers who had come from that country soon taught us the manner of proceeding; and idlers were often enlisted as volunteers when a grand muster was to be effected, or some particularly wild heifer to be found and driven in. The stock-whip, a very necessary instrument for this work, requires some description for English readers. A stout wooden handle a foot in length is attached to a heavy thong of plaited hide, about fifteen feet long from the handle to the end of the lash. This whip is whirled two or three times round the head, and cracked with a report as loud as that of a pistol in the face of a stubborn animal. The wildest cattle when charging you will turn from it, if it be used with skill; but an inexperienced hand is very apt to slice his own face or injure his horse severely, without at all alarming the cattle.

About the middle of May, Mr. William Gordon Bell, a stout Scotch farmer, showed a noble example of enterprise by driving the first herd of cattle to Wanganui. Mr. Bell had enjoyed farming experience in several parts of the world. While connected with an estate in the West Indies, he had married a woman of colour, by whom he had a fine hardy family of two sons and two daughters. After residing some time in various parts of the Australian colonies, he had crossed over to this country, with Mr. James Watt, who had been the first to attempt agriculture at Port Nicholson. Long before the town was distributed, Mr. Bell had begun to farm a piece of land between the harbour and the sea for Mr. Watt;* and had been the first to use the plough in Cook Strait. The land in question was of a poor clayey nature, and in a spot swept by both the prevailing winds; so that the crop of wheat, though good in quality, was scanty. The industry of Bell and his family, while working for an employer, had been most remarkable. He owned two or three sections in the second series, including the seventh choice; and having completed his engagement with Mr. Watt, he determined to start for Wanganui with his family, a cow, and six fine oxen which he had bought. The bridle-road to Porirua was only partly finished; and the crossing of the various rivers seemed to offer some difficulty; but the old man had walked over the whole route to satisfy himself, and on his return declared his determination to get the cattle there.

* i.e., Miramar peninsula

His departure was a fine sight. The cow and the six bullocks yoked in a team, with packs on their backs, were attended by old Bell and his two sons. He was known by every one to possess an unlimited stock of perseverance, firmness, and energy. In coming from Watt's farm to the beginning of the Porirua road, he had to pass through the whole town; and all the spectators flocked to shake his iron fist, and wish him every sucess. He answered in broad Scotch dialect, that 'they *should* go—he would take care to succeed'. And many an eye watched them file up the steep path from Kaiwharawhara, and disappear among the woods on the top. I had furnished him with letters to various chiefs along the road with whom I was acquainted, requiring their help at the rivers and their friendly assistance along the road. His ploughs, drays, bags of seed, and other implements and articles of bulk, were put on board the *Sandfly* and another schooner, in which the women of his family also proceeded.

[*Mr. Bell arrived safely at Wanganui with his cattle. The Taupo war-party ravaged Waitotara, and came down the coast to threaten the tribes at Otaki. Wakefield writes of Mr. Hadfield's peacemaking efforts.*]

Turnbull Library

C. Heaphy. Water-colour

NELSON, FEBRUARY 1842

S. C. Brees, Engraving

BARRETT'S HOTEL, WELLINGTON

CHAPTER XI

Pigs: Lawlessness at Wanganui

TOWARDS THE end of May, I sent the *Sandfly* on to Kapiti, and started to join her by land; wishing to see the progress of the road, and to visit the wreck of the *Jewess*. I was accompanied by Lieutenant Thomas, who had engaged in the survey department of the Company's service. The bridle-road had been completed to the distance of about seven miles from Port Nicholson. We slept at Paremata; and the next day I travelled on to the wreck, Mr. Thomas staying to collect some of his things still remaining at the whaling station.

The *Jewess* had been driven ashore on the sand, only about half-a-mile north of the rocky coast. I here found the captain, who had not yet deserted her. The vessel was still whole, and we slept in the bunks of the cabin that night, though the high tide, causing rather a smart surf after we had got to sleep, rocked her about, and washed into the cabin through the holes in her bottom. Between the vessel and near Waikanae I met a large body of Port Nicholson natives, who had been to a conference at Waikanae on the subject of a threatened attack of the Taupo war-party.

It appeared that after ravaging Waitotara, from which all the inhabitants had again fled, except a few too old and infirm who were taken, killed, and eaten, the *taua* of the Ngatipehi had come down to Otaki; and that a union of their force with that of the Ngatiraukawa had been proposed, in order to revenge the defeat at Waikanae in October 1839. The Port Nicholson natives, on the receipt of this news, had mustered 200 or 300 men under Wharepouri, Te Puni and Taringakuri, and hastened to join their relations. Mr Hadfield had succeeded in frustrating all these warlike preparations. This gentleman had, after very laborious efforts, and in one instance at the peril of his life, managed to acquire a very extensive and honourable influence over the hitherto fierce chiefs of the Ngatiraukawa. Whatanui and part of his family had become *mihinare*, as well as several other chiefs of rank; and Mr. Hadfield had wisely managed to introduce the new doctrine without destroying the native aristocracy. He thus dissuaded Whatanui, and through him the great part of the tribe, from fighting. Heuheu, I heard, had been furious at this successful interference with his designs; but had ended by confessing himself fairly beaten, when Mr. Hadfield calmly and courageously presented himself before him in the midst of his anger, overthrew his reasoning, and reproached the old chief in the conclave of his people with a want of the dignity and deliberation suitable to his place of *kaumatua* or 'patriarch'.

I had not yet been introduced to Mr. Hadfield's acquaintance; but I already began to feel sorry for the prejudices which I had entertained against him on first hearing that he had come with Mr. Williams. All the natives, whether converts or not, spoke in the highest terms of his conduct in every particular. I knew, intimately, many of his more immediate followers at Waikanae, some of them of high rank among the tribe; and could not help imbibing from them some of that respectful admiration for his character which they were proud of acknowledging. Even the corrupt and profane beachcombers and whalers of Kapiti would go out of their way to say a good word or do a service for Mr. Hadfield. 'He is a missionary,' they would say, with an oath; 'but he's a gentleman every inch of him; and when he can do a poor fellow a good turn with the Maoris, why he will!'

The whaling was at this time going on with great spirit; and I sailed away from Kapiti one morning in the midst of an animated chase, the whale and the boats having crossed my bows more than once.

I now remained at Wanganui for some time; and sent the *Sandfly* backwards and forwards under the charge of a steady sailor whom I had engaged.

My house was full of goods of various kinds belonging to the settlers, who had not yet got their houses ready to receive them;

and I soon found myself as it were forced into keeping what would be called a 'store' in America, or a 'shop' in England. In trading with the natives, I was obliged to procure all sorts of things from Wellington; and I had numerous applications from people who wanted small quantities, and could not get them anywhere else. The same with tea, sugar, flour, and other articles of food, which I took advantage of the trips of the schooner to bring up in bags, casks, or cases; so that I was very soon a shopkeeper in spite of myself. However, I had by this time learned to be anything that might be required; and the 'shop' was for some time as amusing an employment as anything else. I have no doubt my books, kept in my own way, would have afforded much matter of laughter to any one brought up as a tradesman. I seldom received money payments. Pigs from one, labour from another, wine from a third; stationery or wooden planks, spades, cart-wheels, or window-frames from some other customer: such was the kind of barter which prevailed. I think that the only customer from whom I ever received cash for a long while was Mr. Mason, the missionary, who paid me in hard silver for two kegs of tobacco.

I had a large herd of swine running in the swamps and fern-ridges at the back of the settlement. For a long while I had turned out all those which I bought young or in bad condition from the natives, after branding them over the tail. They got very fat as they grew, the feed being excellent about here. The succulent root of the *raupo*, or bulrush, is a very favourite food of the hog, and the fern was also of good quality.

When I wanted to catch a number to send to Wellington, or to kill and salt down, a grand hunt took place. I had bought one or two good dogs, and bred them to the sport. They soon learn to beat the ground, and follow the scent of a pig; and take great delight in the chase. If large and strong, and found in open ground, a hog will often give a run of some miles, and you follow the dogs on foot through high fern, reeds, wood, scrub, and swamp, till their barking and the snorting of 'porker' give notice that he is at bay. The pig-dogs are of rather a mongrel breed, partaking largely of the bull-dog, but mixed with the cross of mastiff and greyhound, which forms the New South Wales kangaroo-dog. The great nurseries for good dogs have been the whaling stations, where they bred them for fighting. It soon became a fashion for travelling settlers like myself to have a pack of pig-dogs, known for their strength, skill, and courage, whether in fighting or hunting. At a rude settlement such as Wanganui, they served also to protect the house from the depredations of the wandering sawyers, and other loose adventurers, who were getting more daring in their undertakings, and from the annoyance of a few among the natives who began to pilfer, or to breed quarrels by rude and insulting behaviour, and a good watch-dog or two were no despicable guardians of a house, and were very desirable companions out-of-doors at night.

But to return to the hunt. The hog once at bay, bold and unskilled dogs rush straight in for his nose, and are often severely wounded by his long tusks or his hoofs. An experienced dog, without allowing him to escape, watches his opportunity to seize the jowl or the root of the ear. A dog that persists in seizing the legs, or any other part, is generally shot by his owner, as the practice spoils the hams, and is considered contrary to rule. When the dogs are fast, no struggle of the hog, no dragging of the dogs through bushes or swamp, succeeds in shaking them off; and the native lads run up and fasten thongs of the flax-leaf round the hind-legs. If the animal is very wild, they also bind the fore-legs and even the muzzle, as the weight of the dogs, and fatigue, prevent much resistance. The pig is rarely killed in the field, as it is considered more sportsmanlike to bring him in and show him off alive; so that the hunting-knife or rifle, although sometimes carried in case of necessity, is rarely made use of.

This was comparatively tame work to the wild and fatiguing chases, which I have at times enjoyed with Kuru and a troop of the Maori lads, in districts near the river where the hogs had been undisturbed for many years, and were claimed by any one who caught them. Especially in the district between the Wanganui and Wangaehu rivers, we used to spend whole days in this pursuit. Kuru was a keen sportsman, and well skilled in pig-hunting. He took great pride in my excellent dogs; and also in beating me, which he generally did from his superior activity and knowledge of the country. I have often been completely thrown behind, and lost my way among some of the wooded hollows into which we have descended from the open table-lands; and when I at length found my way to the river, and got home an hour or two after dark, dead-beat and faint with hunger, having been afoot since my breakfast at sunrise, I would find Kuru smoking his pipe after a comfortable meal, swelling with triumph at having returned some hours before, with two or three fine *poaka*.

I found that the settlers had to complain more and more of the annoying conduct of a great number of the natives. The surveyors were more often stopped in their work. This continued at still more frequent intervals after Messrs. Thomas and Carrington had returned to complete the survey.

[*During a ride to the* pa *on the* Whenuakura *river,* Wakefield *was caused considerable amusement by the panic of the Maoris at their first sight of a horse.*]

As I had got a mile or two in advance of the pedestrians, and rode fast along the last part of the beach, I was not seen by the inhabitants of the *pa*, until close to the river. They then ran down on to the beach. By this time I had plunged into the river, which here flows over soft and shifting sands. The horse's body was nearly hidden; and though many of my old friends here had recognized me, and shouted '*Tiraweke! Haere mai!*' they evidently thought that a native was carrying me on his shoulders. There were now nearly a hundred natives collected, many of whom had never seen a horse before, crowding over each other to give me the first greeting.

With two or three vigorous plunges the horse suddenly emerged from the water, and bore me into the middle of them. Such a complete panic can hardly be imagined. They fled yelling in all directions without looking behind them; and as fast as I galloped past those who were running across the sandy flat and up the steep path leading to the *pa* of Te Hoe, they fairly lay down on their faces, and gave themselves up for lost. Half-way up the hill I dismounted, and they plucked up courage to come and look at the *kuri nui*, or 'large dog'. The most amusing questions were put to me as to its habits and disposition. 'Can he talk?' said one; 'Does he like boiled potatoes?' said another; and a third, 'Mustn't he have a blanket to lie down upon at night?' This unbounded respect and admiration lasted all the time that I remained. The horse was taken into the central courtyard of the *pa;* a dozen hands were always offering him Indian corn, and grass, and sow-thistles, when they had learned what he really did eat; and a wooden bowl full of water was kept constantly replenished close to him. And little knots of curious observers sat round the circle of his tether-rope, remarking, and conjecturing, and disputing, about the meaning and intention of every whisk of his tail or shake of his ears.

The lawless state of the place [Wanganui] became daily more annoying. I had to lash my cook, who had travelled hither with the Taupo party, and who delighted in the *sobriquet* of 'Coffee', to the big post in the middle of the house, with my dog-chains, for theft; intending to send him to Wellington in a schooner, which was to sail the next morning. But he proved to me that I did not understand thief-taking, or at any rate thief-keeping; for he slipped his irons in the night, and started to the northward.

I had another rather serious instance of the disadvantages of being without law. Three or four loose characters, who had arrived from England in the *London,* kept the licensed grog-shop which was near my house, and encouraged all kinds of ruffians, as a kind of feudal retinue, by liberal distributions of spirits. It was frequently hinted to me that they salted down a great many more pigs than they ever bought from the natives, or turned out with their brand. My dog had got so fond of the sport, that he would follow any one who held up a rope to him as a sign that they were going to catch a pig; and many of the large hogs were not to be caught by inferior dogs. I detected my neighbours of the grog-shop hunting and killing my pigs as coolly as if they had been their own; and one morning one of the members of the worthy firm came and enticed my dog for the purpose of doing it with more *gusto.* As soon as I found this out, I went down to the grog-shop, where the hunting-party were consoling themselves with copious draughts of gin for their sorrow at having been deprived of two large pigs bearing my brand by my agent, who had caught them in the act. I entered into the joke, and cheerfully begged that the innocent amusement of robbing me might now cease, as the pleasant excitement of doing it without my knowledge could no longer be said to exist. One of the firm grandiloquently offered me satisfaction with 'swords, pistols, or any other weapon', for what he had done. When I quietly declined this kind offer of satisfaction for stealing my property, and told the hero that he might think himself lucky if I did not put him into gaol for felony, he laughed, and said, 'There was no law in New Zealand; there was no fear of his getting put into gaol!' I then gave him fair warning that I would try my best; but by the time I got to Port Nicholson, he had decamped on board an American whaler lying at Kapiti.

CHAPTER XII

Wellington and Hobson

ABOUT THE beginning of August, I received intelligence that the *Sandfly* had struck on a rock in making the anchorage at Kapiti on a dark night, and had sunk with all her cargo. As there was some chance of getting her up again, I proceeded by land to Waikanae, with two native lads to carry my blankets and provisions.

After finding all efforts to raise the vessel vain, I proceeded to Wellington, where progress had been made in the signs of civilization. A large and well-furnished chemist's shop, with the due allowance of red bottles and blue bottles, and glass jars full of tooth-brushes and sponges, and gay labels of quack pills and ointments, showed a broad front to the beach near Barrett's hotel. As this shop, which gloried in the sonorous title of 'Medical Hall', was close to the usual place of disembarkation for passengers, it became a much-frequented morning lounge; especially as Dr. Dorset and another of our oldest medical friends were partners in the establishment. Many other equally gay shops began to ornament the bustling beach. Two clever rope-makers had begun the pursuit of their trade on a large scale, using the *phormium tenax* as prepared by the natives; and they received ample support from all classes there being a considerable demand for small rope for the running rigging of ships, fishing-nets, and whale-lines for the stations in the Strait.

Rangihaeata and his followers had destroyed some of the bridges on the Porirua bridle-road, and in some places trees were purposely felled across the narrow path with a view to prevent the easy passage of travellers.

In the town itself, the want of authority vested in the sole legal officer was producing great mischief. Numerous persons were squatting on the lands reserved for public purposes, and destroying the ornamental timber upon them. They were not ejected, as the Police Magistrate probably thought that such a course 'might be inexpedient, even if strictly legal'.

The indignation at Captain Hobson's neglect of the settlement was fast increasing in violence among the settlers. Daily examples of its evil effects were presented to each member of the community. For instance, the whole provision for justice had been, for eighteen months from the arrival of the Lieutenant-Governor, a single police court, with undefined authority and scanty jurisdiction. Thus, in the wretched hut which served for a jail—where prisoners were heavily ironed, in order to prevent them from walking through the straw walls—two men, committed for trial, and who, until fully convicted, were to be considered as innocent, had been incarcerated upwards of eleven months. And in a community in which much property was daily changing hands, and very numerous commercial transactions took place, debts remained unpaid, and contracts unfulfilled; wills were unproved and unexecuted; and trespassing, in its various forms, occurred daily and with impunity.

The natives had begun to ridicule the idea that 'Wide-awake's' white men were cared for by the Governor or the Queen.

Towards the end of July (1841) we had a batch of news from 'Hobson's Choice', as Auckland was very generally called. This came by a cattle-ship from Sydney, as our dates from that place were two months later than those from our own metropolis.

From Adelaide, Port Philip, and Hobart Town we had also two months' later news than from the seat of Government, which Captain Hobson had chosen on account of 'its centrical position'.

The three islands had been proclaimed, in accordance with instructions from the Colonial Office, as New Ulster, New Munster, and New Leinster. Except in official papers, these names have never been used, from their great similarity and inconvenience. I doubt whether, even at this day, the great majority of European inhabitants know which is which without looking at a map.

The proclamation had been accompanied by another, recommending the Europeans to be 'kind to the natives'. This advice came with peculiar grace and *naïveté* from the Auckland Government, which had not yet pretended to produce a farthing of revenue from the valuable reserves of the natives at Wellington. It had not made the slightest provision for their education or comfort. It had not cared whether they were hungry or fed, naked or clothed, clean or dirty. They were still living in filthy villages, subject to disease from the accumulation of dirt, and their residence in ill-ventilated and closely crowded dunghills; still left at the mercy of wars, cannibalism, infanticide, and frequent scarcity of food from unskilful cultivation; still clothed badly and inadequately; still ignorant of all that it was absolutely necessary at this time for them to know. The neglected settlers at Port Nicholson had already done far more than the Government towards the moral and physical improvement of the equally neglected natives.

There was at this time scarcely a settler in Port Nicholson of any class who had not a whole family of natives forming a part of his own. Te Puni would frequently walk the six miles from Petone, in order to call on Colonel Wakefield, and his other friends in the town. And this not on a begging visit, for he had now too much property of all kinds to beg of anybody, but because he began to enjoy the pleasure of civilized intercourse, and took pride in the friendship and example of his *rangatira pakeha*. Thus he would stay with my uncle for an hour, chatting about the improvements which he was carrying on at Petone, in imitation of those in the town, watching with admiration the progress of the garden, or the preparation of the lawn for seed, talking over the news from Auckland, learning something of our laws and institutions which was not beyond his understanding, and becoming more fit, at each visit, for being raised to the social station of his friends. He seemed to take especial pleasure in having the opportunity to teach his sons and younger relations a lesson in good behaviour by these visits to well-behaved people. Te Puni himself was a gentleman in every sense of the word, and would have been recognized as such in any society. I never saw him do an action, make use of a gesture, or betray a feeling, inconsistent with the most refined good manners. It needed no recommendation from Auckland to make one kind to him and his. There was an influence in his very look and speech, which must have disarmed the most ungenerous despiser of savages.

Captain Daniell and Mr. George Duppa returned just at this time from an expedition in the *Balley*, having been requested by Colonel Wakefield to observe and report upon the country and harbours in and near Banks's Peninsula, with a view to the selection of a site for the expected colony of 'Nelson'. They had coasted from Kaikoura, or the Lookers-on, to the north side of the peninsula, and Mr. Duppa had ascended the banks of one of the rivers which flow into Pegasus Bay, for eight miles from its mouth. They described the isthmus, which connects the peninsula with the main, to be not a sandy neck, as hitherto represented in the charts, but a broad extension of the level, low, and fertile country which reaches from the broken ground of the peninsula to the foot of the snowy range of Southern Alps, and extends far to the north and south, watered by several small rivers. They united in describing this tract of country as affording rich pasturage and excellent soil, and sprinkled with numerous groves of pine timber. They also spoke in the highest terms of the harbour of Port Cooper, and Port Levy, now called Port Ashley.*

On the 19th of August, a little vessel came round the point about four miles from the town.

'Emigrant ship!' cried one of the loiterers on the beach.

'Whaler!' shouted another.

'No! it's a large schooner or a brig,' said some knowing hand, looking with a telescope from the coffee-room of Barrett's hotel.

'Oh! a cattle-vessel from Sydney perhaps—or a Yankee full of *notions*,' suggested some one in the gazing crowd which began to collect.

'Too small,' said the captains and other nautical oracles; 'no hay on the quarter for cattle—not smart enough for a Yankee!'

'Perhaps only pigs and potatoes from Hawke's Bay or Wanganui, after all,' said a passer-by, who had been attracted by the numerous levelled telescopes and the crowd of conjecturing gossips—and he walked on.

'Now, she's in irons!' cried some sailor, as the vessel missed stays and drifted astern near the mouth of Evans Bay; 'What a lubberly craft!'

* The name 'Port Ashley' was rarely used. A subsequent attempt, in 1850, to name the harbour 'Port Albert' was also unsuccessful. The only change is from Levi to Levy.

At length the unknown vessel approached the inner harbour, and the red ensign was made out at the peak, and the union-jack at the mainmast-head. It became evident that she *must* be the Government brig! She anchored off the hotel; union-jacks were hoisted at Colonel .Wakefield's house, and at the straw hut in the Pipitea *pa* which served as a police-office and government-house. Boats put off from all parts of the bay, including the police boat with the whole resident staff, namely, the Police Magistrate, the Health Officer, and the Postmaster; and a return boat soon brought word that it was positively the Governor.

The natives who heard of it laughed at the report. They said the ship was not half so big as the ship in which 'Wide-awake's' *tutua* (common) white people came, and it could not be the *Kawana* (Governor). They pointed to the diminutive size and slovenly appearance of the craft; which certainly did look small among the two large emigrant barques, an American whaler, and two or three fine brigs and schooners, lying near her, and only deserved to be ranked as leader of the mosquito fleet of coasters which lay near the shore. They were sure we were telling them *tito,* 'lies'; or *hangareka,* 'making fun of them'. 'We had said so often that the Governor was coming; they would wait till they saw the Great Chief themselves.'

The settlers at each other's homes, at the hotels, or at the workshops, according to their respective classes, quietly commented on the arrival of Captain Hobson. But little gladness arose from the discussion, as they were convinced that they had an enemy to meet, instead of a kind guardian to greet with welcome. An admirable feeling of respect for their own dignity induced all to scout the idea of hissing the Governor on his landing, or making any other active demonstration of dislike; but it was sorrowfully whispered how passionate a welcome from the true hearts of some thousand Englishmen would have echoed along the hills, had they been about to receive a ruler who had deserved common respect or gratitude.

The next day at noon, having engaged apartments at Barrett's hotel, his Excellency landed on the beach, close to the door. A considerable assemblage of the first people in the place had been standing on the road near the hotel and Medical Hall, previous to this time, talking over the rumoured intentions of Captain Hobson; but as his boat neared the shore, they stepped silently into the houses in a marked manner. I well remember that I was rebuked by a large party who had retreated into Dr. Dorset's sitting-room for even looking out at the window; but I was determined to have a good view of the expected 'power and dignity'. I was not disappointed.

As the boat grated on the silent and almost deserted beach, some nameless tuft-hunter came up just in time with a mob of about forty ragged labourers, whom he had collected among the idlers at a public-house, and they raised a very faint cheer, probably because badly paid for. Two still less reputable characters formed part of the deputation to receive his Excellency. These were Mr. Davy, and a drunken Sydney horse-breaker, named Bob Barrett, who had fastened a smart cavalry saddle-cloth on to a wretched old nag, and who rode into the water by the side of the boat, splashing the Governor and his suite all over, and begging him to ride in procession on the horse. Beyond this, I will venture to say that no land-owner, no holder of capital, no respectable mechanic or decent tradesman, no person who had a name to lose, assisted at the disembarkation. Captain Hobson at last got rid of the troublesome jockey, and walked from the boat to the hotel, looking much mortified. He was attended by Lieutenant Smart as his aide-de-camp, by his private secretary, Edward Shortland, and by a 'mounted policeman on foot', as an orderly. The whole affair looked as little like dignity and power as it possibly could. Five or six natives from Pipitea *pa* told us, as they went homewards, that they were much disappointed; that he did not look like a chief at all; and that they could not understand why he was said to have so much authority over all the white people.

A levee, held on the Tuesday following, was an equally complete failure. Besides the officers of the Government and of the Company, the latter headed by Colonel Wakefield, only about forty persons attended, chiefly new arrivals; and several of even this small number were butchers or shopmen dressed up for the occasion, who were delighted to be able to attend a levee at any price. But the real leaders of the community, whether by birth, influence, talents, education, wealth, or honourable feelings, did not afford his Excellency an opportunity of meeting them. One was at his farm, another fishing or shooting, a third building a chimney, or riding after cattle, another planing a plank, and all going on with their usual avocations, as though no Governor had been there. I passed the door of the hotel on horseback a few minutes after the levee had begun: I could see through the window that the room was nearly empty; and the aide-de-camp, who had to present the cards of visitors, stood on the steps of the outer door jingling his spurs, and sunning his gay uniform, without being able to catch a single other customer for a peep at the lions.

Among the passengers in the Government brig were the three-epaulet Surveyor-general, Mr. Felton Mathew and Mr. George Clarke, the lay agent of the Church Missionary Society in New Zealand, and formerly a catechist and gunsmith of some skill, now appearing as the Chief Protector of the Aborigines! It was said that he came to make the necessary arrangements for the placing of the native reserves on some advantageous footing.

This gentleman kept very much in the back-ground; but there was a general inquiry as to who the man could be, that was always to be seen prowling about in the *pas*, and holding much private talk with the discontented among the natives. He seemed to become a part and parcel of the Pipitea and Te Aro villages, though not one of the settlers even knew who he was.

During the Governor's visit Mr. Richard Hanson was gazetted as Crown Prosecutor for the District of Port Nicholson; to which office was attached a salary of £250 per annum. Six days later, Mr. G. B. Earp was gazetted as a Justice of the Peace, and Member of the Legislative Council. In order to be qualified for the latter office, he had been placed at the head of the list, so that he might appear as one of the three senior Magistrates.

The going over of these two gentlemen to the enemy was one of the earliest instances of what afterwards came to be called 'catching the Government fever'. This idea of some Wellington wit very pithily expressed the manner in which the oldest settlers and most unprejudiced officials from England generally imbibed the distinctive manners, the vulgar haughtiness and importance, and the opinionated partisanship, of the Auckland staff, with their first draught from the Auckland treasury.

Mr. Murphy had requested me to put in writing a description which I had made to him of the wretched state of Wanganui, through the absence of any authorized person to restrain the excesses of the lawless vagabonds who infested that part of the country, in order that he might lay it before the Governor. His Excellency, in consequence, sent for me, and requested me to become a Magistrate, together with three other gentlemen living at that place. He also assured me that Mr. Dawson would include Wanganui in his itinerary visits about Cook's Strait: and that he hoped these measures, and the appointment of a small constabulary force, would allay the evil. I had felt much reluctance in allowing my name to be included in the commission of the peace, not unmindful of the dismissal of two gentlemen for the free expression of their political opinions. But as I had hitherto carefully avoided any active expression of my opinion of local politics, lest my relationship to Colonel Wakefield should be used to accuse me of undue prejudice in favour of the Company, I was persuaded to accept the appointment, in the hope of doing some good to my favourite settlement.

On the 28th August a fast brig arrived from Plymouth in 93 days, beating in at night under double-reefed topsails against a strong gale. This was the *Arrow*, a store-ship forming one of the preliminary expedition of the proposed 'Nelson' colony. She announced that two barques, containing the rest of the pioneers, might be daily expected, having sailed in company with her. It was proposed to found this colony on some part of the Middle Island.

On the 8th of September, the *Will Watch* arrived, bearing Mr. F. Tuckett as Chief Surveyor, and a whole staff of assistants and labouring men for the new settlement.

Colonel Wakefield immediately applied to the Governor, requesting him to point out a site fit for the colony, according to the conditions agreed upon between Lord John Russell and the Company. His Excellency suggested a place called Mahurangi, situated about fifty miles from the capital at Auckland. But the negotiations on the subject were interrupted by the departure of the Governor on a trip to Akaroa, on the 11th of September.

On the 18th, the *Whitby* arrived, bearing my lamented uncle

H

Captain Arthur Wakefield of the Royal Navy, as Agent for Nelson, and the rest of his staff; and also Captain F. Liardet of the Royal Navy, as Agent for New Plymouth.

I went on board the ship as she came in; and was much pleased to greet among the crew, besides my dear and good uncle, several younger relations and school-fellows who had engaged as subordinates in the surveying staff of the new settlement.

On the 20th, a public dinner was given to commemorate the arrival of the expedition. The honoured guests were Captain Wakefield and Captain Liardet, and two officers of the French corvette lying at Akaroa, who had come up to buy provisions for their countrymen settled there. Seventy of the *élite* of the colony sat down, the chair having been taken by Dr. Evans. I shall not relate all the toasts which paid the due compliments to our guests, or proved our eager welcome of the new colonists who were about to join us on so large a scale. 'Te Puni, Wharepouri, and the Chiefs of Port Nicholson' were not forgotten, although they had escaped the notice of Captain Hobson. But when the chairman, without comment, proposed 'the Governor of New Zealand', only about half-a-dozen persons besides the Company's officers rose to do honour to the toast, and made a feeble attempt to raise a cheer, which was drowned in the respectful silence of the great body of independent settlers, who sat still with their empty glasses upturned on the board.

Captain Hobson returned from Akaroa on the 24th, and the negotiation as to the site of the 'Nelson' settlement was renewed. The Governor obstinately named Mahurangi as the fittest site; the agents of the Company suggested Port Cooper, of which Messrs. Daniell and Duppa had brought back so promising an account. But his Excellency declared with some warmth that he would 'not colonize New Munster'. He disapproved of Port Cooper in a conclusive but somewhat intemperate despatch. Colonel Wakefield closed the negotiation by a despatch explaining the motives which induced him to fall back upon the original permission to select any site within the territory claimed by the Company, and named Blind Bay as a spot likely to be approved of by Captain Wakefield on due examination.

Captain Hobson had at length condescended to spend twenty-

seven days among that part of his population which he had himself
officially described as 'from their rank, their numbers, and their
wealth, by far the most important in the colony'.

His further doings, during this short stay, may be gathered
from a list of proclamations published by his command in the
Wellington Gazette. These proclamations gave official notice of his
approval of the town of Wellington, and a definition of its boundaries; of the approval of the jail as a common jail (and a very
common jail it was); of the establishment of bonded stores; of
the application of the New South Wales Police Act for towns to
New Zealand; of the authority of the Crown Prosecutor to prosecute
in his own name; of the institution of an overland mail to Wanganui;
of the tenders to be made for the building of a pound; of the
illegality of squatting on the Public or on the Native Reserves; of
the establishment of a Court of Requests; of a description of the
Reserves made by the Crown for public purposes; and of a prohibition against the cutting of timber in the belt of land reserved
for the ornament of the town and recreation of the townspeople.

[*Wakefield then lists Hobson's sins of omission, among them his neglect
of Wellington's needs.*]

No harbour-master had been appointed. Auckland had been
provided with a harbour-master almost before any vessels entered
that port; while Wellington, after receiving 200 vessels, and a
daily increasing shipping-list, was still without such an officer.

And yet the shipping had never been more busy than during
the Governor's stay at Barrett's hotel. Ships, brigs, barques, and
schooners were constantly dropping their anchor, or getting under
way, or tacking just under his bed-room window. Vessels from
Sydney and the other Australian colonies, from South America,
from England, whalers for refreshments, and a numerous flotilla
of coasters were daily turning the point, sometimes with fair,
sometimes against contrary winds. The wharfs and beaches were
almost obstructed by the landing of goods and the activity of a
port. Indeed those who did hold communication with his Excellency often heard him acknowledge that, as a port, nothing could
surpass Port Nicholson, and that 'they must not expect to see
anything like it at Auckland'.

No Government buildings were appointed to be erected. The jail remained a straw hut, very much like a part of the adjoining native *pa*. The great barn which served for police-court, post-office, church, and court-house, still stood in the same state in which it had been deserted by the surveying staff—dilapidated, nearly tumbling down, and perfectly pervious to the wind in every quarter, with straw walls and earthen floor. But the large income to be drawn from the settlement by the newly enforced customs duties appeared doomed to be spent on Auckland.

The Governor could not refrain from frequent admiration of the site and capabilities of Wellington, though he never went beyond the immediate neighbourhood of the town, not even visiting the Hutt. He very much qualified the expressions which he thus loudly made use of in words, when he got to Auckland and began to write home. His Excellency did not scruple to misrepresent matters in order to defend his senseless choice of a capital to the Colonial Minister. Every one who heard him in Wellington felt convinced that he deeply regretted having made his election on the hearsay evidence of others. His visit to Akaroa had undeceived him completely as to one opinion which he had very rashly formed, that Auckland was a 'centrical' position, because the Middle Island was hardly habitable, and not fit to be colonized; and the ease with which the shipping came and departed on their various errands in opposite directions, must have convinced him, as a practical naval man, that Cook's Strait, with its excellent harbours, and room for the evolutions of a navy, is a much more advantageous communication between the two coasts than the isthmus of three or four miles which separates the port of Auckland from the bar-harbour of Manukau, a port often closed for weeks together by the prevailing westerly winds.

One allowance was perhaps due, and was by many people made, for the hostile and ruinous policy of the Governor. It was clear that he had never recovered the unimpaired use of his faculties, since his unfortunate attack of paralysis, soon after he first arrived at the Bay of Islands. His appearance in walking was that of extreme bodily infirmity; and his manner and speech were full of the whimsical obstinacy and crotchety churlishness of an irritable and debilitated mind.

CHAPTER XIII

By the River Route to Taupo

I NOW PROPOSED to make a journey to Taupo, to see my old friends there. A chief of the Patutokoto tribe, named Para, agreed to accompany me, with his attendants and family; and Kuru sent me word that his Taupo wife and his elder brother would also join me with their suite. After preparing all the arms, goods for barter, provisions, and other requisites, I started up the river [i.e., from the Wanganui settlement] in my light canoe, accompanied by Para in a large one of his own, on the 9th of November. We were bound to Kuru's country settlement at Tata, 100 miles up the river, in the first instance. I have already described the scenery as far as Pukehika, about 70 miles up. The only new feature was the sight of Te Kauarapawa *pa* in ruins; the houses, and fences, and trees, having been destroyed by the Taupo war-party on its return. Nine miles above Pukehika, after passing through some more delightful scenery, rather more wild and less inhabited in its characters, we reached a large stockaded village called Pipiriki. Two fortified hills constitute the defences in case of war; but the inhabitants generally reside on the cultivated flat between the two. They were all *mihinare*; but their former head chief, Kai, being the principal teacher and leader of religious exercises, I found them an exceedingly well-behaved and orderly community. The whole population, including the chief, being nearly related to Kuru and Rangitauwira, received me very kindly. They were all among those who, having assisted at the bargain, have never attempted to secede from its fulfilment. They sincerely condoled with me on the dishonesty of the other natives. 'In the old times,' said Kai, 'we should have fought to maintain you in possession of the land, against those who fairly sold, and have since repented and told lies; but now we are missionaries, and we can only be sorry.'

I was much struck with the severe discipline which this curious specimen of a warlike and influential chief, turned into a stern religious pastor, maintained over his people, who may have amounted to 200 of all sexes and ages. The houses and the *pa* were cleanly and well kept. Almost perfect silence prevailed during the whole day. Everything was done apparently by some rule. The ovens were made up, the firewood cut, the court-yard swept out, as though by clockwork; and none of that noisy and merry chatter was ever heard, which generally distinguishes the Maori village. Each week-day was kept with the solemnity of Sunday; and jokes, songs, dances, or romping, were entirely banished. The very children seemed prematurely grown into little old men and women. While I was greeting the chief and his family, the rest of the community sat at a distance. None of the usual crowding round, and if it were not for its hilarity, almost intrusive rushing to shake hands; no shouts; not even a smile.

In the midst of this remarkable stillness, one among the mutes, could refrain no longer, and laughed outright at some cheerful observation which I made to the chief.

'Who laughed?' shouted Kai, in his deepest tones.

No answer—long faces—and repressed tittering among the ranks of the half-hidden children at the back.

'Who was it laughed?' repeated he, seeking to find the culprit. But the gay joker could not summon courage to acknowledge his crime; and so Kai treated the assemblage to a long sermon on the sin of laughing. He had perfectly by rote the greater part of the New Testament; and quoted from it in order to support almost everything he asserted. 'A man that hath looked on a woman,' said he, 'has already committed adultery in his heart: so he that laugheth, hath already stolen; for the thief laughs to your face while he steals your property. Laugh ye not! for it is the way to sin.'

Such was the intense religious enthusiasm of this extraordinary man; and such the extravagance of speech and doctrine to which he was carried by it. Benevolent and high-minded, of a character to lead other men, endowed with much firmness and kindness of heart, and even wise on many points, Kai had early embraced the new doctrine with fervour, and had appointed to himself the task of leading all his tribe in the way that they should go. He reminded me of some old patriarch of the Cameronians by his rigorous discipline and intensity of purpose; and, though I thought his doctrine carried out in practice to much too saddening a degree for such merry men as his followers, I could not refuse him my high admiration for the admirable success of his plans, for his great consistency, and for having inculcated a very unusual observance of the moral virtues as well as the mere forms of the Christian religion among his flock. The Pipiriki people were certainly the best-behaved natives whom I had yet seen under the new *régime*.

From Pipiriki to Tata, a distance of 20 miles, the scenery assumes a new and magnificent character, the river flowing between cliffs 100 to 200 feet in height, fringed with graceful ferns and mosses down to the water's edge, while the wood on the top hangs far over the precipice from both sides. In this part, the only path to the settlements consists of a rude but strong ladder, consisting of trees and *kareao*, or supple-jack, reaching from the water to the top. It is this district of the country which is called by the natives Te Wahipari, or 'The Place of Cliffs'.

About half-way between the two places we passed Mangeao, an almost impregnable position, from which the Wanganui people have been accustomed to look down with security and contempt upon passing war-parties of the Waikato and other invading tribes.

Coming suddenly round a sharp bend in the river, you are in a rapid reach about half-a-mile long, beyond which the river again turns to the right. The cliffs increase in height as you advance into the reach, so that the forest-trees on their edge seem like feathers; the song of the birds among them is only faintly heard, and the streams which rush over the steep are frittered into the thinnest spray long before they reach the water. Facing you, the cliff is surmounted by a steep hill of the additional height of some 500 or 600 feet, which seems to tower proudly over the trench in which the river flows; and on its top, the natives told me afterwards, are cultivations, springs of water, and woods of large timber, and ample room to support many hundred people when compelled to take refuge there.

Though the river has a considerable descent here, and the polers have to work hard throughout the distance in ascending, the gradual increase in the height of the cliffs combines with the way in which the strata strike the water-line, to produce a remarkable optical deception. It seems as though you were rapidly descending; and I have more than once noticed that, in returning towards the sea at the rate of ten miles an hour, you appear to be going up hill at this particular spot. Add to this, that out of a dark cavern in either cliff, near the water's edge, a large stream comes roaring, and echoing, and foaming into the river; that an augmenting darkness is produced, as you advance, by the height of the cliffs and the comparative narrowness of the cleft in which the river flows; and that some old legend or superstition makes the natives speak in whispers and compose their features to seriousness; and the sublimity of the whole scene may be imagined. Such was the intense excitement produced on me by this burst of nature's majesty, when I first went through the pass, that I relieved myself involuntarily by a deep sigh and a rushing of tears to my eyes, when we had passed on into the comparatively tame and reposing scenery which immediately follows.

Just before we arrived at Tata, we gave notice of our approach by a rattling salute. The reports reverberated far along the steep walls of the river's channel, and rolled up the wooded hills above, mingled with the sharper tones of the answering salute from the settlement. At length we reached the foot of one of the sky-scraping ladders which I have before described, leading to the top of the cliff, here about 200 feet high, while the river is not more than 40 yards broad. The natives clambered carelessly up, with heavy chests, and guns, and paddles, and my great dog in their arms, while I was ascending cautiously, step by step, with uncertain footing, and hands aching with the efforts which I made to clench hard the vibrating rounds of the ladder. At the bottom they had shown me the spot where 'two or three foolish old women', they said, 'had been smashed quite flat, having missed a step while going down in the dark to the canoes.'

At last I reached the top in safety. Here Kuru, with all his family and adherents, were drawn up to receive me. The next day I was guided by him to a mountain called Aurupu, close to the river, about two miles higher up, from which I got a view of Tongariro and Mount Egmont.

§

It was not till the 19th November that our party was ready to start. The loads were packed and distributed among the natives. I had with me a large quantity of goods, both for the purchase of mats and for presents to my friends. So one carrier had a large kit full of blankets, and another a bundle of half-a-dozen pieces of printed calico. A hundred-weight of tobacco formed another load; a tin-box, containing tea, sugar, and bottles of pepper, salt, and mustard; another, containing journal-books, sketch-book, pencils, and other necessary nick-nacks; pipes among the blankets, spare boots or baked legs of pork fastened to the top of baskets full of shirts; bags of shot, tinder-boxes, cartouch-boxes, canisters of powder, hand-lamps, a bottle of oil, tomahawks, leathern valises with spare clothes, pea-jackets, and a light tent, figured among the baggage. One man looked like Atlas, as he went long with a huge damper on the top of his pack. This is a loaf baked in the ashes, which has the advantage of never getting much harder than on the day it is baked.

The tent packed into very small space. It was composed of unbleached calico. It stretched over two uprights four feet high, and a ridge pole six feet long, to the breadth of about four or five feet. The necessary poles and the pegs for the bottom were cut at the encampment each night, or carried from the wood in passing when we had to encamp in the open country. When rolled up, the tent was not so bulky as a greatcoat, and yet, when well stretched, it afforded ample shelter from a night's heavy rain to two people.

On the 19th, then, we got into the canoes, to the number of about 35, men, women and children. We pulled down four miles to the place where a tributary, called Manganui, or 'large branch', flows into the Wanganui. This we ascended about two miles, the natives jumping out and tracking the canoes up rapids, several of which had a fall of six feet. The Manganui also runs between cliffs, nearly 200 feet in height, and is inhabited as far up as we went that night. We encamped at a settlement called Moeawatea, or 'Sleep-in-the-day-time', and proceeded the next morning, after crossing the river twice immediately above, through hilly forest-land for about five miles. Here the boys were tired with their heavy loads, and stopped in a patch of fern for the night. But it would be tedious to relate each day's journey separately. Suffice it to say that, although I had been told it was but two days' walk from the Wanganui to Taupo, at noon on the 23rd November the natives said it was still two or three days' walk. We had proceeded but slowly. Our path lay chiefly along the valley of the Manganui, which keeps an average of two miles wide, and is intersected by a deep cleft in which the river runs. Many parts of the valley are clear, and in some places we passed over small plains of grass; in others, we plunged into the forest, and crossed steep ridges, apparently in order to avoid circuitous bends of the valley. We had forded the river five times; and the assistance of the natives was most welcome in overcoming the difficulties occasioned by the rapidity of the stream, and the slippery rocky footing. This road must be perfectly impassable in winter, when the river is swollen by freshets. The heavy loads had made our progress very slow: so that the potatoes began to run short, and they all stopped to dig fern in one of the open places. Fortunately the river abounded with a kind of bird between a coot and a widgeon, called *whiorau*, of which we shot about half-a-dozen at each ford.

I now selected two natives to carry my tent and bedding, and Mr. Niblett* and I determined to push on by a forced march. We accordingly left the rest to roast fern to their heart's content, and bring up the heavy baggage at their leisure.

We pushed on about six miles more to-day through forest, and encamped at dark under an old *rata* tree of renown, which glories in the name of *Korako*. We had forded the river twice; and ascended its bank the last time by means of a rickety *kareao* ladder, about 30 feet high, which is fixed to the cliff at the exact spot where a small waterfall spouts over the edge, and renders the ascent far from safe or pleasant.

It rained moderately all night and poured at daylight; but we had now no other alternative than to push on, defying the weather.

*A traveller who joined the party at Pukehika.

Ten miles, over a level table-land covered with wood, brought us to the Manganui, where it is swollen by three smaller streams. We descended at least 1500 feet to the stream, crossed it and two of its tributaries, and then ascended a ragged ridge, to the opposite bank of the dark, deep dell in which the stream flows. This dell, with its various branches, presents a very picturesque appearance, from the steepness and height of its banks, which are covered almost wholly with the *tawai*. This tree has very small dark leaves. It is used for ship-building, and is called by Englishmen the 'black birch'. It generally grows in elevated situations. Five miles more along a forest, consisting of nothing but *tawai*, brought us to a level grass plain, which continues at the same height as the table forest-land. The plain seemed about four miles in width, and was bounded on either side by wooded hills, whose summits were hidden by thick masses of clouds. This kind of prairie is called *mania* by the natives. It is covered with a poor tufty grass of very delicate blade, though here and there are excellent patches of other grasses well fitted for pasture. At twilight we prepared to encamp at the edge of a point of wood which projected like a promontory from the eastern edge of the prairie. We had some difficulty in lighting a fire, as it had poured incessantly the whole day; and we were obliged to fare on short commons, and sit wrapped in our blankets by the fire until the warmth made us sleepy enough to turn in, notwithstanding the wet, which had completely soaked through tent, blankets, and everything else.

Two young *weka*, or wood-hens, about as large as sparrows, which my dog pulled out of their nest in a burrow under a fallen tree, were esteemed a valuable addition to our scanty supper.

The rain had continued all night, and gave no signs of mercy in the morning; but as one *whiorau* and twelve potatoes were our whole stock of provisions, and we were still far from our journey's end, delay was out of the question. At the first dawn of day we pulled on our wet clothes, and walked eight miles along the prairie, which is in many parts swampy and covered with rushes. We now crossed a small tributary of the Wanganui, and, after two miles' walk through a belt of *tawai* forest, a larger tributary called the Tawai. The plains now seemed to extend on every side; and as the weather cleared up, and the clouds lifted, we saw the majestic forms of Ruapehu, and the Paratetaitonga volcano, within a few miles of us to the eastward. Furthest to the southward lay Ruapehu, covered with snow. *Para te tai Tonga* is the mountain which Mr. Bidwill ascended in 1838, and calls 'Tonga Dido'. Tongariro, however, is a generic name applied to the whole mountain mass.

To the north-east of the volcano, two peaks, apparently extinct volcanoes, complete the gigantic group. This double peak is called Pukeonake.

After eating a quarter of a *whiorau* and two potatoes each, for breakfast and dinner, we pushed on 12 miles over a barren plain to the northern spur of Pukeonake; on the highest part of which we divided about two ounces of sugar, our last atom of food, among the four of us, and ate it with much relish.

Here, too, we took a good rest, and looked about us. We had crossed the Whakapapa, a large tributary of the Wanganui. This stream takes its rise from a small lake, which is at the bottom of a circular basin of rocks, five or six miles in diameter, stated by the natives to have once been the site of Mount Egmont.

On quarrelling with his friend Tongariro about the affection of a small volcanic mountain in the neighbourhood, which is described as a lady mountain of most fascinating appearance, old Taranaki is said to have torn up his rocky foundations from this basin, and left the ragged and splintered edges to it, which are pointed out as proofs of the fact. He then clove a path through mountain and wood to the sea-coast, and the Wanganui sprang up in his ancient site, and followed his footsteps to the sea. So runs the native legend; and the basin is called to this day Rua Taranaki, or 'Taranaki's Dyke'. It most likely refers to some tremendous eruptions of nature which have doubtless torn these islands at some distant date.

From this open and elevated spot we could distinguish numerous glades like that by which we had entered the *mania*, shooting into the wooded country like the fingers of an outstretched hand, diverging from the volcano in various directions, and of different lengths and breadths. On the edges of that along which we had travelled, the trees were dead, and many of them scathed and blackened. And in the very centre of the broad glade, especially among the swampy parts, we constantly came upon the trunks of huge trees, black as charcoal, and half buried in the soil. From these appearances, I concluded that the glades had been formed, at the time of these convulsions, by the irruption of streams of burning lava into the woods. At present, Paratetaitonga only vomits clouds of steam, and that only now and then; but it had probably, at a former period, and will again, discharge more dangerous materials.

On the north-eastern side of the spur, we crossed the Wanganui itself, where it just trickles between the stones which form its winter bed, and was not above a yard wide. From the highest point of our path, we could trace the broken country formed by its valley for many miles almost directly towards Mount Egmont, which glittered gaily over the far horizon. The whole country to W. and S.W. seems one sea of wooded mountain. The northern side of Pukeonaki slopes down very suddenly to the shores of a small lake, called Rotoaira, or 'Lake Yes-indeed'.

From the spot where we jumped over the Wanganui to the west shore of Rotoaira is about five miles, the last two through a swamp in which we sank up to our knees at every step. I remember being much exhausted by this last exertion at the close of the hard day's journey. We were faint with hunger, sore-footed, and speechless from fatigue; but we could not help smiling at the absurdity of each other's appearance, when occasionally resting by standing still up to our knees in water, unable to sit or lie down. A canoe from the eastern shore soon answered our salutes, and took us over to a settlement called Tukutuku, where they set abundance of boiled potatoes before us; but I fell asleep in my clothes after eating two or three, more tired than hungry, notwithstanding the jabber of at least fifty natives of both sexes, who crowded into the house to stare at the new *pakehas*, and hear the news from Wanganui.

Tukutuku is a pretty settlement, in the N.E. corner of the lake. The underwood has been cut away, but the tall forest trees, chiefly *matai* or *mai*, remain standing and still alive; the plantations and villages are disposed among their trunks, on the acclivity which rises from the side of the lake to Pihanga. They grow all their potatoes here by throwing up the soil in heaps, about four feet in diameter, and a foot high; so that the whole cultivation takes place above the surface in artificial beds. The soil is a rich brown loam, mingled, however, with a large proportion of powdered pumice-stone.

§

On the 30th November, having rested three days at Tukutuku, we passed over the low wooded neck which unites Kakaramea to Pihanga, and emerged into fern ground, from which we enjoyed a magnificent view of Lake Taupo and the surrounding country. Descending from the high ground, we now crossed the Tokaanu, a stream which flows from the northern side of the Pihanga, and came suddenly on a novel scene.

A space of about 10 acres on either side of the Tokaanu stream is perforated with holes and cavities of various sizes, from which steam issues in large quantities. Some part of this space is barren, and whitened by the sulphureous exhalations from the hot springs; but in other places, *manuka* and rich grass grow to the very edge of a boiling cavity. In some places, a small hole only is perceptible, from which issues a stream of steam: here the natives form their ovens, and cook food very nicely with great expedition. In other spots, cavities from ten to thirty feet in diameter are filled with water of various temperatures; some nearly boiling, others tempered by the cold stream which runs through one part of them. In one of the latter we all had a delicious bath. The cavity was too deep to reach the bottom, though we dived off a bank eight feet high; and the temperature varied from 70 degrees to 100 degrees as you approached or not the embouchure of the different springs that supply the bath. In all directions steam or hot water issues from the ground; and the clouds of steam which cover the spot, and the gurgling of the different hot fountains around you, add to the wonder excited by the strange sight. A stranger requires to be careful as to where he steps. We were shown two deep basins full of nearly boiling water, into one of which a man threw his slave for stealing potatoes; while a pig had forced a man who was pursuing him into the other. They said that the bones of both were plainly visible a year or two since, but have been completely destroyed by the action of the water.

It is from this and similar spots, which abound between Lake

Taupo and the Bay of Plenty, that the denizens of this volcanic region have assumed the generic name of Waikoropupu, or 'Boiling Water'.

Half a mile from the springs, we reached the settlement of Tokaanu, where 300 people were assembled to receive us.

My companion fell ill soon after we arrived at Tokaanu; so that I was detained a month here, instead of pushing on, as I intended, to Auckland by way of Waikato and Manukau. I ascertained that in eight days I might easily have reached Auckland from Taupo, by that route. During my sojourn, I visited the different settlements.

The terraced flat between a steaming gorge at the western extremity of Kakaramea and the lake is covered with plantations and isolated houses. Among these latter, that of Te Heuheu* is prominent. It is about 40 feet long, 15 broad, and of a proportionate height: a narrow veranda ornaments the northern front, before which a square is reserved from the *kumara* grounds which surround it on three sides. On the day that we went, by previous appointment, to pay our first visit to the old man, about 200 people had assembled in the little square; and Te Heuheu, who sat at one end of the veranda, attended by his principal wife, motioned us to a seat while he went through the necessary *tangi* with the Wanganui natives. A splendid feast followed: 200 kits of boiled potatoes and *kumaras*, five pigs skewered like birds and baked whole, eight or ten pots full of white-bait, and three calabashes of pigeons and *tuis* stewed in their own fat were brought in by a long train of slaves, and piled up in the centre of the square. After this had been distributed among the visitors, the chief talked to me about Wanganui, the Governor, and Poneke, [Port Nicholson] and asked me to come and see him again before I left the neighbourhood. In the meanwhile, he gave me five pigs for food while I remained at Tokaanu, and said he was ashamed of having no food to offer me such as white men liked. He expressed great gratitude for my reception of him and his war-party at Wanganui the autumn before; and begged me to look about the country and call it my own, and the people my people. But he accompanied this with a

* Te Heuheu II had already met Wakefield at the conference on the Wanganui River. He refused to sign the Treaty of Waitangi, and resisted *pakeha* encroachment.

warning not to try and buy the land from him, for he had determined never to sell either that or his chieftainship.

He concluded the interview by saying that he remembered I
was fond of hearing the songs and seeing the dances of the natives.
So, like a baron of olden time shouting 'A hall, a hall!' he yelled,
'*He haka, he haka mo Tiraweke!*' ('A dance, a dance for Tiraweke');
and 100 men and women, headed by his wife Hokokai, went
through some spirited *hakas* and *waiatas* for an hour.

From Te Rapa* to Tokaanu the shore is formed by a swamp,
which reaches to the hills. The principal and easternmost channel of
the Waikato forms a long low peninsula, on which is built a very
strong *pa*, called Waitahanui. Across the eastern end is a strong
double fence, 15 feet high, and a like fence protects the western
point. In the *pa* are the finest native houses that I have yet seen.
The *wharepuni*, or sleeping-houses, are most of them 10 or 12 feet
in height, and very spacious: the veranda, or open space in front,
would easily accommodate ten sleepers, and the whole front is
carved and painted with most elaborate designs. The *kauta*, or
cooking-houses, are proportionably large. In that part of the *pa*
belonging especially to Te Heuheu, there is a row of cooking-houses
40 feet long by 15 broad, and 10 feet high in the walls, which are
constructed of enormous slabs, well fitted together. Round windows, with sliding shutters, admit the light and let out the smoke.
The *pa* is 500 yards long and 100 broad; and is used as a city of
refuge by all the inhabitants of Taupo and Rotoaira. Each division
of the tribe had its own separate quarters. There was no one in
the *pa* on the occasion of my visit, and the fences were ruinous
in many places; but they talked of renovating the fortification as
soon as the harvest should be gathered in, to provide against
apprehended invasion from Waikato.

While at Tokaanu, I could not but observe the excellent conduct
of the natives. This was as much owing to their own friendly
disposition as to the authority of their chief. I was never annoyed,
as I had often been at more civilized or more Christianized settlements. My wishes seemed a law to them; and they were always
making voluntary efforts to procure me any food or amusement
which they thought would be agreeable. The only exceptions to

* Te Heuheu's village, Te Rapa, was overwhelmed by a landslide in 1846.

this rule were invariably among the few missionary families, who seemed to take pride in being less courteous than the others, and more over-reaching in their barter for the different little things, such as shallots, craw-fish, ducks' eggs, which they brought in exchange for pipes or tobacco.

Close to my house was a warm spring, so shallow that you could lie down on the sandy bottom, holding your head out of water. In this bath all the natives assembled, morning and evening; and, indeed, I never found a time, late or early, that there were not some in the water. I soon learned to join them; and used to remain there for hours, smoking and playing at draughts, at which game all the natives have learned to be extremely expert. To their frequent use of these baths I attribute the cleanliness and good health of the natives of this part of the country; who are totally free from the cutaneous diseases so universal among the coast tribes, and generally a cleaner and handsomer race.

After I had been at the lake about a fortnight, a chief and his train arrived from a place called Te Whaiti, in the district of Urewera with pigs and mats. The report that there were plenty of double-barrelled guns to be got at Wanganui had induced him to start with his stock and goods on a journey of nearly 300 miles, in order to procure what he could not get from the traders on the east coast. He had previously despatched a messenger to me, begging me to bring some *tupara*, or 'two-barrel', for him if I came to Taupo, and we accordingly met by a sort of appointment. A very famous artist in *tattoo* came with the party, and was kept in constant and profitable employment. Everybody, from the renowned warrior to the girl of twelve years old, crowded to be ornamented by the skilful chisel; and shirts, mats, axes, and other articles accumulated in the carver's kits. He was a superior man in many respects. He used to beat everybody at draughts, and had a store of old legends to amuse his audience. I saw Iwikau,* or 'Skeleton', the head fighting chief of the tribe under Te Heuheu, being chipped on the cheek-bone. The instruments used were not of bone, as they used formerly to be; but a graduated set of iron tools, fitted with handles like adzes, supplied their place. The man spoke to me with perfect nonchalance for a quarter of an hour,

* Brother of Te Heuheu.

although the operator continued to strike the little adzes into his flesh with a light wooden hammer the whole time, and his face was covered with blood. The worst part of the pain seems to be that endured a day or two after the operation, when every part of the wound gathers, and the face is swollen considerably. The staining liquid is made of charcoal. I rarely saw a case in which the scars were not completely well in a week.

Although I had sent messengers for medicine and advice to Wanganui soon after discovering the illness of Mr. Niblett, we heard no tiding of them; and I proceeded to get the invalid carried there by a device suggested by the new-comers*, who had often seen it practised on the east coast. A litter was soon constructed of stout poles and plaited flaxen straps, and four natives were hired to relieve each other as porters.

The day before starting, I went to take my formal leave of old Te Heuheu, pursuant to his request. After the usual greetings had passed, he told me at once that he suspected that our two parties had met, one from Poneke and the other from Waitemata (Auckland), to consult over his land, with a view to buy it or even seize it forcibly at a later season. 'If this be your wish,' said he, 'go back and tell my words to the people who sent you. I am king here, as my fathers were before me, and as King George and his fathers have been over your country. I have not sold my chieftainship to the Governor, as all the chiefs round the sea-coast have done, nor have I sold my land. I will sell neither. A messenger was here from the Governor to buy the land the other day, and I refused: if you are on the same errand I refuse you too. You white people are numerous and strong; you can easily crush us if you choose, and take possession of that which we will not yield; but here is my right arm, and should thousands of you come, you must make me a slave or kill me before I will give up my authority or my land. When you go, you will say I am big-mouthed like all the other Maori who have talked to you; but I am now telling you that by which I mean to abide. Let your people keep the sea-coast, and leave the interior to us, and our mountain, whose name is sacred to the bones of my fathers. Do not bring many white people into the interior, who may encroach on our possessions till we become their servants; but if you can make up your mind

* Messrs White and Blackett who had arrived from the Bay of Plenty.

to come yourself now and then, and visit this mean place, whose people are your slaves, you will find the same welcome. The place and the people are yours. Go to Wanganui.' The old man said all this calmly and without working himself into a state of excitement. I succeeded, after much trouble, in making him understand that we had all come to Taupo out of curiosity only, and with no view of acquiring land.

I asked his permission to ascend Tongariro on my way back; knowing that he had been very angry with Mr. Bidwill for doing so during his absence. But he steadily refused; saying, 'I would do anything else to show you my love and friendship; but you must not ascend my *tupuna*, or "ancestor".' He told me that he had for the same reason refused the same request when made by the two white men who had come from the Governor to buy his land; referring to Dr. Dieffenbach and Captain Symonds, who had been here two or three months before.

This was a curious illustration of the enforcement of the custom of *tapu*, as used to support the dignity of the chief. Te Heuheu constantly identified himself with the mountain, and called it his sacred ancestor.

This legend of an hereditary descent from an object, majestic in itself, and naturally productive of awe, had doubtless been handed down from father to son in the chief's family; and was wisely calculated to maintain the aristocratic position of the leader, by appealing to the weak and superstitious imaginations of the crowd. When I remembered the strong effect produced upon myself by the mere sight of the pass in 'The Place of Cliffs', I inwardly admired the wisdom of the ancestors of these people, who had so contrived to weave up their own precarious dignity with legendary superstition, and the venerable testimony of nature's most kingly works.

Like the first rulers of young Rome, who proclaimed their descent from gods, and imposed laws advised by a celestial nymph, so Te Heuheu backed his other claims to empire by maintaining inviolate the mysterious *tapu* of his mountain ancestor.

On the 1st of January 1842, we left Tokaanu; Mr. Niblett being carried in his litter, and attended by about a dozen natives besides the porters.

[*The return journey to Wanganui* viâ *the Onetapu desert took the party eight days.*]

CHAPTER XIV

Progress and Difficulties at Wanganui and Wellington

AT WANGANUI I found that a considerable addition had been
made to the white population of the settlement. The *Clydeside*,
brought out by her owner, Mr. Mathieson, had entered the river
and ascended as far as Landguard Cliff.* She bore a large party of
passengers from Wellington, with their goods and chattels. Macgregor, in acting as pilot, had put the vessel on the sand-spits
both in entering and in going out; but no serious damage had
been done.

A drove of some fifty head of cattle, too, had arrived by land
for Captain Moses Campbell, who had himself come in the *Clydeside*,
and had been followed to this place by several Scotch settlers.
Many of the surveying labourers, chiefly Scotchmen, had taken a
liking to the country while exploring it, and were preparing for
the reception of some of their friends and relations from Wellington.

Colonel Wakefield had paid this settlement a visit during my
absence, having ridden the whole distance on horseback. He had
come to see if any satisfactory arrangement could be made with
the discontented natives, and had held a meeting with them at
Putikiwharanui, in the presence of Mr. Mason, who interpreted
between the parties. It appeared, however, that nothing could be
done before the affair had been inquired into by the Court of Claims.

I accompanied some Wellington visitors one day to the farm of

* The cliff at Waipuna, two miles from the river's mouth, named 'Landguard' on account of
the post on which Kuru had made me cut Colonel Wakefield's name, and which is still there.
[Wakefield's note.]

Mr. Bell, who was at this time, in the beginning of February, (1842) reaping his first crop of wheat.

He had about thirty acres of land under plough cultivation, but some part of this was in potatoes. Although he had not succeeded in eradicating the fern this first year, and a good deal of it was up among the corn, yet what wheat there was was of excellent quality, and promised well for the next season. Mr. Molesworth, who had just done gathering in a very luxuriant crop on his land in the valley of the Hutt, looked with some contempt on this more moderate production, and cried down the fern land; but old Bell predicted, that in another year he would hardly fear comparison. After partaking of a scone, and a cup of milk in the farm-house, and admiring the excellent condition of the bullocks, who had been fattening on idleness among the rich natural pastures in the neighbourhood, we returned to the settlement.

Bell had managed to locate himself here, notwithstanding considerable opposition from the natives, by an admirable mixture of firmness, good temper, and kindness. He had first paid the natives for putting up the frame of a house; and had then filled up the walls with *kareao* and clay, and whitewashed them. A little garden had succeeded. He had then proceeded to clear off the flax, and fern, and other scrub, which was waist-high on the land which he meant to plough. When he began this operation, the interruption commenced. One perseveringly annoying and ill-tempered chief headed the malcontents; but Bell had made a friend of another, by judicious presents and attentions, and obtained some protection from him whenever the persecution became a little too serious. The friend was Kirikaramu, the chief who had signed the deed at Kapiti, and afterwards accompanied Kuru and myself hither to the grand sale. He was a repudiator of the bargain generally; but had appreciated the advantages of having a good *pakeha* to live near him, and teach him how to plant potatoes and grow wheat. He never did more than remonstrate with Waka, the troublesome neighbour; apparently conniving at extortion, though he would not allow violence to be used.

During the progress of the ploughing, Waka used to come and watch, and keep walking by the side of the old farmer, telling him he should plough no more. But Bell pretended not to understand him, and smiled at him, and '*geed*' the bullocks, and warned Waka to get out of the way of them when they turned, and ploughed on. Waka got furious; but Bell wouldn't look a bit frightened, and told him he didn't understand him; 'He must go to the boys,' meaning his own sons; 'they'd talk Maori to him'; and he '*geed*' the bullocks, and ploughed on. The patience of Waka soon got exhausted, and he retired sulkily towards the house, after putting in some pegs a few yards beyond where Bell had got to, pointing to that as his ultimatum. And while the good-wife gave him a large mess of bread and milk, or a smoking dish of pork and potatoes, and the sons and daughters chatted good-humouredly to him while they built a pigsty or put up a stock-yard, old Bell was ploughing on. And Waka ate and smoked, and basked in the sun, wondering at the industry of the *pakeha*, till he got sleepy, and crept back to his village for the day.

The next morning, however, he would be afoot pretty early to besiege the *pakeha maro*, or 'hard white man', as he called him. But he was never early enough; and the first sight that met his eyes was always the *bête noire*, the team of bullocks and the old man trudging steadily along the fresh furrows. Waka would begin by looking for his pegs, and hunt about for a long while, grumbling and puzzling, before he found out that the plough must have gone over them some hours ago, if not the evening before. And while he was hunting, the plough sped quietly on. Then came the remonstrance, the shrug of the shoulders, and the fury, and the good-humoured indifference, and the reference to the boys, and the meal, and the sleepiness, and the return home, and the careful pegging of the ground as before. The same story over again; no patience could stand it; old Bell and the team went on, slow, sure, and regular as the course of the sun.

And, besides, on one occasion when Waka had brought a large troop of attendants, and threatened to commit some violence, the old man had called his stalwart sons to his side, and taking up a spade or a ploughshare, had said, in broad Scotch, while his resolute looks and prepared attitude interpreted his words into ↑ universally intelligible language, 'Dinna ye think to touch a thing that's here noo; for if ye do, by the God that's abune us, I'll cleave ye to the grund! A bargain's a bargain; I've paid ye richt and fair; and I'll gar ye keep to it.' And then Waka *would* look frightened; and begin to think his good daily meal was better than a blow of old Bell's weapon; and peace was soon restored.

And when the ploughing was done, the planting potatoes was too amusing to be interfered with, for they ridiculed the idea of expecting any crop from potatoes cut into small pieces. 'Bide and see,' said the old man; and they waited with anxiety for the time of crop; and the report spread far and wide that the old *pakeha* with the 'cows' was very good and brave and industrious, but that he was certainly gone *porangi*, or 'mad', for he had cut up his seed potatoes before he put them in. 'Poor old man!' they said, 'his troubles must have turned his head—such a very absurd idea!'

But the crop came better than their own from whole potatoes; and they stared, and found that the foolish old man could teach them some lessons in growing food; and they soon honoured him as much for his knowledge as they had learned to stand in awe of his courage and resolution.

And though they have not yet allowed him to use the whole of his section, he has now fifty acres under plough cultivation, sends grain and grass-seed enough to Wellington to pay for the luxuries which his family require, owns several cows and a flock of sheep, calls himself the 'Laird of Wanganui', and gives harvest-home festivals. He talked of buying a horse, and caring for no man, when I last saw him.

But, unfortunately, all settlers have not the admirable qualities of William Gordon Bell, who had indeed shown a great example of success against the numerous difficulties which staggered lesser men.

A day or two afterwards, I started by land, with 'Yankee Smith', the trader whom I have before mentioned, and two of my 'boys' to carry baggage. We crossed the rivers, and got to Rangitikei late at night, after a tedious walk against a strong southerly wind. Along these sandy beaches, this is a great hindrance in walking— the sand drives sharply against eyes, nose, and mouth, and stings the face. I have often known natives refuse to travel along the coast against a *hau kino*, or 'foul wind'.

Arriving about noon at Manawatu, we found a large party of Ngatiraukawa assembled in the *pa* at the mouth. Among them was a chief of high rank, by name Taratoa, the head of a branch of the tribe called Ngatiparewahawaha; and whose daughter was married to Whatanui's eldest son. I had often heard of him, but had never met him before.

He had also heard of me, it appeared; for after two or three lads, whom I recognized among the crowd as having been engaged at Kapiti during the whaling-season, had whispered to him, he motioned me to a seat by his side on a large log outside the *pa*, and addressed me with the usual greetings, telling me who he was, and that he was well inclined towards me. I answered him, that I was in a hurry to go on, and did not like making new friendships on short acquaintance. I asked him briefly, how much *utu* he wanted for putting us across the river in a canoe; as a white man, who had lately established a ferry a mile higher up on the opposite side, was said to be up the river on a trading excursion. '*Utu!*' said Taratoa, with well-feigned indignation; 'I do not ask *utu* from a great name like Tiraweke; one great chief should never beg *utu* from another. Launch a canoe!' shouted he to some of his assistants. 'Put my white man and his people across the river!' And as the canoe was small, he told me and the Yankee to get in, and the boys should follow with their loads in another trip. I thanked him for his courtesy; but, suspecting that this sudden civility could not be genuine, I sent Smith and the boy who had got his things first, remaining myself with the one who had got mine.

By the time the canoe was half-way across, some of the young men began hinting to me that a suitable present of money would be very desirable from me to the chief. As he acquiesced in this view, I took five shillings out of my pocket, turned round to him, and laid them on the log between us. 'As you wish to make a bargain of your courtesy to a guest,' said I, 'there is a shilling for each of us, and one over; I should only have paid four to go in the boat of the white *tutua*' (common man).

He would not take it up, however, at first; and said, that all other passengers that were *rangatira*, or chiefs, had given him 'money gold' (sovereigns or half-sovereigns) for ferrying them across. He instanced 'Wide-awake', and the three other gentlemen who had returned with their horses some days before me. 'You ought to make a large present,' said he, 'in consideration of your great name.' I was firm, however, and when the canoe came back he told me to get in.

But the man who had guided it across demanded a shilling for himself as we were going to embark. I threw one to him, and was shouting the customary farewell, when another man came up and asked two shillings more, as the owner of the canoe. I refused; he called some of the bystanders, and hauled the canoe up high and dry on the bank.

I took no notice of this insult. Waving my hand to Smith, I shouted to him, in Maori, to proceed without me. *'Haere ki Poneke!'* ('Go to Port Nicholson!') I sang out, so that all the bystanders might think I was bidding him farewell.

I then told my carrier to untie his kit, and to spread one of my blankets on the sunny side of the log, close to Taratoa. I reclined upon the blanket in chieftain-like comfort, cut up some tobacco, filled my pipe, called out to the slaves with an air of authority to bring fire, and, after lighting my pipe and taking two or three puffs, handed it familiarly to the chief. He took it from me, but forgot to use it, for he was aghast at my coolness. The pipe remained in his extended hand; his mouth was half open; his features expressed the utmost astonishment. The rest of the people, about a hundred in number, pressed closer round the log, anxious to see the upshot of my singular conduct. At last I got up and addressed the chief.

'The great chief of the Ngatiparewahawaha,' I said, 'is kind to his friend. He has said that the name of Tiraweke is marked on his heart. He sees that his friend is tired with the long walk, and he does not wish to send him across the river till his legs are rested. It is good: Tiraweke will be a *manuhiri* (honoured guest) of Taratoa till he is strong to pursue his path. The great chief of Manawatu will clean out a house in his village for his visitor, and strew the floor with young fern. He will tell his wives and his slave-women to prepare the ovens, and to lay out a feast worthy of a great name. He will send his young men to the sea for fish, and to the fresh-water creeks for the fat eels of the swamp. He will gather the finest *kumara* from the gardens, and bid his guest get strong on the good food of the land. Tiraweke was a fool not to see into the heart of his brother. He will smoke his pipe for

two weeks in the village of the great chief, and will then carry
to Port Nicholson a story of a great name that has a great heart.
The white chiefs shall know the name of Taratoa. I have done.'

The greatest change was produced by this reflection on the
want of hospitality shown to one whom they had begun by pre-
tending to receive with honour. Shouts of admiration and loud
laughter at the turning of the tables burst from the crowd. The
women ran to the ovens; and the old chief, perfectly delighted at
finding that I had really earned my reputation among the natives
by a knowledge of their customs and feelings, laughed heartily, and
took me cordially by the hand. He insisted on my waiting till
some potatoes were roasted, and then had the canoe launched, and
put the basket of *kai* into it. He escorted me down to the water's
edge, and returned the money to me. 'I know you want to go on
now,' said he, 'or I would ask you to do in earnest what you
proposed in joke. I am much ashamed; but come back soon, and
pay me a long visit, that I may know you are not angry. Go to
Port Nicholson.' I often afterwards spent several days with this
chief at his various residences, and we have been ever since warm
friends.

We reached Otaki at night, after fording the Ohau, at half tide,
up to our chins. I remained two or three days in the house of
Sam Taylor, a European who had long resided in these parts; and
commenced an acquaintance with the Ngatiraukawa people.

They had entered into negotiations with Colonel Wakefield
for the sale of a large tract of land at the Manawatu. A formal
conference had been held here on the subject some time before,
when the chiefs of the Ngatiraukawa had derided and overthrown
objections raised by Rangihaeata to the purchase.

A schooner had carried the goods agreed upon to the Manawatu,
where they had been distributed. Some surveyors were already at
work there, and some more expected every day. Another vessel,
I was told, had carried the machinery of a steam saw-mill belonging
to a private settler there; and numerous landowners had paid visits
to the district. The natives were very anxious for the permanent
residence of a large body of white people among them.

Those of the Otaki natives who had become missionaries were
generally as well-behaved as the people of Pipiriki, though not so

extravagant in their observances; for Mr. Hadfield had managed very wisely to introduce Christianity by the authority of the young chiefs, and to make them consider the new doctrine as a cheerful rather than a saddening and moping innovation. He had introduced among them the growing of wheat; and generally inspired them with friendship towards the white colonists, instead of suspicion and jealousy. Many of them had lately visited Port Nicholson; peace having been at length restored, by Mr. Hadfield's unceasing efforts, between them and the Ngatiawa tribes who inhabited the intervening country. They had returned with the most favourable reports of the treatment which they had experienced from the settlers, and of the advantages to be derived from friendly relations and trade with the *pakeha.*

The increased traffic of white people along the beach had induced two whalers to fit up houses of accommodation for travellers at Waikanae and Te Uruhi, and Toms had built a new wooden house as an hotel at Paremata Point at Porirua. The bridle-road had been completed for some time; the bridges were repaired and the trees removed; and I walked easily in three hours and a half from the head of Porirua harbour to Wellington, where I arrived about the first week in March.

§

The whole five months during which I had been absent had only furnished more matter for complaint against our hostile governor.

Money was drawn in large quantities from Cook's Strait in order to be spent at Auckland. Not an erection of any kind, except a miserable pound, had been made or proposed by the government. The legislation for the colony was going on at a great distance from the principal body of those for whose benefit it was intended; so that no remonstrance or complaint could be heard by the council of the Auckland Pacha*.

I can imagine no position more despicable and wretched than that of one of the original settlers, who, having once fairly caught the 'Government fever', had to perform his unthankful office among his former associates. Perfectly acquiring the haughty repulsiveness of the troop which he had joined, he is doomed to lose the friendship and often even the very acquaintance of those who knew him and

* The reference is to Governor Hobson.

esteemed him in England, and were once partners with him in the noble work of early colonization. He appears to become tainted by the touch of the Auckland dross: he no longer revives old associations, or excites a feeling of sympathy in the minds of his independent fellow-settlers.

Few of the members of such young and frank communities as the Cook's Strait settlements will stoop to conceal their disgust by an outward show of politeness. They revere the motto that 'union is strength'; and the deserter from the bundle of sticks becomes, almost at once, a virtual outcast from good society. Though he may still be invited to large balls and dinner-parties, he seldom afterwards finds himself at the more familiar and friendly picnics, and impromptu dances, and pot-luck dinners. In such intimate society he would be an undoubted wet blanket; for some better man would probably leave the room when he came in, without attempting to disguise his aversion. He hardly walks along the beach but some two or three former friends gallop past him with an open sneer on their faces; and any one who does speak to him, of whatever rank, does it coldly and carefully, as though he dreaded that his words should be taken down and twisted into disaffection at the head-quarters of official enmity.

Notwithstanding all they had to complain of on the part of their rulers, the energetic band of colonists had made very great progress. Villages were in process of formation at two spots on the banks of the Hutt, by land-owners, who divided their sections into small allotments for sale or improving lease. They were named respectively 'Aglionby' and 'Richmond'.* Another village was rapidly being peopled on the country section immediately north of the town. This section, belonging jointly to Mr. Watt and John Wade the auctioneer, was divided off into one-acre and two-acre allotments. The proprietors constructed a dray-road up the steep side facing the harbour, which gave access to the sunny nooks and terracing flats on the N.W. slope; and then they put so many lots up to auction at once. Johnny Wade sold off many allotments at the rate of £20 per acre. And these were not speculating land-jobbing prices, for they were agreed upon by *bonâ fide* occupants,

---

* Both villages were on the west bank of the Hutt River between Railway Avenue and Wakefield Street, Lower Hutt.

chiefly labouring men, who had time given them in which to pay up their purchase-money. They used to work at their little patches of ground after their labour for the day was over; and Wade's Town, which had before looked a very bleak hill, of poor soil, and denuded of timber by the clearing of former years, soon boasted a population of 200 working people, whose neat cottages and smiling cultivations peeped from every nook among the picturesque hills, especially on the N.W. side, which is sheltered from the cold winds, and timbered in pretty patches, overlooking the velvet foliage of the Kaiwharawhara.

In the upland valley of Karori, too, several people had begun to clear. The road had not yet reached this, having to cross a steep part of the Kaiwharawhara valley; but the clearers used to find their way by an old Maori path, and live in the bush for days together. The valley is situated at the elevation of 700 or 800 feet above the level of the sea, about two miles S.W. of Wellington by the present road. The level land in it is about 1000 or 1200 acres, and this tract boasts the very finest *totara* and other timber.

Three wooden jetties now projected into the port at the south side of Lambton Harbour; and alongside of one of them a schooner of 70 tons had loaded the machinery of a steam saw-mill, destined for the banks of the Manawatu.

A fourth pier proved of much convenience opposite Barrett's hotel. It was built by subscription among the two or three people living on the adjoining section.

A small steam saw and flour mill had been at work in Wellington since the beginning of October, and was kept in constant and profitable employment.

A Horticultural Society had been formed, and had held its first show on the 24th of January. Although this period of the year, our warmest weather, was by no means the most favourable for the purpose, the exhibition had been most remarkable. Many new-comers who had been present told me that they had no idea before they saw this collection, chiefly of vegetables, of what could be produced.

Two cabbages grown on mere shingle at Petone, within thirty yards of the sea-beach, weighed respectively 21½ and 12 pounds, being a Hybrid and an early Fulham; although they were kept three weeks after arriving at perfection, in order to appear at the show.

Some of the kidney potatoes grown in the Hutt, from native seed, measured nine inches in length, and were of excellent quality. Specimens of the red flat turnip were shown 19 inches in circumference and weighing 2½ lb.; and of the common white turnip 21 inches in circumference and weighing 3 lb.

The wheat, with remarkably full and large ears, had a straw five feet seven inches in length.

Apples, the first fruits of trees imported from England, were exhibited.

Every other sort of vegetable figured in the list of prizes; and seedling geraniums and dahlias represented the flower-garden.

The supply of poultry was at this time very large. Almost every settler possessed a few, and some as many as two or three hundred head.

The statistics of the consumption of butcher's meat showed how substantially the colonists were already living; for a calculation made from the weekly consumption of pork, beef, and mutton, gave 148 lb. of meat per head, man, woman, and child, in the year. Indeed, it was notorious that no working man would sit down to breakfast without fresh pork; and that they very often ate mutton chops, at 9d. or 10d. per pound, three times a day.

Three hundred and two vessels had entered the port since the beginning of the settlement.

The number of cattle imported during the year 1841 was about 1000 head. Dr. Imlay, a large cattle-holder at Twofold Bay in New South Wales, had lately sent down some very valuable cargoes of a superior breed. Heifers from his stock, eighteen month old, had been sold by auction at £8 10s. per head.

Bricks were now plentifully supplied from several rival kilns; and many buildings were being erected of that material.

The whole of January and the first part of February had been remarkable for a long continuance of fine dry weather. During this space, however, light showers at night were frequent; and there were at no time more than nine days and nights entirely without rain. As this is just the grain harvest time in New Zealand, nothing could be more seasonable; and refreshing rains fell at the end of February to save the pasture on the hills from parching, and to keep the potato-crop from injury.

Mr. Stokes had made another excursion to the Wairarapa plain; and confirmed the former good accounts of its extent and capabilities.

Two landmarks had been put up at the heads of the harbour. One, a three-sided wooden pyramid with open sides, about seventy feet high, on Pencarrow Head, was blown down by a gale of wind soon after; this had been put up by public subscription. Another, on the highest peak between the mouth of the harbour and Lyall's Bay, was more securely fixed by Colonel Wakefield's orders, and remains in its place to this day. It consists of four ton butts, then three, then one, piled above each other, filled with stones and painted white, with a flag-staff on the top. I have distinguished this beacon with a glass from eight or ten miles to seaward.

The *Brougham,* after making a passage of 92 days last year to London with her cargo of oil and bone, had returned on the 9th of February with a new Chief Surveyor for the Company, Mr. Brees, who superseded Captain Smith. He was accompanied by a large suite of young gentlemen, engaged by the Company for three years as 'surveying cadets'. I had met two or three of these on the Porirua road when I came in to town, with labourers and theodolites, and other baggage, starting for the Manawatu. I remember laughing at their dandified appearance, and wondering what new arrivals had thus suddenly and without preparation taken to the bush. Everything about them was so evidently new—their guns just out of their cases, fastened across tight-fitting shooting-jackets by patent leather belts; their forage-caps of superfine cloth; and their white collars relieved by new black silk neckerchiefs. Some positively walked with gloves and dandy-cut trousers; and, to crown all, their faces shone with soap. There had been a little rain, too, the night before; and, having only got about two miles from the town, they were actually picking their way, and stepping carefully over muddy places. I sat down on the stump of a tree and vastly enjoyed the cockney procession; wondering how long the neatness of their appearance and the fastidiousness of their steps would last. They, on the other hand, stared at me, as though they had considered me one of the curiosities of the interior—

turning up their noses with evident contempt at my rough red woollen smock, belted over a coarse cotton check shirt, without neck-cloth, and stout duck trousers, and gaping with horror at my long hair, unshaven beard, and short black pipe, half-hidden under a broad-brimmed and rather dirty Manilla hat. They appeared, too, to view with some distrust a sheath-knife, about eighteen inches in the blade, which I had made my constant companion, and with which I was cutting up negro-head tobacco.

The mutual expressions of astonishment and derision depicted on the respective features of the old hand and the young muffs meeting in the bush would have been nuts to a painter wanting a new idea.

The British population of the Company's settlements was at this time about 5000, including 3000 at Wellington and in the immediate vicinity, 150 at Wanganui, 1000 at Nelson, 600 at New Plymouth, and 200 in other parts of Cook's Strait. Large additions to the Nelson population were expected immediately from England.

I cannot help quoting, from the Wellington newspaper of the 9th of March, the following description of the only Government buildings at Wellington:

'There are now about sixty prisoners in the Wellington gaol, chiefly mutinous or runaway sailors; but there are some felons, and one person at least confined for debt only. They are all huddled together in a wretched Maori building, large enough for twelve or fifteen human beings at the most.

'A decent building for a post-office is also especially required. On Sunday last we saw Mr. Mantell stuffing an old potato-sack amongst the reeds of the dilapidated hut he occupies as Postmaster, to prevent the wind from blowing the letters off the table on which he had assorted them for delivery.

There are no conveniences for the performance of his duties, and it is really unfair to expect regularity and despatch from a public officer to whom the commonest facilities for discharging his duties are denied.

'What makes the neglect of the Government to furnish a good police-office and post-office most discreditable and unjust, is the undoubted fact, that the Port Nicholson contributions to the public treasury amount to many thousands per annum. One-fifteenth part of the revenue collected here and remitted to Auckland would suffice for the buildings needed; but this cannot be had, because of the waste at Government-house and the numerous sinecures at the gulf of Hauraki.'

CHAPTER XV

First Steps at Nelson: Wairarapa
Exploration: Manawatu and Wanganui

ON THE 30th March, the *Martha Ridgway*, a large ship from London with immigrants for Nelson,* anchored at Point Halswell; and the Captain came in to receive his orders from the Company's agent and his consignees in Wellington. Being offered a passage by one of these gentlemen, who was himself going over in the ship, I packed up a small kit, and went on board with him in the pilot-boat. We sailed on the evening of the 31st.

After rounding Cape Stephens, we had made out clearly the entrance of Port Hardy, the southern mouth of the French Pass, which separates D'Urville's Island from the main, the islets at the mouth of Croisille's Harbour, and the bluff promontory formed by Pepin's Island. All this east side of the gulf is backed by high and rugged mountains. The land towards Massacre Bay† rose blue and clear over the distant horizon, until the haze and night closed in; but the low land at the southern end was not yet distinguishable, and the bay, looking like a broad strait, deserved the name of 'Blind' given to it by Captain Cook.

* The 'Nelson' squadron, under Captain Wakefield, had sailed from Port Nicholson on the 2nd of October; and, after visiting Kapiti, and obtaining from Rauparaha and Te Hiko a full acknowledgment that Blind Bay had been fairly bought, had proceeded to explore the coasts of that inlet. After some days' careful examination, a harbour had been discovered in the S.E. corner of the gulf, which had remained before unknown even to many of the white whalers and boatmen who had traded for years in the neighbourhood. Three or four large emigrant ships had called at Port Nicholson to know their destination, and then proceeded with pilots provided by the Company's agent, to the new port. Several coasting-craft now kept up a constant communication with Nelson; whose inhabitants were described as proceeding with great vigour in the work of location. A newspaper was already published there.

† i.e., Tasman's 'Murderers' Bay'. The modern name is Golden Bay.

In the morning, which was calm and cloudless, we found our-selves lying about half-way between Pepin's Island and the entrance of Nelson Haven, and about two miles off shore. The vessels in the harbour and the buildings on the beach had a curious appearance over the low bank of boulders which forms the harbour.

This curious bank, of no great breadth, and raised but few feet above the highest tides, which indeed wash over it in some low spots, runs along parallel with the land for about six miles, thoroughly sheltering a space, which averages a quarter of a mile in width, from the force of the sea.

Our anchorage was outside the bar. In the inner pool is excellent anchorage, as in stormy weather the sea is broken by the bar. The *Bolton*, a ship of 500 tons, lay here when we arrived, and the anchorage was in consequence called Bolton Roads. From thence the navigation to the inner haven requires a practised pilot; as the tides are exceedingly rapid, and the channel very narrow.

A little way inside we saw a group of wooden houses, tents, rough booths, and sheds, disposed about a small hollow in the side of the hill; and Captain Wakefield greeted us as we jumped out of the boat.

The eastern shore of the haven is formed, for a mile from its entrance, by a low steep ridge of hills that are bare of wood. But, beyond this, the haven expands to the eastward into a broad space, which is a lake when covered by the tide, and a mud flat at other times, intersected by the branching channels of a small river called the Maitai. An amphitheatre of about 1000 acres, shelving from the southern shore of this lagoon to the base of abrupt mountains on the east and south-east, seems made for the site of a town; and here Nelson is situated. It is only separated from the entrance of the haven by the ridge of hills which I have mentioned; and a path over its summit forms a short cut between the haven and the town.

The little village was all life and gaiety. Two large wooden stores and a house for immigrants, belonging to the Company, were the centre of business, as labourers came for their rations, or rolled casks and bales into the store. The *Lord Auckland* was discharging immigrants on the beach; the two Deal boats of the Company were being launched or hauled up by their weather-beaten crews,

S. C. Brees. Engraving

MAORI *PA* AT PIPITEA POINT

S. C. Brees. Engraving

COLONEL WAKEFIELD'S HOUSE. On the site of wooden portion of Parliament Buildings

or making trips to the shipping; and knots of whalers, who had come on a cruise to the new settlement, were loitering about on the scattered cannon, ploughs, and cart-wheels. Among these beach-combing wanderers, I recognized many old acquaintances. Some of these eccentric characters seemed curiously divided between contempt for the inexperience of the 'jimmy-grants', as they called the immigrants, and surprise at the general industry and bustle prevailing. The cloudless weather, hotter than I had yet felt it in New Zealand, and the vivacity of the scene, made one think that races or a fair was going on, rather than a serious settlement. All seemed affected by the bright blue sky and lovely scenery around. In the midst of the toil and confusion of landing goods, and looking for relations in the crowd, every countenance beamed with good humour and enjoyment. The very whalers would now and then condescend to show an awkward clodhopper the handiest way of hauling a package up the sloping beach. But few natives figured in the scene, as this spot had not been inhabited for many years.

Near the highest point of the path between the haven and the town was pitched the small square tent in which Captain Wakefield slept. From hence he had only a few steps to walk to the flag-staff, where he communicated with the shipping by means of Marryat's signals; and he was conveniently placed for going to whichever location required his presence.

In the midst of the great amphitheatre was a low isolated mound. Here a long range of wooden houses served as hospital, survey-office, and emigration-barracks; and a constant stream of immigrants, with their bundles, was flowing either way between the summit of this small Acropolis and the nearest point of the lagoon to which the tide would allow the large boats to ascend the channel of the Maitai. Wooden houses, tents, sheds formed of boughs, frames of clay walls and thatched roof, and heaps of goods and chattels of various kinds, were scattered over different parts of the flat. Here and there a newly-arrived party might be seen cutting a square encampment out of the high fern, and erecting their sheds and gipsy fires in the space thus formed. But the principal cluster of the population was along the banks of the Maitai, and on the edge of the wood.

The long straight lines cut by the surveyors through the fern gave an odd appearance to the landscape; and along these glades short posts were stuck into the ground at regular intervals, branded with the numbers of the sections on either side, in readiness for the approaching selection. As I walked along these future streets, quail, either single or in coveys, frequently started up before my steps. They abound all over this part of New Zealand.

During the month that I remained here, the climate was certainly magnificent. There were only three or four days' rain; and the rest of the time cloudless skies and calm air glowed upon the landscape. If I had any complaint to make, it was that I thought it too dry and hot in the day-time; and that the nights were on the contrary very cold, when a light air breathed down from the lofty peaks inland. But I remembered that all these things are to be judged by comparison, and that I had just come from the more temperate tract of land near Wellington, which receives its temperature from a sea-breeze, whichever of the prevailing winds may blow.

The climate in this deep bight of a bay is very remarkable. The wind, which blows almost incessantly one way or the other through Cook's Strait, seems suddenly to lose its power before reaching the southern part of Blind Bay. Thus it is common for a vessel to be under double-reefed topsails in the Strait, and to have her sails all flapping in a calm soon after she has passed D'Urville's Island or Massacre Bay. And I frequently observed that the speed and direction of the scud overhead, and driving masses of black clouds on the northern horizon, indicated a storm outside, when all near Nelson lay calm and slumbering, except a heavier swell than usual rolling on to the shoals at the bottom of the gulf. And in those cases, a little coaster, which had been out in the gale, would confirm our conjectures on arriving a day or two later. During the month, I saw only one day on which it blew a hard breeze; and then two large vessels rode it out in perfect safety in the anchorage outside the bar, although the wind was nearly due north. Now and then a light sea-breeze would bring welcome refreshment for two or three hours during the afternoon. This very remarkable immunity from wind causes an almost incredible difference between the climate of Nelson and that of Wellington, although the two towns are as nearly as possible in the same latitude.

The *Hope*, a vessel of 400 tons from Sydney, had already landed about 100 head of cattle at Nelson. While I was there, the *Brilliant*, of 300 tons, arrived from Twofold Bay with horses and cattle. Dr. Imlay himself was a passenger on board, having come to take a look at the settlements in New Zealand, and to place on a permanent footing the importation of his stock into the country.

I saw only from a distance the valleys of the Waimea and Moutere rivers, in which most of the cultivation near Nelson is now going on, as I had not time to explore any further than the immediate neighbourhood of the town.

Coal and limestone had already been found in large quantities on the shores of Massacre Bay; and a coaster had brought some tons of each article into the harbour. A road was being made by the Company's labourers, round the foot of the dividing ridge, from the haven to the town. In the course of this work they struck at one spot upon a small vein of coal; but this was not found worth working. Coal has since been put on board vessels in Massacre Bay at 10s. per ton, and sold in Nelson at from 27s. to 30s.

The selection of the town-lands at Nelson took place while I was there. I was forcibly struck by the strong colonizing character, if I may so speak, which distinguished the great majority of the leading settlers at Nelson. They seemed to have entered upon their noble task rather with a wish to share in doing good to their poorer fellow-colonists, than with selfish and interested views. A generous and active spirit of benevolence pervaded each thought, each feeling, and action. Most of them were young men of superior education and intellect.

Their gallant ranks have been cruelly thinned by misfortune, and principally by the crowning catastrophe at Wairau. But, in future days, the citizens of Nelson will always remember with pride and sorrow the names of William Curling Young, George Ryecroft Richardson, Patchett, Cotterell, and others now no more, who assisted the first steps of the infant settlement with their manly energies.

If I speak of my own lamented uncle, Arthur Wakefield, to say that he watched over their united efforts and guided their expanding strength as though they had been one family and he their father or their elder brother, it is because I feel sure of being supported to the whole extent of the statement by every colonist who was under his care.

Dr. Imlay had to take some of his cattle on to Wellington, and I accepted his kind offer of a passage in the *Brilliant*. We were baffled for some days off the heads of Port Nicholson by strong northerly breezes, the vessel being very light, and therefore unable to make much progress to windward; but we at length anchored in Lambton Harbour on the 1st of May.

On April 22nd, Mr. Spain, the long-expected Land Commissioner, had at length arrived. He was accompanied by Mr. George Clarke, junior, a son of the Chief Protector of Aborigines, who had been appointed in January Sub-Protector of the Aborigines, and was deputed to watch their interests, especially during the investigations before the Court.

[*Wakefield resumes his narrative after giving a long account of Mr. Spain's investigation of the New Zealand Company's land claims.*]

Nothing could be more encouraging than the mild climate and the unceasing bounty of nature during these winter months. In May, which answers to the chill and foggy November of England, peas were in full bloom, small salads in every stage of growth, and almost all vegetation unchecked by the season. It was likened by Scotchmen to the second month of spring in their former land. No matter how bare, exposed, or rough the spot of ground, excellent vegetables could be produced by the most careless cultivation. The wild pasture on the hills had improved wonderfully under the constant browsing and tread of the cattle. Grass was replacing the fern all over the barren-looking hills that were clear of timber; and in riding after cattle, many spots could hardly be recognized, owing to the great change that had taken place.

Towards the end of May, a sudden melting of the snows on the Tararua range had caused rather a high flood in the valley of the Hutt; and in the middle of June there were a few days of rough gales and heavy rains.

The little steam-mill was grinding and sawing incessantly; several experiments were on foot for inventing machines to prepare the *phormium tenax;* and a brewery was already established, although the hops had yet to be imported from Sydney.

The Mechanics' Institute was in active operation, and lectures were delivered weekly on various subjects to respectable and attentive audiences.

§

About the middle of June, Mr. Charles Kettle, who had been performing the duties of Assistant-Surveyor to the Company at Manawatu, returned to Wellington from an exploring journey into the interior.

He was accompanied by Mr. Alfred Wills, one of the cadets, and a small party of labourers to carry provisions and baggage; and one of the principal chiefs of the Ngatiraukawa, named Ahu, with some members of his family and two or three slaves, had acted as guides to the expedition.

They had ascended the Manawatu to a considerable distance above the gorge between the Tararua and Ruahine ranges, which I have before spoken of as described to me by Jack Duff the trader. Striking to the east and south, they left the river, and crossed some of the low ridges in which the N.E. extremity of the Tararua terminates; and from thence saw a vast extent of *mania*, or grass plain country, interspersed with groves of timber, and watered by the tributaries of the Manawatu, of the rivers which descend into Hawke's Bay, and of the Ruamahanga, which flows into the sea at Wairarapa, or Palliser Bay.

They saw the main branch of the Manawatu stretching towards the North, along the N.E. base of the Ruahine range. The natives told them that it took its rise in the gorges between that and the Kaimanawa range, whose northern extremity abuts on Lake Taupo, and that a canoe might proceed for three weeks further up its course.

Where they left, the Manawatu river was about 90 miles, by its windings, from the sea. But its course is exceedingly tortuous; so much so, that the natives have a legend that it was formed by an *atua*, or evil spirit, who was in the form of a large *totara* tree, and wormed himself along like an eel on his way from the east coast to Cook's Strait.

The expedition now descended the ridge into the upper part of the Ruamahanga or Wairarapa plain, and proceeded along its eastern side, crossing many tributaries of the river which flows down its centre, until they reached a village of the Ngatikahungunu tribe.

After being received very hospitably by these people, they proceeded to the southward, keeping about halfway between the base of the eastern spurs of the Tararua and the main river.

Mr. Kettle described the country between the Manawatu and the Ruamahanga plain as alternate forest and fern land, and conceived that the ridges might have been entirely avoided, had they made a circuit round their north-eastern extremities. Thus, the plain of the upper Manawatu was evidently in easy connexion with those so often described by various travellers about the country which opens on to Hawke's Bay, and also with the vast plain of the Ruamahanga. And through the gorge of the Manawatu, this immense tract of available and almost uninhabited country may be connected with that which lies between Cook's Strait and the Ruahine and Tararua ranges, and around Mount Egmont as far north as Mokau.

Although the party suffered severely from the weather, which was constantly wet at this season of the year where they were travelling, round the spurs of one of the great dividing ranges of the island, yet all concurred in describing the plain of Ruamahanga as a most delightful tract of country.

The plain was described as 60 miles in length, from the ridges which separate it from the upper Manawatu to the sea; and of an average width of 12 miles between the Puketoi range, which divided it from the east coast, and the Tararua range, and that long spur of it the Rimutaka, which lies between the Hutt and the Ruamahanga.

The Wairarapa lake, 10 miles in length, and averaging two in width, fills up the lower part of the plain.

They failed in two successive attempts to discover a passable path over the Rimutaka; and endured considerable hardship from the continued heavy rains among the hills, and from the want of food experienced since they had left the plain, where the numerous pigeons, and an occasional pig caught from the wild herds whose traces they were constantly observing, had for some days supplied them. A third attempt, ascending the Rimutaka nearly due west of the middle of the lake, was more successful; and they found their way to the head of the Pakuratahi, a small tributary of the Hutt running northward for five miles. It joins the Hutt about 15 miles from the beach at Petone. Descending the courses of the tributary and the main stream, they at length arrived at the house of Mr. Mason, the most distant out-settler in the lower valley of the Hutt,* on the 7th of June, thirty-two days after they had started from the survey station at the Manawatu.

They arrived half starved and nearly worn out with fatigue, with but a few rags left on their backs. I met some of them on the road between Wellington and Petone the same evening; and they certainly did look most miserable objects, although they had procured a change of clothing from their friends on the Hutt.

Great credit was due to them for the perseverance which they had shown in attaining their object. They started from the survey station with only a week's provisions; and had only the clothes on their backs when they left the Manawatu, after paying the natives who had poled the canoes up. More than once, the men and the natives had despaired of reaching Wellington, after repeatedly losing their way in the eastern gorges of the Rimutaka; and during several days before reaching the settlements, they had lived on the wild cabbages which they found near the banks of the river. But Mr. Kettle had encouraged them to proceed, by his example as well as his cheerful spirit. Wet through during nearly the whole journey, and lying on the damp ground every night exposed to heavy rains, with the scantiest covering, not a single member of the party, however, suffered any injury to his health; and after a few days' good feeding at Wellington, natives and white men were all as fresh and hearty as ever.

Mr. Kettle's expedition was of great importance, as proving that an immense district of land of the finest character lay in the immediate neighbourhood of Wellington, and must eventually be dependent on the harbour of Port Nicholson for import and export.

It had the advantage of being almost unoccupied; the population of the solitary *pa* being very small, while another scanty tribe lived entirely on the narrow strip of land between Lake Wairarapa and the sea.

* (at Belmont.)

12

Mr. Kettle described the plain of Ruamahanga as resembling in appearance a vast English park on a magnified scale. Alternate tracts of the finest primæval forest, and of pasture-land covered with mixed fern and grass and small shrubs, lay between the numerous streams which are tributary to the Ruamahanga river.

We knew already, since the bridle-road had been made, how easy was the communication, both by land and by sea, with the tract of level land bordering on Cook's Strait, and extending towards Mokau. And it was foreseen that no insurmountable obstacle existed to the formation of roads from the Hutt, over the Rimutaka range, into the plain of the Ruamahanga. To complete the compactness of the district surrounding the little mountainous tract in which lie Port Nicholson and the valley of the Hutt on all sides but the south, the communication between the eastern and western plains was established by the Manawatu to the north of the Tararua range. And the idea, which had been at one time so prevalent, that New Zealand was a very mountainous and rugged country, began to be dispelled. Everybody now acknowledged that the comparatively level and easily accessible country far surpassed the difficult and impracticable part in extent.

§

I made the acquaintance of the chief Ahu [Mr. Kettle's guide] during his stay of two or three weeks in Wellington, and joined him when he returned to his own residence on the Ohau river, as I was again bound for Wanganui.

This old chief is of the highest rank in the Ngatiraukawa tribe, being of an older branch than even Whatanui, though of the same family. He had taken an eager part in the selling of Manawatu to Colonel Wakefield; being exceedingly anxious to obtain for his people the same advantages which were enjoyed by the natives in Port Nicholson from the proximity of a white settlement.

I found him very fond of his rank and conscious of his authority as a great chief; but he had acquired many repulsive qualities as a cruel and merciless warrior, and a considerable share of arrogance and insolence from his early dealings with the rude traders and visitors of the time before us. His character and that of his family is best expressed by the names given to them by those of that rough class who were most acquainted with them. They called Ahu 'The Badger', and Wara and Te Wainuku, his two nearest male relations, 'The Bully' and the 'The Sneak'.

He was easily impressed, however, with the behaviour which he must adopt in order to make himself agreeable to gentlemen. Whether by his conciliating manner towards them, or by the mere fact of his having bought the land and held out hopes that they should have white men amongst them, 'Wide-awake' had become a great favourite with the chiefs of the Ngatiraukawa during his negotiation with them at Otaki. Ahu, who had received ample payment for his men employed in 'Wide-awake's' service, and who had enjoyed the unlimited hospitality of his house at Wellington, seemed determined to show me his gratitude, and always behaved to me as one chief to another.

I was witness to a curious scene on the way. Having walked much faster than the natives, I got a boat at the end of the road, and arrived by myself at Toms's inn at Paremata. Rangihaeata was there, very noisy, asking for spirits as usual; and he requested me to buy him a large quantity, in so arrogant a tone that I refused in rather a decided manner.

He then went on storming about the land; saying that 'Wide-awake' and I should not have any more; that Porirua was not paid for, and that he would never let white people come and live there. He asked whether we wanted it all, that we were so greedy; and said he would never sell it unless he received 'money gold' in casks as high as he could reach. I did not attempt to answer him, as he was much excited with drink, and indeed gave one no opportunity of putting in a word. As he was going out, after finding that I sat still smoking without listening to his bullying and insulting diatribe, I observed that I had been 'all ears, because he was all mouth', and that 'two mouths could not talk where one filled the house'; which amused some of his own followers.

I found him calmer in the *pa* some little time afterwards, and he asked me whether Ahu was coming after me. When I answered that he was, he ran on about Manawatu, and Wanganui, and Taranaki, and all the land being his everywhere; and said he was very angry with the Ngatiraukawa for having sold Manawatu.

'You shall see,' said he, 'how I will *boo-boo-boo* at Ahu about it when he comes'; meaning how he could 'bounce'. I answered very quietly, 'It is good. I will look when the chiefs begin to speak.'

I had a great idea that Rangihaeata would *boo-boo-boo* in vain; for I knew that he had tried to prevent the sale by every argument in his power, both here, when the first surveyors went to Manawatu, accompanied by two or three chiefs of the Ngatiraukawa, and also at the great conference at Otaki, when the sale was finally agreed to; but that Puke and several other of the Ngatiraukawa had laughed at all that he said, and told him to go away, for he had nothing to do with it.

Rangihaeata, however, kept showing me the grimaces of defiance which he meant to make when Te Ahu should come. And the slaves and attendants were all chuckling, and explaining to me every now and then that he was exceedingly angry. I took no notice of all this, till Te Ahu arrived in a canoe which had been sent for him. I then told him of the threat which Rangihaeata had made. He gave a low laugh, and said to me, 'Be a looker-on!'

The greeting was a mixture of friendliness and distant pride, although the two chiefs were very nearly related. Clean fern was strewn in two places, on opposite sides of the court-yard in the midst of the filthy little *pa* which is close to Toms's house. On one of these *whariki*, or 'strewings', Rangihaeata was sitting in state with all his attendants. The visitors were motioned to the other.

While the meal of hospitality was cooking in the iron pots, Rangihaeata rose to speak. His words were a mere repetition of what he had roared in my ears. He began by tracing his own descent and history, and saying all the land was his, and that the white men were greedy and wanted to take it all. The story about the casks of 'money gold' followed. He then warmed gradually up, and spoke louder and more wildly, as he rebuked Te Ahu for having sold Manawatu of his own accord, without consulting him, who was the real owner, and for having invited white men to go and live there. But his speech was moderate and his manner tame compared with what his boasting had led me to expect; although they still partook largely of that bullying tone and undignified character from which his behaviour was never free.

Te Ahu then rose up, and answered him in few, but calm and convincing words. 'You have said that all the land is yours,' said he; 'I do not know; perhaps it is. You relate as an evil deed that I took upon myself to sell Manawatu to the white man. You say that it was not straight. Look at me! I Te Ahu sold Manawatu. I alone, of my own accord. I came not to consult you. I was not good to do so; I am still not good to do so. I care not for your thoughts on the matter. You have described your pedigree and spoken much of your great name. I too had ancestors and a father. I have a name. It is enough; I have done.'

No one ventured to answer this claim, which I believe was true, to a higher descent than that of Rangihaeata; whose fame was derived rather from his constant companionship with Rauparaha, and his bullying and boastful demeanour, than from his rank by blood.

In the morning they seemed very good friends; and we proceeded to Pukerua rather late. We reached that *pa* towards dusk, and had just eaten our meal when the missionary bell rang for prayers. Te Ahu immediately got up, and told the boys to shoulder their loads. He said he could never sleep in this village, as he knew the people would sing hymns and talk '*hanga noa iho*', or nonsense, all night. So we encamped under a natural arch of rock about a mile further along the beach. I rolled myself up in a robe of opossum-skins from New South Wales, and picked out a spot in the shingly beach pretty free from rocky protuberances.

At Wanganui, things were but little altered with the unfortunate little band of settlers. They were living on, however, by means of their gardens and some barter with the natives. Numerous attempts to obtain possession of sections on various spots in the district had failed. The most friendly professions of those who offered to put settlers in possession for a consideration had proved hollow and of no avail; for, after the settler had begun his operations, some new claimant would start up and interrupt, threaten, and bully, till the unfortunate sectionist was obliged to abandon his intentions and put up with his first loss, as the man with whom he had made the bargain generally retired upon the appearance of the new claimant.

I had come hither to break up my establishment, and to pull

down my house; as I wished to show the natives that I considered they had, as a body, broken faith with me. I reminded them that they had pressed me to go to Port Nicholson and bring them payment for the land, and white men; and that they had returned my acceptance of their invitation by not leaving the white men land on which to grow their food. Kuru was much grieved at my decision, but acknowledged its justice. Rangitauwira came from his settlement on purpose to beg me not to pull the house down. He pointed out the rafters which he had himself cut out, and related the history of the *totara* trees from which they were formed. He said, with tears in his eyes, that it would be a bad word for Wanganui that I should pull down 'Whare Wikitoria' because the natives had told lies. But he allowed that I had every right to retreat with anger and indignation from the place; and he regretted that I had not followed his advice, of covering the land with white people immediately after the sale, 'before the slippery hearts of the Maori had had time to change'.

I sold all my goods and chattels by auction; and in about three days afterwards the house was levelled to the ground by my gang of boys.

I have omitted to state, that the laying out of a town at Wanganui, in quarter-acre sections, had been approved by the directors of the Company; and a selection had taken place, every alternate town-section being reserved for the Company. The town was named after Lord Petre, who was a most unfailing friend of the colony in England, and one of the directors of the Company.

On my way back to Port Nicholson, I was accompanied by Kuru and a large train of his relatives. The chief wished to see Colonel Wakefield and Mr. Spain.

CHAPTER XVI

Te Rauparaha Makes Trouble : Elections : Races : Puffers and Grumblers

AT WAIKANAE, Te Rauparaha told me that he had resolved to prevent the white people from spreading any further up the valley of the Hutt, as it belonged to him, and he had not been paid for it. I rather laughed at this at first, as I did not see how he could stop it. I knew that he had never visited Port Nicholson, because he was still afraid of the Ngatiawa, whom he had so often threatened to invade. Frequently when I had pressed him to pay us a visit there, to come to 'Wide-awake's' house, and make acquaintance with the *rangatira* or 'chiefs' of the white people, he had answered snappishly, that he had nothing to do with the white people at Poneke, and that if he were to go the natives would all say he had gone to beg.

He now told me that he had sent a number of his people over to clear land and settle in the Hutt, and that 'Dog's Ear', or Taringakuri, from Kaiwharawhara, had agreed to go and join them in this object. I was somewhat startled to hear that the obstruction was likely to begin so near home from a totally new quarter, and hardly believed what he told me.

On arriving at Port Nicholson, however, I found it was true enough. A large party of stranger natives had been for some time clearing a large extent of land on the banks of the river Hutt, and preventing settlers from occupying other parts, which they stated it was their intention to clear. They kept up a constant communication with Porirua, by means of a path over the dividing ridge which leads to the north arm of Porirua harbour. They had first come over soon after my departure with Te Ahu.

Taringakuri had settled immediately in the neighbourhood of Mr. William Swainson, the eminent entomologist; and his people had begun to clear the forest indiscriminately on a section of which Mr. Swainson had taken a lease, and on which he had commenced cultivation.

I met 'Dog's Ear' shortly after my arrival; and he coolly began to abuse Rauparaha and Rangihaeata just as usual, saying that they were very bad to drive white people off land which they had sold; and that now they had begun to do the same on the Hutt, to which they had no right. He was surprised to find that I did not greet him or make any answer, and ran for some distance along by the side of my horse, asking why I was angry with him. I told him that he and the two great enemies of the white people were of one heart, and that he too had begun to break his faith and to drive the settlers off the land. He stoutly denied it, and said that he had only gone to grow potatoes for the white people for one season, when he would come away. But he was astonished when I told him that my ears had received the whole story from Rauparaha himself, and that I knew him to be that chief's obedient servant. He acknowledged that he had told me a lie, but did not seem at all abashed. On the contrary, he treated it as a good joke, and tried to laugh it off, repeating that he only went for a time, and all for the good of the white people.

The Maori generally are singular on this point. They have little shame in telling a lie; and it is no insult among them to tell a man that he is *tito*, or a liar. It even takes some time to make them understand that no deeper insult can be offered to a white man. The same word *tito* is also applied to improviso or inventive singing; and a famous poet among them is thus renowned as a 'great liar'. They are generally amused at the ingenuity of the person who proves to them that they have failed to conceal the truth, but are seldom ashamed or confused at the public exposure of their falsehood. A very few, like Kuru and Te Puni, have an idea of that sense of honour which makes lying one of the worst crimes which an English gentleman can commit. But I always considered these men startling exceptions, in many points of character, to the generality of their countrymen.

On the 5th of July, an 'awful conflagration' had taken place.

The building which had so long done duty as Police-office, Post-office, Court of Justice, and Church, took fire, and was burnt to the ground in half an hour. Fortunately, Mr. Halswell and the Police Magistrate had for a long while doubted the security of the edifice, and kept their documents at their respective homes; some carpenters who were at work near the spot saved what was lying or blowing about in the post-office corner of the rickety hut; and the whole damage done was estimated at nearly *five pounds!*

On the 9th July, a rather smart shock of an earthquake was felt.

A schooner of 10 tons was launched this month, which had been built to the order of Richard Davis, the native teacher. He invited several of the settlers to a well-managed fête which he gave on the occasion.

Next to the building-yard whence this vessel had glided into the water, a man from Deal was driving a very profitable trade in the construction of whale-boats. The competition at the stations was now so great that speed became an indispensable quality; and six-oared and seven-oared boats were fast adopted. This man's boats got a reputation all over the coast; and I have often been told by the most experienced headsmen that they were far superior to any which they got from Sydney or from the whaling-ships.

On the 13th of August, two settlers from New Plymouth arrived in Wellington by land, to make arrangements for buying and forwarding some cattle to Taranaki.

The general progress of that settlement was described as most satisfactory. Everybody spoke in ecstasies of the country and climate. But the natives had given considerable trouble, and had only been checked by very decisive measures.

During this and the last month, whales had been more than once seen inside the harbour at Port Nicholson. Inefficient crews, with incomplete apparatus, had sallied out in chase from the beach, but had proved unsuccessful. I remember one party of amateurs pulling out a long way, furnished with such a harpoon as small porpoises are speared with, and about 20 yards of line. It was probably fortunate for them that they did not get a chance of tickling the whale with their harmless weapon.

Since the destruction of the barn-of-all-work, the Church of England congregation had met in a house occupied by the Mechanics'

Institute, inside the public reserve on which Colonel Wakefield's house stood. At this time, the Scotch Presbyterian congregation met in the Exchange, and the Wesleyan congregation in a large store closely adjoining.

Early in September, Mr. W. Deans, who had formed one of the exploring party which travelled by land from Wellington to Taranaki about two years before, returned from a trip to the east coast of the Middle Island. He was so pleased with the district near Port Cooper, which had been described by Messrs. Daniell and Duppa, that he began making preparations for squatting there with a herd of cattle. He had been cultivating, in the interval, a patch of some 10 acres at a place called Okiwi, nearly abreast of Ward Island on the east shore of the harbour, but wished for a more extended field of operations. In the course of the next two months he disposed of his lease and improvements, and fulfilled his intentions. He visited Port Nicholson towards the end of the next year, and spoke in raptures of the country where he had been living. He was in quiet possession of a vast tract of rich pasture, where he could ride about and see his cattle increase and prosper rapidly; and he soon returned to his chosen location, disgusted with the tangled web of difficulties in which he found his old fellow-settlers still involved.

News came from Auckland that Captain Hobson was too ill to see any one, and even unable to affix his signature to a written answer. This was indeed his death-illness; for on the 28th of September, the Government brig, bringing the Chief Justice to hold a sitting of the Supreme Court at Wellington, bore the news of the Governor's death on the 10th of that month.

In the virtues of private life, the first Governor of New Zealand was allowed by all to have been exemplary. He was carried off by the same harassing and enfeebling disease, of which the first symptoms had appeared on his earliest arrival to assume his office. Let the blame of the evils which were gathered for the country during his reign fall on the worthless advisers who did not scruple to presume on the weak state of his bodily and mental faculties.

And the colonists listened anxiously for his first words.

On the 3rd of October, the election took place for the Aldermen and Mayor of the borough of Wellington.

S. C. Brees Engraving

NEW PLYMOUTH, about 1845

S. C. Brees. Engraving

PORIRUA HARBOUR. From the site of the Taupo *Pa*

Ever since the proclamation of the borough in August, great excitement had prevailed on this subject.

The Act provided that all male inhabitants should be entitled to register their votes with the Sub-Sheriff by paying one pound sterling each: 350 availed themselves of this privilege.

The usual competition took place between the gentry and the working men. Each party formed a committee, which suggested a list of aldermen for election, held meetings, and canvassed voters.

Placards, advertisements, electioneering cards and squibs, were in as great profusion as on the occasion of a contested election for a borough in England.

On the day of poll, flags and a band of music paraded the beach with some of the popular candidates; distinctive cockades were worn; and the straw hut inside the *pa*, generally used as a police-office, but now as the booth of the returning officer, was surrounded by agents of both parties, eager to force cards with their own list into the hands of each voter as he arrived.

All the usual tricks and intrigues were resorted to; and bribery, in the shape of glasses of grog, was largely at work. But notwithstanding many such tricks, the 'gentry' secured a very good Council, and the aldermen might be held to represent the community very fairly.

At the top of the poll, and therefore first Mayor of Wellington, was Mr. George Hunter, one of the early colonists from England. The other eleven aldermen were elected in the following order: Mr. William Lyon, a shopkeeper; Mr. Fitzherbert, a merchant and auctioneer from England; Johnny Wade, the auctioneer and man of the people; George Scott, a thriving, industrious, and well-educated carpenter; Mr. Molesworth; Dr. Dorset, who had been in our early expedition; Robert Waitt, William Guyton, and Abraham Hort, the three principal merchants of the town; Edward Johnson, a wholesale and retail shopkeeper; and Robert Jenkins, a publican from New South Wales.

The most extraordinary elevation was perhaps that of Robert Jenkins. He had come in one of the vessels from Sydney at the same time as the first colonists from England. Soon after the move to Thorndon, he bought a barrel of beer, and set it on tap in a miserable little hut on the beach. He had then crept on from one thing to the other, until he had a pretty neat grog-shop, with the sign of the 'New Zealander'. When the town sections were given out, he took a lease of part of one of the most valuable sections near Te Aro, and built on it a large brick house, which quite looked down upon the wooden cottage beside it in which the bank was situated. Here he did a thriving business; having his bar full of boatmen and sailors, whalers, bullock-drivers, stockmen, and others of the thirsty class, and a neat parlour in which commercial transactions and sales of cattle and horses were often concluded over a jug of beer. At length he built extensive stables, with four stalls and five loose boxes; speculated a little in buying cattle and setting up a butcher next door to him; took in horses to livery and to be broken in; and became the owner of considerable property both in land and stock. When I left, he was paying a rent of £20 a year for 100 acres of hill-pasture near the town; had made an excellent road up the steepest hill in the neighbourhood to his section; had fenced in half of it; and had a fine troop of brood mares running on the farm.

'Old Jenkins', as he is generally called, is quite a character. He can suit his conversation and manners to any class of society, and there is not a gentleman in Wellington who will not willingly chat over the news of the day with him at the door of his tavern, and often be glad to profit by his experience and knowledge of the world. For, although of unknown origin, and ignorant even of writing, he has many sterling qualities. Though a public-house keeper, he is an absolute observer of temperance without having taken the pledge; and he can boast an uncommon share of vigour, manly independence, and public spirit. He is one of those men who must be in a new community to obtain the estimation which they deserve.

A grand race had been appointed to come off on the 20th of October on the beach at Petone. Nine of the best horses had been entered some months before at 10 guineas each; and now all was the bustle of preparation. The horses were in regular training; jockey jackets and caps were in process of manufacture; top-boots and whips were actively sought after; and betting-books were pulled out at the hotels, at the club, and at other lounges.

I had been appointed Clerk of the Course; and rode over the

day before with 'Old Jenkins', the most active Steward, to superintend the putting up of the necessary posts on the course. A day
had been selected on which a very low spring-tide would leave
a hard sandy beach uncovered; and the distance was about a mile
and three-quarters, from the mouth of the Hutt to Petone *pa*.
It poured with rain on the 19th, and we augured badly for the
weather on the next day. Mr. Molesworth's house, where I spent
the night, was full of sporting characters, including two or three
of the gentlemen riders for the next day, very busy drying themselves after the soaking they had got in coming from town.

In the morning, the village of Aglionby, on the opposite side
of the river, was in an uncommon state of agitation; the stable-
yard of the neat little inn was full of grooms and horses; and
clodhoppers, dressed in their best, were coming down the path
along the river-bank, with their wives and children; for a general
holiday had been agreed upon.

By dint of begging and borrowing, I had managed to dress
myself out in very great style for the performance of my duties;
and when I rode out of the inn-yard in full Clerk-of-the-Course's
uniform, the pink coat—the only one in the colony, belonging to
Mr. Watt—excited universal admiration. I was thinking to myself
at the time, how awkwardly I should be situated if every one were
to claim his own on the course.

Soon after I had seen that the course was in due order—here
and there getting a large pebble or a glass bottle picked out of
the sand, and begging Te Puni to have the natives' dogs carefully
tied up and to keep the pigs at home—the company began to
arrive from Wellington. Carts, waggons, bullock-drays, were all
pressed into the service to-day, and the line of road was a miniature
representation of that to Epsom. Six or eight of the ladies came
over in a spring-cart containing chairs covered with flags; and the
only gig in Wellington, an importation from New South Wales,
brought over the chemist of Medical Hall and two other shopkeepers. One waggon contained the band of music; and a large
flotilla of boats, of all shapes and sizes, brought over those who
had no carts or horses or were too lazy to walk. Booths, tents,
and stalls were rapidly put up; and one man wheeled a barrow
about selling 'ginger-pop'.

The 'coming in' was close to Colonel Wakefield's old house; and there a cold collation had been provided for the ladies. The grand stand consisted of a few planks on the top of eight or ten water-butts outside the fence, supporting the chairs out of the carts.

And now my duties began to multiply. Here I had to explain to a party of natives why they could not lie basking on the middle of the beach; there to beg a party of whalers to haul their boat right up or push her nose off the beach; to get the sails of another boat, moored close off, furled so as not to flap about in the horses' eyes; and finally to stop the persevering band as the horses were 'coming'.

It was one of our brilliant cloudless days, with the heat of the sun just tempered by a light air from the southward as the tide made. Five or six hundred people were assembled by eleven o'clock when the horses started; and it was truly exhilarating to see so English a sport well supported, under the more genial climate and amidst the beautiful scenery of New Zealand.

Seven horses started; as one had paid forfeit, and another had been unfortunately killed some weeks before by a bullock, which scoured the beach of the town in the paroxysm of fury which the cattle often display upon being landed after a long voyage.

I cannot do better than copy the report of the sport from the newspaper of two days afterwards; premising that the favourite among the natives was Mr. Molesworth's Calmuc Tartar, because he resided near them on the Hutt; and that among the white people was Figaro, the thorough-bred horse which Mr. Watt had brought from Sydney as a yearling early in 1840.

PITONE RACES

THURSDAY, OCTOBER 20, 1842

Sweepstakes for ten guineas each. Gentlemen riders. Heats of one mile and three-quarters.

The following horses started—

Mr. Watt's ch. h.	*Figaro,* ridden by Owner		1	1
Mr. Molesworth's bk. h.	*Calmuc Tartar,* ditto		2	2
Mr. Virtue's gr. g.	*Marksman,* ditto		3	0
Mr. G. Hunter's b. m.	*Temperance,* ditto	Dorset	4	4
Mr. Bannister's ch. g.	*Sulky,* ditto	Wade	5	3

| Capt. Buckley's br. g. | *Daylight,* | ditto | Owner | 6 dr. |
| Mr. Revans's gr. h. | *Mazeppa,* | ditto | Tyser | dist. |

Figaro's superior blood enabled him to win both heats with the greatest ease. He was the favourite throughout, and freely backed at 5 to 1 after the first heat.

Several other matches were afterwards made up on the spot, of which we believe the following to be a correct account.

Sweepstakes for one pound each. One mile—

Mr. Revans's bk. g.	*Dandy,* ridden by Dr. Dorset		1
Col. Wakefield's ch. g.	*Beau,* ditto	Mr. Watt	2
Mr. G. Hunter's br. g.	*Wai-ake-ake,*	Owner	3
Mr. Allen's gr. g.	ditto	ditto	4
Mr. Virtue's b. m.			5

Matches for one pound a side, distance one mile—

Mr. C. Von Alzdorf's bk. g. *Black Billy* beat Mr. Machattie's bay pony.
Mr. Lyon's cart-horse beat Mr. Virtue's cart-horse.

Match for five pounds a side. One mile—

Colonel Wakefield's ch. g. *Beau* beat Mr. Virtue's bay mare.

About thirty gentlemen on horseback followed in procession behind the ladies' cart on the road to town in the afternoon; and we closed the day with a race-dinner at Barrett's hotel.

Some industrious mechanics had found a spot, on a large tributary of the Kaiwharawhara, fit for the erection of a mill; and it was now at work.

In the bottom of a thickly wooded valley, only accessible over a steep ridge, a natural fall in the narrow rocky gully of the stream afforded great facilities for erecting a dam. A platform and rough shed extended from side to side of the gully over the dam-head; the wheel and machinery were working underneath; and two or three circular saws were kept in constant employment. The open sides of the workshop displayed this curious work of art in the midst of nature's wildest scenery. Two trees mingled their branches overhead above the rough mill, and several others seemed to grow out of the pool formed by the dam underneath their arching boughs. The stern craggy sides of the gully might be imagined to frown upon so strange a neighbour as the fretting wheel. Two or three long-huts under the forest sent up their curl of smoke; while the neat housewives, with their flaxen-haired children, stood at the doors to receive with joyful pride the praises bestowed by visitors on the untiring industry of their husbands.

Captain Daniell had found a spot in this valley suitable for a farm; and while others were agitating and calling upon the Company to make more roads, each to his own section, he had himself engaged some labourers to make a bridle-road from Kaiwharawhara up to his discovery, which cost him about £30. The millers, who became tenants of his with certain rights as to cutting timber, continued the road to the mill. It was afterwards found that Captain Daniell's bridle-road might be continued into that leading to Porirua, so as to avoid some hundred feet of ascent over the first hill out of Port Nicholson by about a mile of circuit; and the Company completed this line so as to admit the passage of a dray. The entrance into Wellington by this road is singularly beautiful. As you wind round the sides of the rocky spurs, beneath gigantic boughs and luxuriant foliage, you obtain peeps of the velvet woods of the valley of Kaiwharawhara and its tributaries; then a view of the western face of Wade's Town, with its cottages and bright green gardens; and, lastly, the wide expanse of Port Nicholson, with its ships, its peaked mountains, and its glistening town.

§

On the 7th of November, the *George Fyfe* arrived from England with immigrants for Nelson, and a large batch of cabin-passengers. Happening to be in Wellington at the time, I went on board to greet Mr. Dillon, whom I had known before I left England. I remember being impressed with the curious scene which took place on board.

We had hardly shaken hands, when my friend burst out with a series of questions. 'Have you got 100,000 acres of the finest land in the world up the Hutt?' and 'Is it true that you've had to live upon rats for some time?' were among them. I looked round the cabin-table at those who had preceded me on board, and at once answered, 'I see you have had the *grumblers* and *puffers* on board: listen to but little of what you hear from the people who are in the habit of rushing on board fresh emigrant ships; come on shore, and judge a good deal for yourself until you have secured an impartial informant.'

The *puffers* are, perhaps, the most mischievous of these two classes, who both seem to delight in perplexing and tormenting the new-comers almost before the anchor of the ship is down. They are people who seek to give themselves an air of consequence by dwelling on the length of time that they have been in the colony, on the important station which they individually hold among its founders, on their perfect and exclusive knowledge of the capabilities of the country and the politics of the place, and on the advantages to be derived from making their acquaintance, and thus gaining a share of their notability and experience. I remember once hearing one take extraordinary credit to himself, before a knot of gaping and bewildered passengers under the break of the poop, because 'the ship was at that precise moment,' as he declared 'passing over the identical spot where *his* schooner, which *he* had ordered, and *he* had built, and *he* had manned, and *he* intended to send round to *his* whaling-station for *his* oil and *his* bone, and which was the fastest schooner on the coast, had turned over and sunk some months before!' They generally support their vulgar rhodomontade by the most exaggerated accounts of people and things; and, of course, the man from England thinks that a person who knows such wonderful facts must be better informed than the newspaper, or the people who write home. Then perhaps a *grumbler* steps over the gangway; and the puzzled emigrant is met by totally different accounts. The *grumbler* shrugs his shoulders and sneers at almost every answer that he makes; and looks at his querist as much as to say. 'Well, you *are* a fool.' He dribbles out words of doubt and discouragement, looks forward to difficulties, and puts everything in the light of a deception. He says the land is all over 12 miles of hills like those; that it blows and rains worse than any part of the world; that the people are nearly starving; that the farms on the Hutt, about which you have read so much, are only model-farms of the Company, managed under some good name so as to act as a trap for land-purchasers; and ends by telling you that the Company are a set of swindlers, the Government nò better, and both leagued together to take in every new-comer and do for him. And then, perhaps, a violent and ill-bred discussion ensues between the *puffer* and the *grumbler* across the table, and the poor settler retires to his cabin half distracted between the two.

The *grumblers* are, indeed, an extensive class, and do not all come on board ship. They are chiefly to be met with in the parlours of the hotels, smoking and drinking; pitching stones into the sea off the jetty; wandering lazily from one resort of idlers to the other; in the billiard-rooms, and near the public-houses. But the stranger who frequents these places deserves his fate, and no pity is felt for him. He often becomes a *grumbler* himself, by constant association with his tormentors.

The *grumbler* takes pride in sneering at every sanguine hope, in ridiculing every energetic effort to progress; and will hear of no attempt to examine into the discouraging circumstances which do really exist, or of any reason for their existence except the systematic deceit practised by the founders of the colony and by those whom the *grumblers* are please to look upon as first their victims and finally their accomplices.

They are, of course, disappointed men; many of whom have some cause for their disappointment, but no courage to exert themselves or to seek for means of overcoming the difficulties in their way.

A large portion of the class consists of the worthless idlers, of whom their families have thought to rid themselves by sending them to the other side of the world with a few hundred pounds, a land-order, and no friend or adviser. No language can be too strong for reproving such parents or guardians. The exiled scamp (for he has generally deserved that name in England) arrives on the beach, expecting to find everything as complete and comfortable as at home, only a good deal more like an earthly Paradise or Eldorado. He has probably been told that in a few years he may come home with a fortune; and he thinks that this is to be done by standing still with his hands in his pockets. He has had no education to fit him for a colonial life; he has not the slightest knowledge of the value of money; and is one of the unfortunate people who can do 'anything'.

He finds that his section is some miles off, and covered with timber; that he will have to live for some time almost by himself, to have nothing done for him, and in short to work, without many of the comforts and luxuries of an old society. And he is shocked to find that the gentlemen of the place do not disdain to be busy and occasionally to handle an axe or a hammer themselves; and that the really good and pleasant circle of society which does exist will not acknowledge him or receive him amongst them till he has proved his qualifications to join them by roughing it like a gentleman and a 'good colonist'. He is required to assume the *esprit de corps* before he is allowed to put on the uniform.

So he resolves to wait till a road is made to his section, and till there are some people living near it; he dawdles about the beach; sets down the gentlemen for a clique of proud, disagreeable people; gradually gets into the habit of frequenting the billiard-rooms and the hotels; and thinks he has found out a particularly jolly set of fellows in their permanent inhabitants. He drinks, smokes, and sings; perhaps sells his land-order, without having seen his section or even been outside the town; and enjoys the thing vastly until his money is spent in doing nothing. He goes on for some time on credit. But the duns begin to gather round him; he is perhaps deserted by the set at the hotel for some newer hand; and he begins to think that, after all, this sort of life is managed better in London. Of course, there is a great dearth in Wellington of the amusements which would suit his taste: the industrious colonists only indulge now and then in recreation, and even at those times it is short and moderate, and they return to their work.

He is now a confirmed grumbler, and applies the maxims and principles which he has picked up over the brandy-bottle at the hotel to everything which he sees or hears of. He finds excuses in everything for his own misconduct: the wind is too violent, the rain is too heavy, the sun too scorching, the timber too abundant, the land too barren, the houses too slight, the roads too bad, the food too nasty—he never could have got on; in short, 'it is a wretched hole': and he starts off one morning for Sydney or India, having borrowed money or drawn a doubtful bill for his passage. He returns to England, generally a worse scamp than before, to explain why he could not possibly have succeeded by painting everything in the blackest colours.

The grumblers are a dangerous shoal, upon which the newly-arrived colonist is very apt to founder. But the danger requires no buoying off to the old colonist. He keeps in the straight channel of brave perseverance and endurance, beating steadily to windward between the sands to whose formation he has been a witness, and occasionally warning a stranger of their whereabouts.

This leads me to speak of another class of people, sometimes met with in the colony, of whom the oldest colonists are not at first aware. They come from England as well as from the sister colonies; and bring with them letters of introduction as well as personal recommendations which introduce them at an early period to the familiar friendship of the best society in the colony. And it is not, perhaps, till long afterwards that some disreputable history or disgraceful circumstance of their former life is discovered, which explains their exile from the old world.

Against this class we early made some provision by the institution of the Club, on which I dwelt shortly in my former pages. Any new-comer is admissible as an honorary member for three months, on being presented and seconded by two members and approved of by the committee. If he wish to become a member, his name has to be posted with that of his proposer and seconder for a month, and he is then balloted for.

So near the penal colonies of Australia, where loose characters abound, this was a most necessary measure. Although very quiet and hidden in its operation, it has tended very much to preserve a high British tone in the society of Wellington, and even of the other settlements of Cook's Strait, whose best inhabitants become honorary members of the Club during their visits to Wellington. Although this club was at first assailed with much derision and loud abuse of its aristocratic character as unsuited to the tastes and feelings of the majority, it has steadily maintained its station; and possesses by this time an undoubted power of determining the claim of a new man to the respect and confidence of society. It has, in fact, scarcely any other object; for several married men belong to it, who hardly ever use it as a club except when some visitors of importance are invited guests, or when some business matter requires their attendance. Some idea may be formed of its exclusive character, when it is known that there are to this day only twenty-five members, although the number is not limited. This club has probably contributed in great measure to preserve the tone of Wellington from becoming quarrelsome and ignoble like that of Auckland, or vulgar and bargain-driving like that of a young town in the west of the United States, because it has cherished the great safeguard of society, honour.

§

On the night of the 9th of November, a fire swept part of the beach at Wellington. The houses were chiefly roofed with thatch, and many of the walls of the same material. A smart north-west breeze was blowing at the time, and the fire spread with fearful rapidity, the pieces of blazing thatch flying along to other houses 100 yards off, and igniting them immediately. I formed one of a party who tried to save the fire from spreading by pulling down houses along the line; but, though we began far to leeward, the house would frequently light under our hands, or sparks flew over our heads to houses still further off. Fortunately, a large number of sailors from the shipping acted well in concert under their commanders—several houses were torn or cut down, and the thatch carried bodily into the sea. The people, too, of the houses to the south of the Flag-staff Point* had been alarmed in time to wet their roofs; and though the fire ran along a dry brush fence on the top of the hill, it was thus prevented from spreading to the bonded warehouses and large stores at the back of Te Aro beach. If this had happened, the damage would have been immense, as nothing could have escaped the conflagration of the bonded spirits. As it was, the damage was estimated at £16,000. Twenty-three houses of thatch were burnt and three pulled down; and upwards of twenty wooden houses of various sizes were also burnt. Some curious escapes were observed. In one case, the whole wooden wall was scorched into charcoal, round the window of a room in which there was four hundred-weight of gunpowder in kegs; and all the surrounding houses were burnt to the ground. After the fire had ceased, all the young settlers still remained till daylight, rolled in blankets on the floors of some of the large stores at Te Aro,

* The hill above Stewart Dawson's corner, then known as 'Clay Point' or 'Windy Point'.

watching lest some new outbreak should threaten that part of the town.

The greatest humanity and good feeling for the sufferers prevailed. Many people willingly put themselves to inconvenience to shelter their houseless neighbours; and very large subscriptions were collected at Wellington, Nelson, and New Plymouth, and even little Wanganui added its mite, for the relief of those really distressed by the event.

In some respects the fire did good. Many of the peddling shopkeepers whom I have described were driven into the bush, where they might have gone long before; and these seemed surprised to find how easy it was to settle, even with their reduced circumstances. Two villages, with cultivations and clearings of moderate size, soon sprang up along the Porirua bridle-road, at distances of four and six miles from the town; many settled in the upland vale of the Karori; and a more wholesome spirit was thus given to those who remained in the town.

Perhaps the most surprising thing was the rapidity with which, notwithstanding so many discouraging circumstances, the beach was again covered with a better growth of buildings. Out of the ashes of the *raupo* thatch sprang substantial brick and wooden stores and taverns, with slate or shingle roofs; and heaps of melted glass and other rubbish were cleared away from the site of one of the merchant's stores, to make room for the foundations of the Scotch church. Within two or three months, this part of the beach was more thickly populated than before, and no vestige of the fire remained.

On the 23rd of November, Captain Mein Smith returned from an expedition to the Middle Island on the Company's service. Colonel Wakefield had despatched him in a small cutter, about the time that he himself sailed for Auckland, to examine and report upon the coast, the harbours, and adjoining country along the whole east coast of the Middle Island. He had made a very careful and interesting report, with accurate sketches and maps of the principal harbours and rivers. Unfortunately, the cutter, in entering the port of Akaroa on her return, had been suddenly upset by a squall and sunk in deep water; so that all his maps, books, journals, and valuable instruments were irretrievably lost. Captain Smith's report to the Company, made partly from memory and partly from materials which he had sent to Wellington by another opportunity, proved that a very large and promising field was open for colonization in the Middle Island, with excellent harbours and inland water communication, scarcely any native occupants, and a climate, perhaps not so warm as that of Cook's Strait, but equally productive.

Two boys' schools were now established at Wellington; one under the superintendence of the Mechanics' Institute, the other founded in opposition by a private individual. The two schools had about 150 scholars.

Picnics and balls began to multiply as the season of the anniversary approached. Among the most pleasing of these was a picnic given by Messrs. Clifford and Vavasour, who had set an excellent example by clearing away at their section, half a mile beyond Captain Daniell's farm on the Porirua road, immediately that they arrived. They were in time to ask their fellow-passengers in the *Fyfe*, who were going on to Nelson to lunch in a tent in the midst of their first clearing; and a party of the ladies of Wellington joined the merry throng, and cheered them to perseverance in their good work.

Another export was now much talked of. This was the bark of the *hinau*, a large forest-tree which abounds all over the country near Cook's Strait. The natives extract from this bark the black dye for their mats. A considerable quantity of this bark was now collected and sent to England, that its value might be ascertained.

The berry of the *titoki* tree might also be turned to account. The natives extract a very fine oil from it; and a small quantity, which was sent to England as a sample, has been described as of great value for the finer parts of machinery.

Poor Mr. Swainson was at this time more distressed than ever by 'Dog's Ear' and Rauparaha's other native emissaries. He had hired three sections, of 100 acres each, of untouched forest-land on the banks of the Hutt. He had fondly made plans for laying this out according to principles of his own, by leaving belts of timber to shelter the patches of cultivation from the wind, clumps in various spots for ornament, an orchard here, a flower-garden there. He had built a substantial farm-house for his family and another for his labourers. And he had begun with a clearing of about two acres, in which a fine crop of wheat for seed was just coming to perfection. Taringakuri, who had established himself close to the house, at first promised to cut only what Mr. Swainson pointed out to him, and pretended only to want one crop in return for his trouble. But, notwithstanding repeated mediations of Mr. Spain or of Mr. Clarke junior, which only seemed to make matters worse instead of restoring peace, the deceitful chief had cleared all the wood indiscriminately off a large tract of ground. Belt after belt, clump after clump, fell beneath the merciless axes of his followers; and the native clearing at length reached to within a few yards of the house and the little patch of wheat. They now openly laughed at their victim, and told him to 'look out', for as the dry weather came on, they should set fire to the fallen wood. His appeals to the Police Magistrate for interference, to the Crown Prosecutor for an indictment, to the Court for an injunction, had been all of no avail.

In October of last year the natives were not only living there permanently, but encroaching still further on a large portion of the valley, in any part of which they forbade white men from settling. The clearing of the Ngatirangatahi, Rauparaha's especial servants, extended nearly a mile along the banks; and they carefully stopped every white man who began to clear or saw even in parts that had never before been occupied.

I spent my Christmas at Otaki, and dined off a haunch of goat venison instead of a sirloin of beef. But I heard that the festival had been celebrated with 'right merrie' sports in Wellington. A cricket-match between two clubs which had practised for some months, quoits, swings, and other diversions, were numerously attended on Te Aro flat.

On New Year's Day, 1843, the concluding selection of preliminary country sections took place. The new districts laid open were the valley of the Upper Hutt, above a gorge six miles from the sea; a large district between the Manawatu river, and a line drawn east from Lake Horowhenua to the Tararua range; a varied and rather inaccessible district between Port Nicholson and the coast of Cook's Strait, which extends from Mana to Cape Terawhiti; and some new valleys in the neighbourhood of Porirua, and between that district and the valley of the Hutt.

Every one appeared well satisfied with the choice which he had made. The different maps were laid on a long table in the open air outside the survey-office; and the crowd of bustling agents and tormented surveyors' assistants formed a gay scene.

On the 11th January, the colonial brig arrived, bringing Lieutenant Shortland, the Acting Governor, with his suite and Mr. Spain. Notwithstanding his former faults, he was received in a very forgiving disposition, in consequence of Colonel Wakefield's reports of his earnest promises that the land-claims should be speedily settled. I really believe that he was at this time well inclined to do justice to the Cook's Strait settlers. His Excellency at least conferred one substantial benefit on the town, by directing the erection of a substantial and roomy gaol. Numerous escapes had recently proved the perfect inefficiency of the Maori hut and its stockade.

At this time [January 1843] the Company's agent issued a contract for the clearing of the Porirua bridle-road to a width of six feet, and the felling of the timber for 10 feet on either side along the whole 12 miles, so as to admit the sun and wind upon the swampy and muddy portions. The contractors engaged a large gang of Hutt axe-men, headed by a renowned Yankee backwoodsman, who used to pocket many a half-crown by making bets with new-comers as to the number of minutes he would take to get through a tree. They got expeditiously and creditably through their contract.

I was at Otaki on the 4th March, when the splendid comet of 1843 was first seen in the south-west. The first night some natives rushed into the house to ask for explanation of the extraordinary sight. After watching it for some hours, I foretold that it would be seen again for many nights; which they would not believe, telling me that I was *porangi*, or 'foolish', to think that the *atua*, or 'spirit', would appear when I liked. And I was much laughed at till the next night, when there it was still! It was seen for nearly a month; and the clearness of the atmosphere added to its beautiful appearance. The nucleus was distinctly visible, like a small star; and the tail, of uncommon brilliancy, subtended an angle of 36° as observed from Wellington, and of 45° as observed from Wanganui.

About this time I had occasion to go in a boat from Otaki to

K

Rauparaha's islet near Kapiti. I had not seen Rauparaha or Rangi-haeata at Otaki for some days; but I found them both here. It appeared that they were receiving the visit of Karetai, a head chief of the Ngaitahu tribe, who had come from Otago* in a fine large sealing-boat, in order to make overtures for the reconcili-ation of the two tribes. It was said, that if this could be effected on a sure footing, Taiaroa and 'Bloody Jack', Rauparaha's former inveterate enemies, were coming to confer with him on various affairs. The southern chief was dressed in an old dragoon helmet, and black tail-coat without trousers under his dirty mats. His manner was very insolent and undignified; and his language a mixture of Maori 'bounce' and whaling 'slang', which showed that he was tainted by the character of the coarse Europeans among whom he had lived.

Rauparaha began to talk to me about the land with much violence; Rangihaeata, too, as usual excited by drink, ran up and down for a little while using very violent language on the subject; but he went back to lie down in his hut when I laughed, lit my pipe, and passed some merry joke upon his large mouth having it all to himself.

Rauparaha then pursued the subject in a conversational style, as I lay on the shingly beach close by him, among his basking train.

'Do you mean to take all the land?' said he; 'you are driving the natives first from one place and then from another; are you and Wide-awake to have it all?' He went on for some time, posi-tively as though the natives were being driven out instead of the white people, as was really the case in all the settlements; and he declared he would stop it.

I knew it was useless to argue the point with him, as I felt sure that some sinister influence had been at work upon him recently, from his irritated manner and tone. So I answered jokingly. He repeated that he would stop the white people: he didn't care for Wide-awake or the Governor either. They shouldn't have Porirua, and they shouldn't have the Hutt; and they shouldn't have Wairau, which he informed me was being surveyed by people from Nelson. He declared none of those places were paid for. I told him that we should always be of two opinions about that, and that it was

*Spelled 'Otako' by Wakefield.

of no use discussing it, as we could not agree. And I again tried to joke off the dispute, saying that the white people would creep on and get their right at last. I remember being struck with the hyena-like scream with which he said, 'Then we'll fight about it!' But I still laughed at his obstinacy, and showed him how unequal a battle it would be if he trusted to force instead of justice. He said, however, that he did not care; 'it must be one for one, till either the Maori or the *pakeha* were *kua pau*', or 'exhausted'.

As I rose to get into my boat, Rauparaha told me that he and Rangihaeata were going to Nelson soon to tell the 'Wide-awake' of that place not to survey Wairau, as it had not been paid for.

CHAPTER XVII

New Plymouth Interlude

I T WAS not till the beginning of April that I got a letter from Colonel Wakefield, dated from Wellington, instructing me to go on to Wanganui and manage the Company's case before Mr. Spain. But I found that Mr. Spain had got impatient at the delay in the arrival of either Colonel Wakefield or myself; had held his Court and closed it, after three days' examination of witnesses.

I now proceeded by land to Taranaki, accompanied by Wahine-iti and one or two 'boys' to carry baggage and provisions. As far as Whenuakura we also travelled in company with a New Plymouth settler, who was driving a flock of 300 sheep and six or eight bullocks thither from Wellington, after a rest of a week at Wanganui.

The Agent of the New Plymouth settlement had determined to cut a bridle-road inland of Mount Egmont, to connect New Plymouth with the coast of Cook's Strait, somewhere between Waimate and Patea, by an easier and a shorter route than that round the coast. This object had at length been effected, notwithstanding the opposition of the great body of natives on this side, entirely by native labour. We met a party of the workmen who were on their way to show their friends the double-barrelled fowling-pieces, in which they had insisted on receiving the principal part of the payment. Along this bridle-road we proceeded.

After all the beautiful spots and districts which I had already seen in New Zealand, I was struck with the surpassing beauty and luxuriant productiveness of the country hereabouts, just after entering the wood, which is at first like an immense shrubbery with occasional large trees. The abundance of the second crops in the existing native gardens, the rankness and yet softness of the grass which had sprung up in the old deserted patches, surrounded with flowering shrubs amidst which countless flocks of singing-birds were chasing each other, all combined with the genial atmosphere, although it was approaching to the middle of winter, to remind me touchingly of Shakespeare's sweet picture of the perfection of agriculture. Just such a country and climate is des-cribed by him, if worked by happy and industrious farmers:

> *Earth's increase and foyson plenty,*
> *Barns and garners never empty;*
> *Vines with clust'ring branches growing;*
> *Plants with goodly burden bowing;*
> *Spring come to you at the farthest*
> *In the very end of harvest!*
> *Scarcity and want shall shun you,*
> *Ceres' blessing so is on you!*

A long trudge through the forest, of which the trees increased in size as we advanced, presented but little variety till we emerged on the picturesque broken country which stretches northwards from Mount Egmont at a distance of 10 or 12 miles from the coast. We had slept two nights in the bush, and the third we reached a hut in a small cultivation on the western edge of the forest. The journey had proved very tedious, from the extraordinary number of gullies and streams which we had to cross. Among these were the Patea and several of its tributaries, which take their rise in the side of Mount Egmont.

In the open lands, a scrub called the *tutu*, to which I have else-where referred, is rather dangerous to cattle. The natives make a sickly beverage from the berries, which are very small, in bunches like currants, and of which the seed is highly poisonous. The leaves, and especially the young and tender shoots, are much liked by the cattle, and often deadly in their effects. But this seems a very irregular occurrence. I have often known cattle eat the *tutu* without being at all affected. At other times, and especially in newly-arrived cattle, a very small quantity causes a disease very much resembling that produced by an excess of clover. Instant and severe bleeding is the only chance of saving the stock affected. The *tutu* is very abundant among fern and dry grass pasture, and is exceedingly difficult to exterminate. Horses and sheep either do not eat this plant or are never affected by its noxious qualities.

Descending from the broken country, we found ourselves on the plains of New Plymouth, which are almost entirely covered with fern, varying in height from three to ten feet. Scattered groves of timber and gentle undulations from the plain into the valleys of the water-courses and their tributaries diversify the view agreeably.

At length we got into a line of road through the fern. One or two strong wooden bridges over the streams, and three or four neat houses and fields in various directions, soon told of the neighbourhood of a European settlement. We crossed a rough suspension-bridge in process of erection, of which the chains were supported on the round trunks of four large trees; then some smiling gardens, neatly hedged and ditched; a forge; a row of labourers' cottages; some cob houses in various stages of progress; and we reached the house of Mr. Cooke, who had invited me, when he was at Wellington, to come and find him out.

From thence to the mouth of the Uatoki river, about a mile north of the Sugarloaf islands, the houses and gardens thicken apace; and there a little nucleus of dwellings forms the town.

The absence of a port had been of great advantage to the 1100 people who had settled at New Plymouth. The commerce of a shipping town had not encouraged a race of small shopkeepers and petty merchants; but the colonists had at once struck the plough or the spade into the ground. I found that a very large proportion of the people were scattered about in different directions on promising farms; and a numerous race of small farmers or yeomen is rapidly springing up there. A great many of this class originally arrived at this settlement from the west of England; and they have had no temptation to change their pursuit for one to which they were less accustomed.

The soil of this undulating and very pretty country is for the most part excellent for agricultural purposes; but the growth of pure fern is not suited for the immediate maintenance of cattle and sheep. While I was staying at Mr. Cooke's house none of his cattle could be found for nearly three days, as they had strayed many miles in search of pasture. The population of New Plymouth seemed a particularly happy set of people. As they are little troubled with politics, I rarely saw many of them in the town, which is as dull a place, except to look at, as you can imagine. But on going to their little farms a mile off in one direction or two miles in another, I found them hard at work, delighted with the fertility of the soil which they were turning over, with hardly a complaint to make, and spending homely English evenings round a huge farm-house chimney; rising early, and not long out of their beds after their tea and pipes. I could not help reflecting, while spending an evening or two in this domestic way as a visitor at one of these farm-houses, that New Zealand is just the country for people like these, the better class of English yeomen. The climate is better adapted to an English constitution than that of almost any other of our colonies, although without a distinct winter, or frost, or fogs, or raw easterly winds, to check vegetation or make you house your cattle. The amazing productiveness of the soil, or rather of the air—for almost all land, if sufficiently turned over and exposed for a time, gives abundant crops—must tend to make agriculture the most pleasant of occupations.

It is rather a colony for persons of contented mind to enjoy life better with the same means, than for fortune-hunters to acquire a great and rapid increase of means wherewith to go back and enjoy life in the old country. But in the enjoyment of life in the colony, I include the constant pleasure of seeing scenery through a clear atmosphere, of breathing pure and invigorating air, of sleeping nine months in the year with your bed-room window open, and yet never feeling it too warm for fire when rain or a gale of wind keeps you indoors. For otherwise you are always out of doors, watching the robust growth of your plants or the brilliant rising and setting of the sun, the surprising condition of the cattle without any great care, or the constantly varying but constantly beautiful appearances of the landscape, be it ever so meagre, which is open to your view.

On my way back to Wanganui round the shore, I saw but little that was new. On arriving at Wanganui, I went up to Tata, and spent a very pleasant week or two with Kuru and his family. The chief was living a most happy and contented life among his potato-gardens.

CHAPTER XVIII

The Wairau Massacre

TOWARDS THE end of June I descended the river in company with Kuru.

When we reached Tunuharere, about fifteen miles from the sea, strange reports were shouted to us from the *pas* and potato-gardens as we glided lazily along in the glowing sunset. The natives have generally a number of exaggerated stories which they delight to shout out in this way to people who have been away for some time; and I paid no attention to these cries at first, as they seemed no more than customary.

But suddenly Kuru sprang up from the couch on which he was reclining by my side, the boys ceased paddling, and all signed to me to listen. A shout came clear and distinct over the water, and I felt faint at each word. 'There had been a fight,' the harbinger of ill news cried; 'and Rauparaha had killed Wide-awake and 40 white people—no natives had been killed; that was all he knew!'*

I tried to laugh it off; and Kuru, too, kept telling me it was all *tito,* or 'lies'. But from each little settlement or hut the same story still rang, with varying additional circumstances; all agreeing, however, that 'Wide-awake' was dead. I thought they meant my uncle in Port Nicholson, and could not understand how any fighting could have occurred there; I could not make it out; but the reports were too confirmatory of each other in the main circumstance; and every yard seemed a mile till I reached the white settlement.

There was no longer any doubt. An Englishman [Mr. Rowand] had arrived from Wellington who told the following tale. He had

* Twenty-two Europeans, including Captain Arthur Wakefield, Jerningham's uncle, were killed.

seen the Government brig arrive in Wellington and land Mr. Tuckett, the Chief Surveyor of Nelson, and two white men and a native who were dreadfully wounded, but had managed to escape from the combat which had taken place on the Wairau plain near Cloudy Bay. It was supposed that no others had escaped out of a party of 40 Englishmen who had gone from Nelson to the plain of Wairau to assist the Police Magistrate and two other Magistrates in executing a warrant upon Rauparaha and Rangihaeata. He knew no more of the details; but he knew that my uncle Captain Wakefield and Mr. Thompson were among those slain; for he had received an account of this from Rauparaha himself at Otaki on his way hither from Wellington. Rauparaha told him that he had tried hard to save the gentlemen and keep them as slaves; but that Rangihaeata would not listen to him and killed them all. He said nine had been thus killed, after a short deliberation as to what they should do with them. Rauparaha had also made this man promise to deliver me a message, only allowing him to pass on his undertaking to do so. The message was merely to know what I was going to do—whether I was for peace or war—and to ask me to come to Otaki and see him, that he might *korero* with me.

The white people at Otaki said that Rauparaha had sent his canoes up the Manawatu to the care of some of his tributary tribes, and was considering by which route he should retreat to Taupo or Rotorua, in case of pursuit by the white people.

I repeated this distinctly to Kuru; who had declared that he would believe nothing except what I told him was true. When I had done, he took me to a hut where we could be heard by no one else, held me firmly by the hand, and addressed me in a calm and impressive voice so that I remember nearly every word. 'You know,' said he, 'how many men I could count if I were to send my call to the tribes of my wives and those of my father. In two weeks, I can count a thousand men, all well armed. From Taupo, as well as from all the settlements where I have relations on Wanganui, they would all come. Listen! if Rauparaha tries to reach Rotorua by this path, I will put a net over his head and give him to you. Listen! you and I will go into the bush with our warriors, and we will rise up till we have taken him, or got payment for the blood of our fathers. It shall be the sacred war-party of our lives; and we two shall have but one heart. If I am killed first, you will have your brother as well as your father to take payment for. If you are killed first, my arm shall be stronger when thinking of your blood as well as that of my Maori relations. It is enough. I have done!'

As soon as I could speak, I thanked him sincerely for his offer; but explained to him that in these cases white men did not take revenge themselves for the murder of their relations. I told him that we had the Queen, and laws, and governors and magistrates, ships and soldiers to help them, to punish such deeds; and that they would not be reduced to bringing the natives into fresh wars with each other.

I wrote, by a small cutter, and also by land by a native messenger, to Colonel Wakefield, begging for accurate particulars, and for advice as to what was going to be done; as, in case of an attempt to take Rauparaha at Otaki, I felt sure of being able to cut off his retreat to the interior, by means of Kuru. At length I got an answer from Colonel Wakefield that it was not considered advisable to make any attempt to take the murderers now, as without an adequate force the attempt would probably fail, and only lead to retaliation on out-settlers.

On the 8th of June, while I was still at Wanganui, the most severe earthquake occurred that I had yet felt. The day had been dull and calm, and a little rain had fallen about noon. After this, the wind breathed lightly up the river, and then shifted in a sudden squall to north-west with some more rain. After this squall, a curious mist drove swiftly up the river from the sea, such as I had never seen before. It was in a light thin stratum about 60 feet above the ground, and did not extend either to the level of the river or to the top of the hills. Then the mist cleared away, and the afternoon became warm and fine at about three.

Two hours afterwards a sudden waving motion of the earth commenced from the direction of Taranaki, accompanied by a low rumbling noise. The motion continued to increase in force, with occasional wriggles, for about half a minute, and it was at least two minutes before it was entirely quiet. The people ran out of their houses, which were rocking and bending, being most of them built with very elastic poles and light tied roofs. Some were for running to the hills, some to the water; but the motion was just enough to make your footing feel too insecure to run, and some people told me it made them turn sick. The river was covered with bubbles; and a man who was standing at the bank, up to his ankles, washing a shirt, told me the water had suddenly risen to his knees, and then gone down again. In the morning some cracks were found in the mud-flat between high and low-water mark, five or six feet wide, and 100 yards long, and one or two smaller ones on the bank close to the water; as they had filled up with mud, we could not tell how deep they had been at first. Some of them, however, were still six or eight feet in depth.

A few badly-built brick chimneys and clay walls were damaged, but no accident occurred to any one. The natives sat still during the whole affair, apparently quite indifferent; though they afterwards acknowledged that they had never experienced so bad a *ru*, or 'shake'.

The most important effect appeared to have been the raising of many parts of the flat, on which the town is situated, a few inches, as they could now be seen from Putiki for the first time.

I have a notion that the slight shocks, very like the vibration produced by the rumbling of carts in the London streets, which we so often experienced in New Zealand, are gradually raising the whole country, and that much of the present coast has been thus recently raised from under the sea. This earthquake was felt more severely about Wanganui than anywhere else. The cracks were less at Wangaehu and Rangitikei, hardly perceptible at Manawatu, and not to be seen at all at Ohau; and hardly any shock was felt at New Plymouth or Wellington. The cracks all pointed towards Tongariro.

§

I armed myself for the journey to Wellington with a rifle, pistols, and cutlass; and we reached Rangitikei the first night. Here I found Te Ahu [father of Wahine-iti], Billy Whatanui, two or three other young chiefs, and about 12 other armed men, awaiting our arrival.

We slept one night at Manawatu, and the next afternoon, we reached Whatanui's settlement at Horowhenua lake. The patriarch spoke of the Wairau affair, and said Rauparaha and Rangihaeata had acted very badly. 'But,' continued he, 'we have a Queen; for she is my Queen as well as yours. And when her soldiers come to take the bad men, I shall sit still and let them go by. I will not rise up, for the two treacherous chiefs were in the wrong. Go, keep your soreness and your anger in your heart till you have reached Poneke.'

The next day, July 17th, I went on to Otaki, Te Ahu still escorting me with all his train. As I passed between Mr. Hadfield's house and the chapel, on my way to the house of Taylor my agent inland, two or three women recognized me. They jumped from their seats and ran down to the *pa* shouting 'Here is Tiraweke; he has come to shoot Rauparaha. Alas! Alas!'

I gathered from white people and natives here that Rangihaeata was living about six miles up the Waikawa river, where he was fortifying a strong *pa* on a lake; and it was understood that the two chiefs intended to make a stand there, should the authorities attempt to take them by force. Rauparaha was living at the smaller Otaki *pa*, and was busying himself with the formation of a large party of adherents in case of a struggle. He had become a 'missionary' the very day he arrived here from the Wairau massacre, and was allowed to attend the chapel regularly.

Every one who knew Rauparaha at once understood, that he had taken this line in order to secure the alliance of the missionary natives, who were now a very large and influential party among the inhabitants of Otaki and the neighbouring country.

To the other natives he was constantly showing a pair of handcuffs taken from one of the constables who was slain, and exciting them to resistance by saying that these were meant to take the young and strong men first, and not weak old men like himself! His wife and his slave-women wore the rings of the murdered men. His houses were full of their clothes, their arms, and their watches; a tent belonging to them was pitched ostentatiously in the *pa*, and various other articles were hung about as though in triumph after a victory. And yet he went to chapel every morning and evening! Mr. Spain, who had been deputed hither by the Wellington Magistrates to assure the natives that the white people would not attempt to revenge Wairau, but would leave it to the Governor, had reported on his return that all was pacific and quiet; and Mr. Hadfield, who had accompanied Mr. Spain on that mission, and whom I met on my way to Waikanae, made me turn away from him much hurt, when he told me that these poor men had only acted in self-defence against people who did very wrong; and that it would be not only unjust and illegal, but most imprudent, to attempt to take them or try them for their deed.

In passing Ohau, I had been shown the house built by the natives for a Mr. White, whom Te Ahu had invited to come and squat with cattle near his settlement. He had had two cows running there for some time, and was now on his way from Wellington with 20 or 30 more. Te Ahu and two or three other important chiefs of the Ngatiraukawa, were anxiously expecting him at the main *pa*.

Early one morning, Mr. White came to Taylor's, and said that Rauparaha had set his men to drive the cattle back to Waikanae, declaring that not only no cattle should go to Ohau, but that he would have no white people at all there or at Otaki. He would have a clear ground in case it came to fighting. The Ngatiraukawa chiefs were much surprised at this declaration, as they imagined they had a right to do what they liked with their own land. Te Ahu especially appeared to be quite amused, and to think that he could talk this fancy away; for he begged me and the other white people to go down to Rauparaha's *pa* and hear the *korero*. So we went down in a party, natives and white people.

Some little time elapsed before the *korero* began. Rauparaha crept up doubtingly to greet me, and held out his hand.

I refused this offer in a marked manner, and merely answered his greeting by a distant nod.

He acknowledged the propriety of my refusal, said 'It is good,' and returned to his seat.

He then rose to speak. He began with a long history of himself and of his conquest of Cook's Strait; all as proving that he was a great chieftain and the head of the natives. He displayed, as usual, great eloquence; and he was going on to relate all the circumstances of the Wairau affair, but I checked him. I told him I should leave the *pa* if he talked about Wairau; that I was come only to hear about his right and his will to turn white people out of Otaki, as that concerned me.

He then went on to repeat the prohibition which we had heard this morning, saying that all the land was his alone. He said Manawatu was fairly sold; so was Wanganui; so was Taranaki; the white people might go there. But to Ohau they should not go; and those at Otaki must go away to Kapiti or to Port Nicholson. Some of the whalers present laughed at this, having too many friends and relations by their wives to fear being turned out. Taylor, among the number, laughed outright, for he had lived with the tribe for many years, and was a general favourite among them. Rauparaha turned to him and said, 'You must go too, Sammy.'

He concluded by calling himself 'the king of the Maori'. He asked 'What right had they to want to tie his hands? As for Wikitoria,' he said, 'never mind that—*woman*,' was what he said; but with an accent, intonation, and sneer, which gave the word its most insulting meaning. I have already said that the language is not rich, and the word *wahine*, 'woman', is one of those whose sense is qualified by the manner of uttering it. I have no hesitation in saying, that he then expressed the most infamous term that can be applied to a woman. 'Who is she,' continued he, 'that she should send her books and her constables after me? What have I to do with her? She may be Queen over the white people; I am the king of the Maori! If she chooses to have war, let her send me word, and I will stand up against her soldiers. But I must have room; I must have no white people so near.'

I asked him, whether he had not signed a paper to say the Queen was his chief, when Mr. Williams brought it to him, and also on board the man-of-war? He turned round sharply and said, 'Yes! what of that? They gave me a blanket for it. I am still a chief just the same. I am Rauparaha! Give me another blanket to-morrow, and I will sign it again. What is there in writing?'

Thus one of the most powerful of the 512 chiefs spoke of the much vaunted Treaty of Waitangi, which he had signed twice according to all accounts.

I now turned to Te Ahu and the other chiefs, and asked them if it were true that all the land belonged to Rauparaha alone. I reproached them with dishonesty in selling the Manawatu and parts of the Otaki district as though it were their own. I reminded Te Ahu, too, that he had often shown me how much land he possessed about Ohau, and that he had invited Mr. White to settle there; and that no one had ever said before that it belonged to Rauparaha.

Te Ahu answered me, that when the chiefs of the Ngatiraukawa came down from Taupo, they had chosen the district out of Rauparaha's conquest in order to sit upon; and that, while peace lasted, nobody had thought of Rauparaha's supreme control. They had learned to consider the land their own; they had even laughed at the remonstrances of Rangihaeata about selling the Manawatu; and they had wished to get white men amongst them. He even said, that while there was no anger, Rauparaha's claim would not have been acknowledged. But the *riri*, or 'anger', he said, had made a great difference; and the land was gone back again to him who had first taken it. It was true; the Ngatiraukawa had no land but Taupo and Maungatautari (a district between Waikato and the Bay of Plenty).

And then he rose to endeavour to persuade Rauparaha to change his determination. He reminded him of 'the war-parties which he had brought him on his back, to assist him against his enemies, through dangers and troubles more than he could count'. He related how 'he had burned the villages of the tribe of Taupo to make them come with him to be by the side of Rauparaha on the sea-coast'. He counted 'how many times they had adhered to him in his feuds with the Ngatiawa', and described 'how much blood of the Ngatiraukawa had been spilt for his name'. Te Ahu had now warmed with his subject, and was running up and down, bounding and yelling at each turn, and beginning to foam at the mouth, as the natives do when they mean to speak impressively. 'Let the cows go!' he cried; 'let them go to my place!'

Rauparaha seemed to consider that Te Ahu's eloquence was becoming too powerful, and he jumped up too. They both continued to run up and down in short parallel lines, yelling at each other, grimacing and foaming, and quivering their hands and smacking them on their thighs, with staring eyes and excited features. As they both spoke together, it became difficult to hear what they said, but I caught a sentence here and there which gave me the sense of their argument. 'No!' cried Rauparaha; 'no cows; I will not have them.' 'Let them go!' yelled Te Ahu. 'Yield me my cows and my white man; the cows will not kill you.' 'No cows, no white men! I am the king! Never mind your war-parties! No cows!' answered Rauparaha. 'The cows cannot take you,' persisted Te Ahu; 'when the soldiers come we will fight for you, but let my cows go!' 'No! no! no indeed!' firmly replied the chief, and he sat down.

Te Ahu remained standing. He took breath for a minute; then he drew himself up to his full height, and addressed his own people in a solemn kind of recitative. 'Ngatiraukawa,' he sang, 'Arise! arise, my sons and my daughters, my elder brothers and my younger brothers, my sisters, my grandchildren, arise! Stand up, the families of the Ngatiraukawa! To Taupo! To Taupo! To Maungatautari! To our old homes which we had burned and deserted; arise and let us go! Carry the little children on your backs as I carried you when I came to fight for this old man, who had called us to fight for him and given us land to sit on, but grudges us white people to be our friends and to give us trade. We have no white people or ships at Maungatautari, but the land is our own there. We need not beg to have a white man or cows yielded to us, if they should want to come. To Maungatautari! Arise my sons, make up your packs, take your guns and your blankets, and let us go! It is enough! I have spoken!' As he sat down, a mournful silence prevailed. An important migration had been proposed by the chief, which no doubt would be agreed to by the greater part of the Otaki, Ohau, and Manawatu natives, on whom was Rauparaha's chief dependence for his defence.

I noticed that he winced when he first heard the purport of Te Ahu's song; but while Te Ahu continued, his countenance gradually resumed its confidence. Much as I abhorred his character, I could not but yield my unbounded admiration to the imperious manner in which he overthrew the whole effect of Te Ahu's beautiful summons to the tribe.

Instead of his usual doubting and suspicious manner, his every gesture became that of a noble chief. He rose with all the majesty of a monarch; and he spoke in the clearest and firmest tones, so that the change from his customary shuffling, cautious, and snarling diction, was of itself sufficient to command the earnest attention of his audience.

'Go!' said he; 'go, all of you!—go, Ngatiraukawa, to Maunga-tautari! Take your children on your backs and go, and leave my land without men. When you are gone, I will stay and fight the soldiers with my own hands. I do not beg you to stop. Rauparaha is not afraid!

'I began to fight when I was as high as my hip. All my days have been spent in fighting, and by fighting I have got my name. Since I seized by war all this land, from Taranaki to Port Nicholson, and from Blind Bay to Cloudy Bay beyond the water, I have been spoken of as a king. I am the king of all this land. I have lived a king, and I will die a king, with my *mere* in my hand. Go! I am no beggar! Rauparaha will fight the soldiers of the Queen when they come, with his own hands and his own name. Go to Maunga-tautari!' Then suddenly changing his strain, he looked on the assemblage of chiefs, bending down towards them with a paternal smile, and softening his voice to kindness and emotion. 'But what do I say?' said he; 'what is my talk about? You are children! It is not for you to talk. You talk of going here, and doing this and doing that. Can one of you talk when I am here? No! I shall rise and speak for you all, and you shall sit dumb; for you are all my children, and Rauparaha is your head chief and your patriarch.' He completely won his point by this fearless rejection of their assistance, ending in an arrogant assumption of absolute authority over their movements. One of the highest chiefs said to me, 'It is true, Tiraweke! he is our father and our *ariki* (superior chief). Rauparaha is the king of the Maori, like your Queen over the white people'; and the others bowed a silent assent, and each seemed to swell with conscious dignity as the follower of such a leader. The cattle were not allowed to pass; but Rauparaha agreed quietly to the request of the chiefs in the course of the day, that the white people already established here should not be sent away.

§

We arrived at Wellington on the evening of the 23rd of July. I now had an opportunity of perusing the depositions taken, and of learning from Colonel Wakefield the particulars of what had been done.

Rauparaha and Rangihaeata had crossed the Strait to Nelson about two months before on a begging expedition. They received presents and kind treatment from Captain Wakefield; but at a conference held there they said he should not have the plain of Wairau. After Captain Wakefield left the conference, Rangihaeata was heard to say by several of the settlers that 'he would *pung-a-pung*, or kill, Wide-awake if he took Wairau'. But Captain Wakefield, to whom this was reported, said Rangihaeata was a mere bully, and that his threats were only noisy vapouring. And he directed the preliminary survey of the Wairau plain to be proceeded with, in order that it might be ready for selection as soon as Mr. Spain should have decided upon the claim.

The lands in the Wairau district were advertised for survey by contract, by Captain Wakefield, in March 1843. The contracting surveyors, Messrs Barnicoat, Parkinson, and Cotterell, with their men, forming in all a party of about forty, started by sea from Nelson on the 15th April, and landed on the Wairau beach on Tuesday the 25th.

Meanwhile, Rauparaha and Rangihaeata, being at Porirua in attendance on the Court of Land Claims, made known their determination to prevent the survey from proceeding. Mr. Spain used his influence to pacify them; agreed to meet them at Port Underwood, to investigate the land claims, as soon as possible after the adjournment of his Court at the end of June; and obtained from them a promise not to enter the Wairau within the time appointed, nor do anything before his arrival.

On the 28th May, Mr. Toms received Rauparaha and his party on board the schooner *Three Brothers*, of which he is captain and owner, at Porirua. They were landed at Port Underwood, in Cloudy Bay, on the 1st of June. They then started with other natives in eight canoes and a whale-boat for the Wairau, where they arrived on the same day.

On the same evening, they went up the river to Mr. Cotterell's station, in number amounting to upwards of 100. Next morning, Rauparaha and Rangihaeata, with about 30 followers, after ordering Mr. Cotterell and his men to leave the place, stripped and burned his hut and that of his men, together with the timber intended for survey-stakes. They then assisted the white men to carry the contents of their huts to their boats, and despatched them to Ocean Bay. Next day, Mr. Tuckett, the Company's Chief Surveyor, arrived, met Mr. Cotterell at the mouth of the Wairau, and sent him to Nelson with a note to Captain Wakefield. Mr. Cotterell laid an information before the Police Magistrate, Mr. Thompson, on the 12th June. Three other Justices of the Peace were on the bench—Captain Wakefield, Captain England, and Alexander M'Donald, Esq. After much deliberation, a warrant was granted against Rauparaha and Rangihaeata on a charge of arson.

The Police Magistrate at Nelson having issued his warrant, and being informed of the numbers of the natives, and of their being armed, resolved to attend the execution of the warrant himself, accompanied by an armed force. He expressed his opinion that such a demonstration would prevent bloodshed, and impress upon the natives a sense of the authority of the law. The Government brig *Victoria* was then in the harbour; and, at the request of Mr. Thompson, Captain Richards consented to carry the party to Wairau. It then consisted of the following persons: Mr. Thompson, Judge of the County Court and Police Magistrate; Captain Wakefield, and Captain Richard England, both Justices of the Peace; Mr. George Ryecroft Richardson, Crown Prosecutor for Nelson; Mr. James Howard, a Warrant Officer in the Navy and New Zealand Company's Storekeeper; Mr. Cotterell, Surveyor; four constables and twelve special constables. John Brooks went as interpreter, having often been similarly employed. The brig sailed on Tuesday, June 13th. In the Gulf, the same day, she met the Company's boat on her return from the Wairau, with Mr. Tuckett, Mr. Patchett, a Merchant and large Land-Agent, and Mr. Bellairs, Surveyor. These gentlemen, at the request of Captain Wakefield, joined his party with the boat's crew.

On the evening of Thursday, June 15, and the following morning, the party landed at Wairau, where Mr. Barnicoat and his men joined them. Muskets, and a cartouche-box of ball-cartridges with each, were served out to the men, and cutlasses to as many as chose to avail themselves of them. On Friday afternoon, they ascended the right bank of the river about five miles. Higher up, it being too late to proceed, the Magistrates and their followers then encamped for the night at a pine-wood called Tua Mautine, and set a watch. Their movements, it appears, had been all along watched and reported by scouts.

On the morning of Saturday, June 17th, two boats having been brought up, the Europeans embarked in them and ascended the river a few miles further. They now amounted to forty-nine, thirty-three of whom were armed with muskets. One or two carried fowling-pieces. Mr. Howard had a cutlass. The remainder were apparently unarmed, but in general were furnished with pocket-pistols.

When mustered, before setting out, Captain Wakefield having called 'Order!' said to them, 'Men, whatever you do, *do not fire* unless you get orders.'

Having ascended the river about four miles, the party perceived some smoke issuing from a wood, and soon heard the voices of the natives, that of Rangihaeata being plainly distinguishable. On advancing, they found them posted in the wood, which is about 50 acres in extent, on the right bank of a deep unfordable rivulet, called Tuamarina, which flows into the Wairau on its left bank, and is at this place about 30 feet wide. They were squatting in groups in front of the dense wood, on about a quarter of an acre of cleared ground, with their canoes drawn up on the bank of the stream. The white men halted on the left bank, with a hill behind them covered with fern and *manuka,* and sloping upwards with several brows or terraces.

All accounts agree in estimating the number of the natives at about 120 or 125, including women and children. The men amounted to 80 or 90, about half of whom were armed with muskets, the rest with native weapons.

At the request of the Magistrates, a canoe was placed across the stream to serve as a bridge, and Mr. Thompson, Captain Wakefield, Messrs. Tuckett, Cotterell, and Patchett, Brooks the interpreter, and Maling the Chief Constable, crossed over.

The Police Magistrate then called on Rauparaha and Rangihaeata. The former alone came forward; and Mr. Thompson told him that he was the Queen's representative, that he had warrants against him and Rangihaeata for the destruction of the property of Mr. Cotterell, and that he must go on board the brig, with such of his followers as he chose, where the matter should be investigated. Rauparaha said that Mr. Spain would inquire into and settle the business in a little while. Mr. Thompson explained, that Mr. Spain's business lay in deciding as to land-claims; that this was a question about destruction of property, and had nothing to do with the ownership of the Wairau. Rauparaha requested to have the matter decided on the spot; and professed his readiness to make the compensation to Mr. Cotterell required by the Magistrates, provided their decision pleased him. Mr. Thompson replied, that the case must be heard on board the Government brig, whither Rauparaha must accompany him. On Rauparaha's reiterated refusal to comply with this proposal, put in direct terms to him, Mr. Thompson declared he would compel him. Rauparaha said he did not want to fight; but that if the white people fought he would fight too. Mr. Thompson, pointing to the armed men, threatened that he and his party should be fired upon. Sixteen natives immediately sprang to their feet and presented fire-arms. Rangihaeata now came forward, and vehemently defied the Magistrates and their power. At last, Mr. Thompson called out, 'Captain England, let the men advance.'

In the meantime, the men left on the other side of the stream had been divided into two bodies, consisting of 16 and 17 respectively; one under the command of Captain England, the other under that of Mr. Howard. When the dispute was at the highest, Captain Wakefield, perceiving the danger of being separated from the men should a collision arise, proceeded to the creek with the intention of bringing them over on a canoe, which, with the consent of the natives, was laid across it. Mr. Thompson, it seems, just then called to Mr. Howard for his men, and he led his party to the stream. In the canoe they met Captain Wakefield, whom the rest of the gentlemen were apparently following. 'Keep your eyes on them, my men; they have their guns pointed at us,' said Captain Wakefield to the advancing men. At this moment (observing some movement among the natives towards Mr. Thompson or the gentlemen), he exclaimed in a loud voice, with great energy, 'Men, forward! Englishmen, forward!' and a shot was fired, according to the explicit and consistent evidence of Joseph Morgan, by one of the natives, which laid his comrade Tyrrell dead at his feet. These two men, with Northam, also killed at almost the same time and spot, were in advance of their party, and on the opposite bank of the stream when this occurred.

It was then, apparently, that Mr. Thompson gave orders to fire, if any were given at all. Before he could be obeyed, however, the natives had fired a volley, which was instantly returned. The gentlemen were crossing while this went on; Captain England, the last of them, wading through the water, into which he had fallen, holding on by the side of the canoe. Those of Mr. Howard's party who had reached the other bank returned at the same time. The firing was kept up briskly on both sides for a few minutes; but in this skirmishing the natives had greatly the advantage, the bushes on their side being much closer and affording far better concealment. This, and their previous confusion from meeting in the canoe, may account for the greater loss of life among the Englishmen.

Immediately after crossing, Mr. Patchett received a shot in his left side. He leapt up, then fell, mortally wounded, on the spot where he had been standing. Northam and Smith fell at this time near the same place. Captain Wakefield, observing his men already retreating, as well, probably, as the disadvantage at which they were fighting, their enemies being almost invisible and themselves exposed, ordered them to retire to form on the hill. At this moment, it is ascertained that the natives were on the point of taking to flight, when Rauparaha, seeing the retreat—for there is no doubt that they retreated immediately—excited his men, who, raising a war-cry, darted across the stream in pursuit of the Europeans. These latter retreated, without order, in the direction of the hill; Mr. Thompson, Captain Wakefield, Captain England, and Mr. Howard, urging them 'for God's sake to keep together', but in vain. Captain Wakefield, therefore, in order to prevent a further sacrifice of life, ordered the firing to cease; and Captain England and Mr. Howard advanced toward the natives with a white handkerchief, in token of peace. The retreating party and the natives continuing to fire, Captain Wakefield and the gentlemen about him were compelled to proceed further up the hill, in order, if possible, to put an end to the conflict. Mr. Cotterell, after accompanying them a short distance, sat down, intending to deliver himself up. As the natives came up, he recognized among them one to whom he had frequently shown acts of kindness; to him he advanced with open arms. The native thereupon discharged his musket in the air; but two others immediately seized him, and dragged him by the hair down the hill into a *manuka* bush. There, as was afterwards found, they despatched him with their tomahawks.

On the second brow of the hill, Captain Wakefield said, 'Your only chance of life is to throw away your arms and lie down.' He and Mr. Thompson and Brooks again shouted '*Kati!*' (peace), and waved a white handkerchief. Besides the last-mentioned persons, there were present Captain England, Mr. Richardson, Mr. Howard, some of the constables, and a few others. Messrs. Tuckett, Barnicoat, and others, went off a little before. The rest fled up the hill in different directions, and were pursued a little way by some of the natives. The natives now ceased firing; and as they came up, the white men delivered up their arms, at Captain Wakefield's order. He himself gave up a pistol to one of them.

The whole party seem to have gone a little further down the hill; where most of the natives, with Rauparaha and Rangihaeata, immediately joined them. The natives having shaken hands with the prisoners, who were standing in a group, loaded their guns, and seated themselves in a half-circle before them, the two chiefs occupying the extremities. Mr. Richardson, who had received a shot in the hip from which the blood flowed freely, requested Mr. Thompson to examine it; which he did. The natives brandished their tomahawks over the heads of some of the defenceless men. Mr. Thompson observing this, said to Rauparaha, '*Kati*'; which he repeated, and the others then desisted. Two natives then approached Captain Wakefield, and, seizing him, attempted to strip off his coat. Colouring highly, it seems he endeavoured to draw another pistol, as Mr. Howard was heard to say, 'For God's sake, sir, do nothing rash!' or words to that effect. Other natives laid hold of Mr. Thompson, and were taking his coat and watch.

Up to this point there is the evidence of white men and eyewitnesses for all that I have stated. The only man that escaped of all who surrendered themselves to the natives, and from whose deposition I have gathered the incidents I have related as occurring after the surrender, was George Bampton; who, at this moment observing the attention of the natives drawn off him, slipped into the bush on a natural pretence, and succeeded in concealing himself.

A native who took part in the affray gave the following evidence before the Magistrates as to what followed:

'The natives pursued them to another rise of the hill, and followed them until they caught them all; and Rauparaha was talking to them, and had secured all the chiefs, when Rangihaeata came up and said, "Rauparaha, remember your daughter," (one of Rangihaeata's wives, shot by a chance-shot during the action). Puaha's wife was down at the settlement, and called out to him, "Puaha, Puaha, save some of the chiefs, so that you may have to say you saved some": but when she cried they were all killed. Rangihaeata killed them all with his own hand, with a tomahawk. I saw him do it. I saw Rangihaeata kill Captain Wakefield, Mr. Thompson, and Mr. Richardson. I saw him kill John Brooks, near the bunch of trees up the hill. I saw him kill Mr. Cotterell.'

The deputation from the Wellington Magistrates, with Dr. Dorset, sailed for Cloudy Bay on Wednesday the 21st. On arriving at Cloudy Bay, they found that Mr. Ironside, the Wesleyan missionary stationed at Cloudy Bay, had been to Wairau with two boats' companies of whalers, had discovered 17 of the dead bodies, and having no alternative, had already commenced their interment on the spot, according to the rites of the Church of England.

The bodies of Captain Wakefield, Mr. Thompson, Captain England, Mr. Richardson, Mr. Howard, Bumforth, Cropper, Gardiner, and Coster, were found near the spot where the last of those who escaped left them alive, lying within 20 yards of each other, in their clothes as they fell. Captain Wakefield's coat and waistcoat alone had been stripped off. The skulls of all had been cleft with tomahawks, and generally disfigured with repeated blows, struck with such ferocity that every one must have been more than sufficient to have produced instantaneous death.

I must also mention, that Te Ahu and various other natives told me that Rangihaeata had used another argument to persuade Rauparaha that the white chiefs should be killed. When he saw the nine or ten dead bodies of the labourers who had been shot in fair fight, he said to Rauparaha, 'We shall be sure to be killed for this, some day; the white people will take *utu;* let us then have some

better blood than that of these *tutua* (common men). We are chiefs;
let us kill the chiefs and take *utu* beforehand for ourselves.'

§

While the Magistrates went to examine witnesses, the people
of Wellington became alarmed at their totally defenceless state,
in case of the outrages of Rauparaha and his followers being continued in this direction, now that he had managed to get to Otaki
in safety.

So the settlers had enrolled themselves as volunteers, under the
express sanction and superintendence of the Mayor, the Justices
of the Peace, and Mr. Macdonogh the Police Magistrate, who
swore them in as special constables. A Committee of Public Safety
had been appointed; a battery built and mounted with two 18-
pounders on the flag-staff hill; officers chosen to command and
drill the volunteers; and the necessary measures taken to place all
the powder in the settlement under the control of the authorities.

Colonel Wakefield told me that he had passed the volunteers
under review on the Sunday morning previous to my arrival, and
that they seemed to have profited very well by their drilling,
except a troop of some 20 cavalry composed of gentry, whose
horses were not yet accustomed to the drums or to the banging
of the sabres about their ribs. There were about 400 bayonets
mustered; but Colonal Wakefield spoke in special praise of the
appearance and evolutions of a rifle corps of about 100. They had
been well drilled by Major Durie.

The Government brig had been despatched to Auckland on the
30th of June, and Dr. Evans had taken a passage in her, deputed
to represent the whole circumstances to the Acting Governor.
The brig made a very quick voyage, and returned just before
daylight on the morning of the 24th July. Among the passengers
in the brig was Major Richmond, one of the Land Commissioners,
now appointed Police Magistrate for Port Nicholson.

Major Richmond had hardly eaten his breakfast when he landed,
and went straight to the house of Major Durie, to request in very
peremptory terms that he would take immediate steps for the
disbanding of the corps of volunteers under his command.

And the following proclamation was stuck about all over the town, when it was found that the Rifle Corps still prepared to go through their daily drill:

Whereas divers persons in the borough of Wellington have unlawfully assembled together for the purpose of being trained and drilled to arms, and of practising military exercises: Now, I have it in command from his Excellency the Officer administering the Government, to give notice, that if any person whatever shall henceforth so unlawfully assemble for the purposes aforesaid, or any of them, in the borough of Wellington, or else-where in the southern district of New Ulster, the assemblage of such persons will be dispersed, and the persons so unlawfully assembling will be proceeded against according to law. Dated this 26th July, 1843.

M. RICHMOND, *Chief Police Magistrate*

The volunteers had been most lawfully organized and drilled, under the express sanction and in answer to the invitation of the Assistant Police Magistrate, the Mayor, and some nine or ten other Justices of the Peace.

It was represented to Major Richmond that reports had come in from all quarters of the danger to be feared from the natives. On the Hutt, scarcely two miles from the village of Aglionby, a constable had tried to apprehend a native who had been clearly guilty of theft in a white man's house; but he had been surrounded by friends of the culprit flourishing spears and tomahawks, very roughly handled, and forced to desist from his attempt. Rauparaha and Rangihaeata were said to be forming a new *pa* at the entrance of Porirua harbour; and to have assembled there some 200 men, including the whole population of Cloudy Bay.

It was agreed that Mr. Petre, Mr. Macdonogh, and I, should go and inquire into the truth of these reports, accompanied by Mr. Meurant the interpreter.

Up the Hutt, we found a very large increase in the number of native inhabitants. Two strong *pas* were being built in the potato-grounds. I recognized a great many of Rangihaeata's especial attendants. Two of the men did not conceal that they had been at Wairau; and, in fact, boasted of it to the sawyers and other white persons who were living by their sufferance in this neigh-bourhood.

On the 28th of August, the following scene occurred within fifty yards of the Police Office and Barracks.

A native residing at Pipitea *pa* entered the house of a Scotchman, named Allan Cameron, when Mrs. Cameron was the only one of the family at home. The intruder opened a box, and without assigning any reason took from it a large piece of printed cotton. Mrs. Cameron remonstrated, and attempted to take the print from him; when the native insulted her, and struck her under the ear and in other places. Several neighbours, alarmed by her screams, entered the house, and observed among other effects of the violence with which she had been assaulted, that one of her hands was covered with blood. A neighbour, Mr. Bee, a baker, having sent for a constable, strove to quiet the native, and advised him in vain, if he thought himself injured, to represent the case to the Police Magistrate; and then recommemded Mrs. Cameron to give up the print, and wait till the constable arrived. The native proceeded to the *pa*, and the constable followed him and compelled him to restore the print. A number of natives were in chapel at the time, but, on hearing the disturbance, they rushed into the *pa*, and casting off their blankets, maltreated the constable, by throwing him down and jumping upon him. On his calling out for assistance, another constable, accompanied by some of the neighbours, came to the spot and attempted to protect him; but the natives were too numerous, and drove them from the *pa*. Before he could be rescued, he was seriously injured.

I was present, though not on the bench, in the Police Court on the day following. The prisoner having first refused to go before Major Richmond, was, after much entreaty, persuaded by Mr. Clarke junior to accompany him, and the other natives were prevailed upon to suffer him to go to the Police Court. Three witnesses proved the identity of the prisoner, and he himself confessed having struck the woman several times, and that he stole the print and ill-treated the constable.

Mr. Clarke junior treated the offence as of a very light character, and told the Chief Police Magistrate 'that it was a very trifling affair'; but the constable who had suffered, surprised at his remarks, stated that 'he had been nearly killed in the affray'.

Major Richmond, after hearing the case, told the aggressor he might go, but if ever he did anything of the kind again, he would be punished for it.

About this time, numerous cases occurred of increasing insolence and outrageous conduct on the part of the natives. Up the Hutt, and in other quarters, many instances occurred; but they did not appear in the Police Court, as it had become a bye-word that there was law against the white and none against the Maori.

On the 31st, H.M.S. *North Star*, Captain Sir Everard Home, arrived from Auckland, whither she had gone from Sydney to obtain orders. Captain (formerly Lieutenant) Best, was in command of a detachment of the 80th Foot, acting as supernumerary marines on board. As we had expected, there were particular instructions that the troops should not land, except if actually needed for active operation.

A day or two after the arrival of the *North Star* I went to Otaki on horseback. At Taupo Bay in Porirua, where the natives had told us, when deputed by the Magistrates, that a *pa* was to be built, we found about 200 natives in a new village, 12 or 15 large canoes, and the Company's boat hauled up among them.

Te Hiko came out on the beach, and beckoned to me to stop. Accordingly we pulled up our horses; and he introduced me to Taiaroa, the chief from Otago in the Middle Island, who had made a friendly alliance with Rauparaha, as reported to Major Richmond. Taiaroa talked to me for some time about land, in a jargon composed of whaling slang, broken French, and bad English; so that I was obliged to beg him to talk Maori, which I could better understand. I then made out that he was angry with 'Wide-awake' and the other white people for taking so much land; and he said he should turn the white people off to the southward, if he did not get plenty of *utu*.

Among others, he mentioned a Mr. John Jones, who had a large farming and whaling establishment at a place called Waikouaiti, between Banks's Peninsula and Otago. We had not been aware till within a few months before that he had 100 acres of land under grain crop, nearly 100 head of horses besides cattle, and several families of cottagers employed as farm-labourers at Waikouaiti, besides a whaling-station.

I now asked Te Hiko about the boat; but he said he had no

command over it, and that those who had would require large *utu* for restoring it.

While I was speaking to him, I pulled out my pocket-handker-chief. He immediately retreated as fast as he could, hiding his head under his blanket. He told me, when re-assured, that he thought I was pulling a pistol out of my pocket to shoot him. I immediately answered, that I scorned to carry hidden arms amongst them; and showed him that I had none but my cutlass and the dagger in my belt, both plainly visible.

We arrived without further occurrence at Otaki, and remained there two days; during which we went to Topeora's *pa*, and saw both Rauparaha and Rangihaeata. They both professed to be very friendly to me, and inquired what the ship was come for—whether it was to take them or not? I told them I did not know; she might be, she might not; I had nothing to do with it. Rauparaha then repeated that he would fight the soldiers if they came: Rangihaeata said he would eat the ship, soldiers and all.

We were a week away from Wellington.

[*Sir Everard Home, having come to the conclusion from the reports of 'the most sound authorities' that 'there was nothing to be appre-hended' from the Maoris, decided to return with the* North Star *to Sydney.*]

CHAPTER XIX

Wairau Aftermath : Governor FitzRoy

SINCE THE fatal catastrophe at Wairau, the thoughts of the reasoning men among the settlers had been directed more seriously than ever to the apparently inevitable overthrow of the noble experiment in which they had come to take a part; namely, that of civilizing and Christianizing the aborigines on a comprehensive and statesmanlike system. At the Club, at each other's houses, while looking over the operations on a farm, or at any other place where they met and discussed their little politics, a sincere regret for this result was generally manifested, and its causes were traced with a view to a remedy if possible.

[*At this point Wakefield reviews the history of the relations between pakeha and Maori, and moves on to discuss the implacable missionary opposition to the New Zealand Company. His dismissal of the Treaty of Waitangi as a 'legal fiction' reflects the bitterness felt by the Company colonists about the land clauses of the Treaty of Waitangi, which denied to them for so long the land they claimed.*]

From the first period of our arrival in Cook's Strait, we had met with but too many instances of missionary hostility, apparently delegated with care to the greater number of the local missionaries, and by them carried out with earnestness during four years, in that part of the country where they only began to preach when we began to colonize. Its prevalence threw a repulsive shade over the whole course of missionary proceedings; for some of the arguments used against the colonists were as unprincipled as they were uncharitable, and as devoid of Christian spirit as they were wanting in manly honour. Apart from this dark stain, the results of the purely missionary system were by no means satisfactory. Besides that the very extensive instruction for which the missionaries really deserve credit was merely religious and in the native language, the chieftainship was destroyed among the missionary tribes, and the political as well as the physical condition of their scholars had clearly retrograded.

I must, of course, except the labours of Mr. Hadfield from these remarks; but even he had steadily objected to their instruction in the English language. And even he was not free from another grave omission made by the missionaries, the Government officers, and the Protectors of Aborigines. Although they professed such warm philanthropy towards the natives, they carried this philanthropy into their social relations with them to a far less degree than the unassuming colonists. The principal teachers under the missionaries are generally their house-servants at the same time; black their shoes, clean their windows, make their beds, groom their horses, and cook their dinner. The missionaries do not admit their most industrious pupils, or the *protégés* to whom they are most attached, to dine with them at the same table, or to walk when they like into their sitting-room, and hold converse on terms of equality and mutual familiarity. I never saw a missionary or a Government officer who treated a native as his brother so entirely as I did Kuru or Wahine-iti, as Colonel Wakefield did Te Puni, or as many other 'devils' did the chief to whom they had become especially attached.

In order to obtain a government at all, the first Governor threw himself unreservedly into the hands of the Rev. Henry Williams and the other missionaries at the Bay of Islands. They were, without a doubt, the authors and interpreters of the Treaty of Waitangi, on which are founded all the relations between the Government and the natives.

The translation of this famous Treaty, which is given officially to the world, is as follows:

HER MAJESTY, Queen Victoria, of the United Kingdom of Great Britain and Ireland, regarding with her royal favour the native chiefs and tribes of New Zealand, and anxious to protect their just rights and property, and to secure to them the enjoyment of peace and good order, has deemed it necessary, in consequence of the great number of her Majesty's subjects who have already settled in New Zealand, and the rapid extension of emigration both from Europe and Australia which is still in progress, to constitute and appoint a functionary properly authorized to treat with the aborigines of New Zealand for the recognition of her Majesty's sovereign authority over the whole or any part of those islands. Her Majesty, therefore, being desirous to establish a settled form of civil government, with a view to avert the evil consequences which must result from the absence of the necessary laws and institutions, alike to the native population and to her subjects, has been graciously pleased to empower and authorize me, William Hobson, a Captain in her Majesty's Royal Navy, Consul and Lieutenant-Governor of such parts of New Zealand as may be, or hereafter shall be, ceded to her Majesty, to invite the confederated and independent chiefs of New Zealand to concur in the following articles and conditions.

ARTICLE I. The chiefs of the confederation of the united tribes of New Zealand, and the separate and independent chiefs who have not become members of the confederation, cede to her Majesty the Queen of England, absolutely and without reservation, all the rights and powers of sovereignty which the said confederation or individual chiefs respectively exercise or possess, or may be supposed to exercise or to possess over their respective territories as the sole sovereigns thereof.

ARTICLE 2. Her Majesty the Queen of England confirms and guarantees to the chiefs and tribes of New Zealand, and to the respective families and individuals thereof, the full, exclusive, and undisturbed possession of their lands and estates, forests, fisheries, and other properties which they may collectively or individually possess, so long as it is their wish and desire to retain the same in their possession; but the chiefs of the united tribes and the individual chiefs yield to her Majesty the exclusive right of preemption over such lands as the proprietors thereof may be disposed to alienate, at such prices as may be agreed upon between the respective proprietors and persons appointed by her Majesty to treat with them on that behalf.

ARTICLE 3. In consideration thereof, her Majesty the Queen of England extends to the natives of New Zealand her royal protection, and imparts to them all the rights and privileges of British subjects.

(Signed) W. HOBSON, *Lieutenant-Governor*

Now, therefore, we, the chiefs of the confederation of the united tribes of New Zealand, being assembled in congress at Victoria in Waitangi, and we, the separate and independent chiefs of New Zealand, claiming authority over the tribes and territories which are specified after our respective names, having been made fully to understand the provisions of the foregoing Treaty, accept and enter into the same in the full spirit and meaning thereof. In witness of which we have attached our signatures or marks at the places and dates respectively specified.

Done at Waitangi this 6th day of February in the year of our Lord 1840

(512 signatures)

The greater part of these complicated and formal expressions could not be translated into Maori, which had no words to express them. Here follows an exact and literal translation of the Maori version which is also published officially:

Here's Victoria the Queen of England, in her gracious remembrance towards the Chiefs and Tribes of New Zealand, and in her desire that their Chieftainships and their lands should be secured to them, and that obedience also should be held by them, and the peaceful state also, had considered it as a just thing to send here some Chief to be a person to arrange with the native men of New Zealand, that the Governorship of the Queen may be assented to by the native Chiefs in all places of the land and of the islands. Because, too, many together are the men of her tribe who have sat down in this land and are coming hither.

Now, it is the Queen who desires that the Governorship may be arranged that evils may not come to the native man, to the white who dwells lawless.

There! Now the Queen has been good that I should be sent, William Hobson, a Captain in the Royal Navy, a Governor for all the places in New Zealand that are yielded now or hereafter to the Queen; she says to the Chiefs of the Assemblage of the Tribes of New Zealand and other Chiefs besides, these laws which shall be spoken now.

Here's the first. Here's the Chiefs of the Assemblage and all the Chiefs also who have not joined the Assemblage mentioned cede to the utmost to the Queen of England for ever continually to the utmost the whole Governorship of their lands.

Here's the second. Here's the Queen of England arranges and confirms to the Chiefs, to all the men of New Zealand, the entire Chieftainship of their lands, their villages, and all their property. But here's the Chiefs of the Assemblage, and all the Chiefs besides, yield to the Queen the buying of those places of land, where the man whose the land is shall be good to the arrangement of the payment which the buyer shall arrange to them who is told by the Queen to buy for her.

Here's the third. This, too, is an arrangement in return for the assent to the Governorship of the Queen. The Queen of England will protect all the native men of New Zealand. She yields to them all the rights one and the same as her doings to the men of England.

(Signed) W. HOBSON, *Lieutenant-Governor*

Now, here's we, here's the Chiefs of the Assemblage of the Tribes of New Zealand, who are congregated at Waitangi; here's we, too, here's the Chiefs of New Zealand who see the meaning of these words, we accept, we entirely agree to all. Truly, we do mark our names and marks.

This is done at Waitangi, on the six of the days of February, in the year One thousand eight hundred and four-tens of our Lord.

Even to express this more simple agreement in the simple tongue of the savages, the writer of the Maori version had to coin several words, such as have been coined by the missionaries in the translation of the Bible. They are words which were before unknown to the native, and therefore not existing in his language. A native, in reading them, would, as nearly as is possible to him, approach to an English pronunciation of the English words; but his appreciation of their meaning would depend entirely upon the explanation made to him at the time of the English word which he had thus attempted to pronounce. Thus,

Wikitoria	stands in the treaty for		Victoria;
Kuini	,,	,,	Queen;
Ingarangi	,,	,,	England;
Nu Tireni	,,	,,	New Zealand;
Wiremu Hopihana		,,	William Hobson;
Kapitana	,,	,,	Captain;
Roiara Newi	,,	,,	Royal Navy;
Kawana	,,	,,	Governor; and
Pepuere	,,	,,	February.

Two important words, *Rangatiratanga* and *Kawanatanga,* also require some explanation. The termination *tanga* and some variations of it are used in the Maori language to produce the abstract notion of any noun or verb to which they are added; thus answering to our *-ing*, *-ness*, *-ship*, *-hood*, etc. For example, *hoko* is Maori for 'to buy'—*hokonga*, for 'buying'; *Rangatira* is Maori for 'Chief', and *Rangatiratanga* is therefore truly rendered 'Chieftainship'. *Kawanatanga* is an adaptation of the same rule to the word *Kawana*, which had itself been coined from the English 'Governor'; and therefore it is truly rendered by 'Governorship'. But the natives could have had, at the time of the Treaty, only very vague ideas as to the meaning of the English word 'Governor' which they nearly pronounced. In the Treaty itself, they were told the 'Hopihana' [Hobson] was a *Kawana*. Without very full explanation, *Kawanatanga* must therefore have represented to their ideas neither more nor less than '*Hobsonness*'.

Fully to understand the value of this contract, the circumstances under which it was procured must be kept in view. Captain Hobson's commission was read at Kororareka, in the Bay of Islands, on the 30th January, the day of his arrival. On the 5th of February, he presented the Treaty to an assembly of the natives of the Bay of Islands; and on the 6th it was signed by 46 chiefs. On the 12th, he met the natives of the Hokianga; and 56 more chiefs signed the treaty. In March, Mr. Shortland, Captain Symonds, and four missionaries, were appointed to secure the adherence of the chiefs of the northern islands to the treaty. One of the missionaries deputed his colleague, Mr. Chapman, and the master of a coasting trader, named Fedarb, to obtain signatures. Copies of the Treaty were thus dispersed about the Northern Island. Some of the chiefs refused to sign it; but at last, between the 6th of February and the 3rd of September, 512 signatures were obtained. Of these signatures, upwards of 200 were those of the chiefs inhabiting the peninsula north of the harbour of Manukau and the estuary of the Thames; leaving only 300 to represent the inhabitants of more than three-fourths of the North Island. There is no evidence whatever that the assent of the powerful and warlike tribes of the interior, in the upper valleys of the Waipa and Waikato, around Lake Taupo and the Rotorua lakes, was ever asked; certainly it was never obtained. The greater part of the signatures were obtained at flying visits, and after one or at the most two interviews. Presents of blankets and tobacco were made to the chiefs who signed; and there cannot exist a doubt that to obtain these presents was with many the motive for signing.

Having not even the name of Governor or Government in their language, it may be supposed that the natives had no very precise or definite ideas of government; a thing unknown in fact to their institutions. Having no collective name for their own country, it may be supposed that they had no distinct idea of different countries, of national distinctions, and therefore none of foreign relations. There is no evidence that adequate means were taken to explain those large and novel ideas to them, so necessary to the proper understanding, not only of any treaty, but even of what a treaty is. Captain Symonds had been only a few months in New Zealand, knew but little of the language, and had not the benefit of the assistance as interpreter of the missionary at Manukau, who was absent; and it may be doubted whether Mr. Fedarb, the master of the trading-vessel (who from his name appears not to have been an Englishman), was capable of understanding the treaty, much less of explaining it to the natives. It was obvious, from these considerations, that the framers of the Treaty purposed to bind the natives to conditions which there were not even the words to convey. And, on the other hand, they accepted of signatures from those who could not know to what they were putting their hands, and professed to the white settlers to have procured a valid adhesion to the compact. The Treaty of Waitangi has been truly described by the House of Commons' Committee of last year as 'little more than a legal fiction'.*

§

Sanguine as ever, the settlers based their hopes on the appointment of some master-mind as Governor. The list of likely men for the appointment was eagerly discussed. It was hoped that some man like Captain Grey, the Governor of South Australia, who had published to the world an admirable essay on the true humanity to be observed in bringing savage nations under British law, might be selected.

With a Governor mildly yet firmly gathering the whole native

* Similar objections apply of course to Wakefield's own transactions with the Maori chiefs.

population under the undoubted pale of British law by such a system; with a well-regulated church of high-minded missionaries like Mr. Hadfield, whose main object should be to unite the two races in one flock as under one law; and with a full, vigorous, and unimpeded revival of the system of Native Reserves and honour to the fading chieftainship; it seemed just possible that the union of all classes of white men in a wisely organized and strenuous effort might yet save the aboriginal population.

Captain FitzRoy's* name was sometimes mentioned. But that officer was known to be so thoroughly prejudiced in favour of the narrow philanthropy of the pure missionary system, unmingled with the concurrent benefits of civilization, that such an appointment was looked upon as probably subversive of the last hope for the natives. I remember one morning hearing several of the best and bravest settlers, collected in Colonel Wakefield's house, agree, 'that when they heard FitzRoy was Governor, it would be time to pack up their things and go'.

The next day, the 13th of September, the *Ursula* arrived from England. Among other passengers was Mr. F. Dillon Bell. He came into the room where nearly the same party as on the previous day were congregated. After the first greetings were over, he said, 'By-the-bye, I suppose you know that FitzRoy is Governor!' Some turned pale, others became flushed or bit their lips, and a chill silence ensued; till one, not the least persevering and energetic of the group, said, 'Well! five years more of troubles and difficulties! I believe that is the time that a Governor's reign lasts.' And he took his hat, mounted his horse, and rode at an angry gallop towards his farm, without waiting to hear more news from the country of his birth.

[*Investigations of the Wairau affair continued, but no punishment was inflicted on the Maoris, to the indignation of the Wellington settlers, who felt that the Maoris would have no further respect for* pakeha *authority.*]

The natives became daily convinced that they could affront, harass, or even kill the settlers, and each other, with impunity. They readily mistook the destructive humanity of the Government

* Wakefield spells the name Fitzroy.

for pusillanimity, and the admirable forbearance and generosity of the settlers for cowardice and weakness. They had Wairau and its authorized impunity, with many lesser, only because not deadly, instances, constantly before their eyes. Te Ahu, and many other of the chiefs at Otaki, who were most friendly to me and the white people generally, did not disguise their utter contempt for the unwarlike habits of the *pakeha*, and their total disbelief of the extraordinary powers of the soldiers. With such children, seeing is believing. Some of them would often say to me, 'You white people are very good for building ships and houses, for buying and selling, for making cattle fat, and for growing bread and cabbages; you are like the rats, always at work. But as to fighting, you are like them too, you only know how to run. Our children learn to handle a spear or a tomahawk when they are quite young; and all natives know how to fire a gun. As to your people, very few of them know how to load one properly. As for your soldiers, have they got four arms and four legs, that they should be better than other men? If I have got a gun like a soldier, I am as good a man as he, though I have only a blanket instead of a red coat. And the ships can do us no harm, if we get away from the coast when we see them coming.' Thus it began to be their firm belief, that the *pakeha* was not only timid but powerless.

I rode up to Otaki about this time [late 1843] and I was going quietly on with my flax-trading, when one morning, before I was up, a native brought a strange report to the house. Rauparaha, he said, had come up very early to the large *pa*, and had stated 'that I was reported to be here for the purpose of watching him and Rangihaeata, in order that twenty men on horseback, whom I expected from Port Nicholson, might be sure to catch them.' He also said that Rangihaeata had threatened to come and burn the house I was sleeping in. I showed the native my rifle and other arms by my bed-side, and told him that I would immediately shoot Rangihaeata, or anybody else, who should attempt to fire the roof over my head. After eating my breakfast, I went unarmed to the *pa* where the two ruffians dwelt. I was accompanied by Taylor and two or three friendly natives.

I found Rauparaha sitting under the tent taken at Wairau. Rangihaeata sprang out of his house in an adjoining court-yard, and made a furious oration.

He was much excited, as though by drink; he foamed at the mouth, leaped high into the air at the end of each run up and down, and made frightful grimaces at me through the fence whenever he stopped opposite to me to turn and run again. He taunted me with being a spy, hiding about inland to watch his doings. He repeated the old question, about whether the soldiers had four arms and four legs that they could take him and put handcuffs on his wrists. He applied the most insulting expressions to the Queen, to all the Governors, and to all the white people. He got to his highest pitch of excitement, when he at length challenged me to stand out and fight him manfully, hand to hand, instead of crouching about in ambush. He roared out his own name, and his known bravery, and his known strength, and his known skill, and his contempt for the whites as fighting men. All this with occasional interjectional yells, grinding of the teeth, protruding of the tongue, quivering head and limbs, and the usual slapping on the thigh.

It was a complete instance of what he called, in whaling slang, his *boo-boo-boo*, or 'bounce'; and, unarmed as I was, I should probably have thought myself in some danger, even with the fence between us, had not Rauparaha and the other natives continued to whisper to me during the whole time of his harangue, 'Don't listen to him! Don't answer! Don't be afraid, they're only words! Don't mind him, Tiraweke!' I looked steadily at him without saying a word; and he at length appeared to get tired, or to be convinced that I would not be intimidated. He finished one of his angry runs by returning into his hut.

I now turned to Rauparaha, and distinctly denied every part of the story which had been reported to him. We then held a long conversation; Rauparaha taking pains to impress upon me his power. He instanced two cases of murders committed by natives in the neighbourhood of Wellington of which the whites never had any sign or suspicion.

He praised my prudence in carrying arms wherever I went; for, he said, the constables and the soldiers had no strength to take care of me here. The Maori all carried arms, and were ready to take care of themselves; why should not I? It was the custom among the Maori chiefs; why not amongst the whites when they travelled in Maori territory? 'Carry your arms,' he concluded, 'and look about you as you ride through the Porirua bush. You might be attacked, perhaps, by some of your own Ngatiawa people.'

He then urged me to return to Port Nicholson, as he acknowledged that my stay caused fears to him and to Rangihaeata.

This was the last I saw of Rauparaha and Rangihaeata. When I returned to Wellington I published an exact account in the paper of what Rauparaha had said to me.

A long correspondence ensued between Mr. Clarke junior and Wi Tako on the one part, and myself on the other. They charged me with reporting untruths, and unnecessarily alarming the community.

About this time, the road was finished a mile above the gorge of the Hutt, so that you could ride thither on horseback; and a bridge was nearly completed by the Company over the river just above Mr. Molesworth's large barn and thrashing-machine. In various spots on the lower valley, settlers were daily being driven off land which they attempted to occupy, by the natives living near Mr. Swainson's curtailed farm. The *pas* there had become the rendezvous for all the worst characters from many of the tribes, as well as for the immediate followers of Rauparaha and Rangihaeata.

§

On the evening of the 26th January 1844, just a twelvemonth since Wellington had been graced with the presence of an Excellency of any sort, H.M.S. *North Star* again entered the harbour, with Captain FitzRoy on board. Immediately on the arrival of the frigate, a notice was sent on shore and circulated, that a levee would be held by the Governor on Saturday, the next day, at two o'clock.

Considering the short notice, the levee was very numerously attended. On landing, the Governor was greeted with cordial acclamations of welcome from a large assemblage of the best settlers in the colony. They appeared determined to prove their confidence in his favourable intentions towards them.

The arrangements for the levee were rather undignified; no aide-de-camp, sentries, or constables had been appointed to keep the ingress through the french window of the large room in the hotel free; and I got jostled in by the eager crowd, along with two or three other settlers, to a spot nearly under his Excellency's nose. He had just done thanking the members of a deputation from a public meeting for their congratulatory address on the safe arrival of himself and his family. He was proceeding to enlarge upon some other topics as I got within hearing; and a general stillness, a sort of chill or damp, seemed to creep over the noisy bustle of the crowd as his opinions were gradually made known. He said that all parties might rely on receiving justice, and nothing but justice at his hands. He then deprecated, in the strongest terms, the feelings displayed by the settlers at Wellington against the native population, of which he judged by what appeared in their newspapers. He stated that he considered the opposition to the natives to have emanated from young, indiscreet men; but he trusted that as they had years before them, they would yet learn experience. One of the first measures to which he would turn his attention, would be the settlement of the land question, which ought to have been settled two years ago. He had great cause of complaint against the Editor of the *New Zealand Gazette* (the Wellington newspaper), which he had carefully read for a long time, and believed to contain most pernicious statements against the natives. The natives should be protected. Justice should be done.

Several of the settlers, and among others Colonel Wakefield, were then presented to him by Major Richmond; and he addressed a few short words of usage to some, and only bowed to others. I followed, as soon as I could extricate myself from the crush, and handed my card to Major Richmond. I had made my bow and had passed on into the crowd on the other side, when the Governor called me back by name. I returned and stood in front of him; when he used nearly the following words, with a frown on his face, and the tone of the commander of a frigate reprimanding his youngest midshipman: 'When you are twenty years older, you will have a great deal more prudence and discretion. Your conduct has been most indiscreet. In the observations which I made to this assembly just now, I referred almost entirely to you. I strongly disapprove and very much regret everything that you have written and done regarding the missionaries and the natives in New Zealand. I repeat that your conduct has been most indiscreet.'

I was so perfectly astounded, that I gained some credit for forbearance, which I should otherwise not have deserved. I looked steadily in the Governor's face while he spoke; and when he had done, walked away in silence without bowing again, and left the room. I walked into the billiard-room adjoining. Two officers of the frigate left the room, apparently fearing lest they should become unwilling listeners to treason, so violently did some of the principal settlers express their feelings.

I again took a peep into the presence-room. It was fast thinning. A large number of the most respectable settlers, feeling that their sentiments were the same as mine, had put their cards in their pockets and left the room without being presented. In a few minutes his Excellency remained standing with only the officers of the frigate and of the troops looking at each other. He then advanced to the open window, and began to address the mob of labourers and others of the lower classes. He preached on the same text. 'Live and let live!' he shouted to them; and the labourers cheered vociferously, for they thought he was alluding to a recent dispute about the rate of wages between the employers and the workmen. But when some one in the crowd explained that the allusion was meant as regarded the natives, and when some more clear expressions branded the white population with cherishing unjust hatred and revengeful and oppressive feelings towards them, even this audience melted away, and the Governor was left talking to the winds and a few wondering natives. He then walked across the deserted street and beach to his boat, and returned to the ship without a single cheer or murmur, or expression of feeling of any sort; except when a rude laugh followed the blowing of his cocked hat into the water by a puff of wind.

On Tuesday I had an interview with the Governor which I had requested. His Private Secretary and Major Richmond were in the room. The Police Magistrate rose to retire, but his Excellency desired him to remain.

He began by telling me, that had he not imagined that I was about to leave town immediately after the levee, he would have taken a less public opportunity of expressing his disapprobation of my conduct.

After reading to me some passages from his instructions as

Governor, and from the charter of the colony, in order to show me that he had a right to reprove misconduct, he referred to letters which I had written at different times since the first formation of the colony, and which had been published in the *New Zealand Journal* of London; remarking that they were filled with sneers and sarcasms levelled at the missionaries; and that I had shown myself, in thus writing, a decided enemy to their proceedings *and to religion!*

He then told me that my name would be one of several to be struck off the Commission of the Peace; and that, although this would appear in public as a simple reduction of the number of the magistrates of the territory, it was his duty to inform me in private, that he 'considered I had been included in the Commission most inadvertently by the late Governor, on account of my youth and indiscretion, on account of the bad example I had set the natives, and on account of my being known as one of those who entertained an especial hatred and animosity towards them.'

He proceeded to blame me severely for having, since the Wairau massacre, worn arms while travelling among the natives who had partaken in that affair, although I had been warned against such a proceeding by the Chief Police Magistrate, Major Richmond. He said that such a course was calculated to encourage distrust and suspicion among the natives, and was, moreover, mere childish bravado; and that he should 'not be surprised if on some future occasion they should take my sword from me and beat me with the flat of it, or duck me in a pond, by way of joke.'

He then censured, in most unmeasured terms, my letters in the paper, reporting Rauparaha's statements. He rated me for attempting by this means to excite the feelings of the Europeans against the natives.

All this was accompanied with the most overbearing gesture, the most arrogant expression of countenance, and the most dictatorial tone. Even if its substance had been true, I could hardly have endured the quarter-deck manner of the lecture from my own father. It gave me the idea that Captain FitzRoy was taking advantage of his high station to lay aside all the feeling and demeanour of a gentleman.

And at the end of the violent attack he rose, and wanted to

bow me out of the room, saying, 'Now, my time is very precious; I've a great deal of business to transact'; and so on. I insisted, in as polite terms as I could, on being heard at least in defence. But I had better have left the room at once; for I was interrupted at every three words, contradicted, brow-beaten, unheard, and worse insulted than before. He told me repeatedly, 'that he knew his duty and he would do it, without caring for public feeling; that he would not be dictated to; that he came here to govern, and not to be governed'; none of which I had attempted to deny.

I was not allowed to explain how unjust and ungenerous a charge was that, against me in particular, of bearing animosity towards the natives.

On the 3rd of February Captain FitzRoy sailed for Nelson. He returned on the 16th. At Nelson he had behaved still more violently than here; so rebuking the Magistrates who had signed the warrants against Rauparaha and Rangihaeata, that they instantly threw up their commissions in a body. Captain FitzRoy had made, both at public meetings and at private interviews, the same declarations, that he knew his duty, and that he came to govern and not to be governed. He had branded the whole population, more deeply than at Wellington even, with the name of wishing to oppress and exterminate the natives. With scarcely an exception, the whole settlement of Nelson had overflowed with the greatest indignation at the treatment they received. The few exceptions were placed in the vacant seats of the Magistrates.

As to Captain FitzRoy's opinion that the savages were innocent, I will not lay myself open to the charge of making a cry for vengeance on the murderers of a near and dear relative. But as he declared that the *white men were in the wrong*, I must claim indulgence for stating the opinion of many thousand British subjects now living in New Zealand, that the *white men were in the right*.

For my part, I could stay no more in the country with comfort under this Government; for so long as Captain FitzRoy ruled, I must always appear to a certain degree as a disgraced member of the society. However much I felt sure of the sympathy of the settlers, the pleasure of my friendly relation with the natives must necessarily be fatally impaired, when they heard that the highest authority in the colony had degraded me because I was their bitter enemy.

I wrote and published a letter to the Governor, defending myself from his opprobrious charges, in order that I might still enjoy the respect of the settlers with whom I had spent four happy years. I got an acknowledgment of the receipt of this letter, but of course no further notice or answer; and two days afterwards I embarked in a ship that was bound for Valparaiso.

I left Cook's Strait with the conviction that the brave colony of Englishmen planted on its sunny shores had taken a firm root in the fertile soil; that no blight, however blasting, would be able to wither it; that no cold winds would be able to kill its vigorous shoots; that no grubbing would eradicate it; that no cherishing of noxious weeds would be able to smother its ultimate growth into a flourishing and happy nation: so plentiful are the resources of the country, and those of the stalwart and invincible colonists who have chosen it for their abode.

But I foresaw for them at least many months more of harassing delays, doubts, and torments, under the tread of a ruler who seemed well inclined to adopt, as far as regarded the delicate native question, the whole determination of the intolerant portion of the missionaries to 'thwart them by every means in their power'.

And I grieved when I felt sure that the poor natives must inevitably descend one step nearer towards a miserable end.

The last hope appeared still to be that some really great man might be despatched in time to remedy the evils which were accumulating for both white people and natives. Some such man as Lord Metcalfe or Sir Henry Pottinger, able and willing to grasp with his master-mind the task of uniting two races in one nation, might yet heal the wounds inflicted by a prejudiced incapable.* A firm and unwavering course of foreseeing philanthropy could alone lay sound foundations for a gentle and permanent union.

We were thirty-seven days in reaching Valparaiso: I remained five weeks at that port and in the neighbouring part of Chile; and then rounded Cape Horn in a French merchantman, which made the voyage to Bordeaux in ninety-two days.

And since my arrival in England I have written the foregoing

---

* Captain FitzRoy was recalled and Captain (later Sir George) Grey appointed in 1845.

narrative. I hope it is not unbecoming in me to say that my intention in every part of it has been to relate truly and exactly the scenes which I saw, and the things which were of paramount interest to me at the time. So earnest has been this intention, that I have often dwelt over-minutely on trivial details, and have fallen almost unawares into the language, while I acquire the unavoidable spirit, of a partisan.

Index